Explosive, crackling, compelling, fascinating. Coogan has ventured where academics, and Americans, fear to tread. The book reminds us to never ever write off another human being. Instead, let's read what he has actually written—look deeply into his heart—and then our own.

– Drew Leader, author of *The Soul Knows No Bars: Inmates Reflect on Life, Death, and Hope*

A remarkable journey into the soul of America in a time of growing segregation by race, class, and education. All are changed, including Coogan, who discovers the gritty, real-world underside of life in his own city, and a new respect for the hard-won insights, know-how, and sometimes eloquence of men a world removed.

– Harry Boyte, Senior Scholar in Public Work Philosophy, Augsburg College, and author of *The Backyard Revolution* and *Everyday Politics: Reconnecting Citizens and Public Life*

This is a book that will urge you to pay attention, to wake from the oblivious daze engendered by TV crime shows and gated communities.

– Eli Goldblatt, author of *Writing Home: A Literacy Autobiography*

These troubling, complex, and challenging accounts have the potential to teach us all something about what lies before and behind a prison sentence. And while writing is a radically insufficient tool for changing systemic inequality, if justice is our goal, these stories, and more like them, should be shared widely.

– Paula Mathieu, author of *Tactics of Hope: The Public Turn in English Composition*

In the stories offered here, there are few heroes, many potential villains, and even characters who somehow seem both. These are stories worth listening to.

– Diana George, writing center director, Virginia Polytechnic University

Always powerful, sometimes funny, and regularly heart-breaking, *Writing Our Way Out* offers readers glimpses into one of the great dramas of contemporary American life: how the disenfranchised cope with hardship while struggling to create new selves and better communities.

– Stephen Hartnett, author of *Working for Justice: A Handbook of Prison Education and Activism*

This book reads like an intellectual drama, a moving traveler's guide in how to have [in Coogan's words] "a life-affirming dialogue" across differences.

– Linda Flower, author of *Community Literacy and the Rhetoric of Public Engagement*

WRITING OUR WAY OUT

WRITING OUR WAY OUT

MEMOIRS FROM JAIL

David Coogan
with
Kelvin Belton
Karl Black
Stanley Craddock
Ronald Fountain
Bradley Greene
Tony Martin
Naji Mujahid
Terence Scruggs
Andre Simpson
Dean Turner

Brandylane Publishers, Inc.
WWW.BRANDYLANEPUBLISHERS.COM

Printed in the United States
ISBN: 978-1-9399305-9-0
LCCN: 2015951867

Brandylane Publishers, Inc.
WWW.BRANDYLANEPUBLISHERS.COM

This book is dedicated to my grandmother Yolanda Dagata, Noni, who at the time of this writing is one hundred and three years old, who wrote her first memoir in her eighties simply because I asked and, in so doing, showed me what happens when courage meets talent in a writer. She never had the benefit of a formal education, yet she was the person who first showed me the power and beauty of memoir. When I asked recently if she ever found writing hard, she shot back, "There's nothing to writing! You just tell the truth and get out of the way!" I hope we did, Noni. For you, I hope we did.

David Coogan

Contents

ACKNOWLEDGEMENTS

I owe a debt of gratitude to former director of Offender Aid and Restoration (OAR) Barbara Slayden and her staff, who encouraged me to go to the Richmond City Jail to teach the class that would become this book.

I am grateful to my students at Virginia Commonwealth University—too many to name here—who helped me type the men's handwritten drafts and, in sharing their own stories, helped me see how much common ground we all share.

I was lucky to get honest, insightful readings of earlier versions of this manuscript from people who helped me tell my own story; who told me what I needed to hear when I most needed to hear it: Wallace Adams-Riley, Jason Boone, Don Campbell, Alex Graf, Stephen Hartnett, Harrison Fletcher, Linda Flower, Terry Marquez, Chris Moore, Dave Robbins, and Tamurlaine Melby. Morgan Huff gets a warm mention, too, for creating the book's website: www.davidcoogan.com.

This project changed me in ways that would have been hard to appreciate, much less celebrate, without my wife Joan, who listened to me when I most needed to talk about it. And I did talk often.

ABOUT THIS BOOK

This is a work of creative nonfiction. It's my memoir of teaching a writing class to prisoners. And it's ten prisoners' memoirs, written with this hope in mind: that each man might understand the story of his life, and in so doing, change its course. The first eleven chapters take place at the Richmond City Jail, and correspond more or less to our first year together, between the summer of 2006 and the late spring of 2007. The next eight chapters cover the men's years in prison and their lives after prison, between 2008 and 2011.

The "our" in Writing Our Way Out refers to all of us participating in this life-affirming dialogue, teaching one another how to see life. All of us, however, have never been in the same room at the same time. Some know each other very well. Others have never met. Even at the jail where this story begins with Kelvin, Stan, Dean, Ron, Naji, and Andre, there were court dates, family visits, lockdowns, releases, transfers—all of which made a mockery of the usual expectation of beginning and ending a workshop with the same people moving through the same lessons. When my students got "shipped" to prison, as they always described it, many went on to recruit new writers. That's how Karl, Brad, Tony, and Terence joined us. And that's how I went from being a teacher with a Saturday afternoon class at the jail to a professor with pen pals in Virginia penitentiaries.

When I realized the men would not have access to computers, I offered to type up their handwritten drafts and return them "as is" alongside a lightly cleaned up version. I then invited them to discuss the two versions. Few of them commented except to thank me for typing and correcting their mistakes. Eventually, I conceded that with the constraints in our class time, the interruptions, transfers to prison, and the impossibility of office hours or back-and-forth e-mailing, I would have to sacrifice the teachable moments at the sentence-level in order to keep the project on track. I took off my teacher's hat and began just returning the lightly edited version. The more I dwelled in their drafts and listened to their voices, the more comfortable I became editing their work. Gradually, I just seemed to know when fixing the grammar would help readers comprehend the man, and when leaving it alone would help them hear his voice. I rearranged or cut some men's material more than others' as I blended our voices into this story. All gave final approval for the way their work appears here.

The stories we tell are true. This is what we remember about what transpired in our lives. We have changed some of the names to protect those persons' privacy. And one of the authors, who has been released and whose felony conviction is no longer a matter of public record, has chosen to publish his story under a pseudonym, Karl Black, to protect his career. No memoir, no matter how truthful, can change the fact that some employers still discriminate, legally, against ex-offenders.

INTRODUCTION

CREATING A CLASSROOM IN JAIL

Before I met the men whose stories you're about to encounter—before I even knew where to find the Richmond City Jail—I was volunteering with my students from Virginia Commonwealth University (VCU) at Offender Aid and Restoration (OAR). OAR is a nonprofit that provides life-skills classes and counseling to ex-offenders laboring with the stigma of a felony conviction—and often with homelessness, poverty, mental illness, substance abuse, and the kind of enduring racism that makes it hard for people coming home from prison to find a job.[1]

It was the coordinator of volunteers at OAR who suggested I start a writing workshop at the jail over the summer, follow up with the men at OAR a month or so later, and then put together their writings in a self-published booklet to raise awareness in the city about prisoner reentry.

I quickly agreed to the idea. I could see the win-win-win in it. The workshop would offer prisoners a chance to reclaim their lives in writing. It would offer OAR a chance to generate greater public support for its work. And it would offer me a chance to make a difference through my teaching and writing.[2]

Going public with these writings did not seem all that unusual to me, in spite of the sensitive nature of the material. Among scholars of rhetoric, composition, and communication, and teachers of writing and public speaking, there is a long-standing concern that intelligent public discourse—a vital component of active citizenship and a healthy democracy—has been declining since the early twentieth

---

1 See www.oarric.org for more on this nonprofit. For a more in-depth discussion of this service learning volunteer project, see David Coogan, "Moving Students into Social Movements: Prisoner Reentry and the Research Paper," in *Active Voices: Composing a Rhetoric of Social Movements*, ed. Patricia Malesh and Sharon Stevens (New York, NY: SUNY Press, 2009), 149–165.

2 For more about the discipline of rhetoric as a catalyst for social change, see John Ackerman and David Coogan, *The Public Work of Rhetoric: Citizen Scholars and Civic Engagement* (Columbia, SC: University of South Carolina Press, 2010).

century.³ In his book *The Cultural Prison*, a critical analysis of public discourse about prisoners, John Sloop has shown that the emergence of negative public discourse about prisoners (particularly minority prisoners) that frames them as unredeemable and animalistic correlates with the dramatic rise in America's prison population during the later part of the twentieth century. Our twenty-first-century culture of media spectacle only exacerbates the problem, as the media critic Bill Yousman has shown: while actual incidences of violent crime have gone down in recent years, violent crime dramas and prison dramas have effectively concentrated the public's collective fears of violent black men into a fetish.⁴

A dominant view in public discourse is never entirely dominant, though. Rhetorical theorists Gerald Hauser and Michael Warner have both shown that smaller, more organic communities—"counterpublics," Warner calls them—can arise to challenge the dominant public view by inviting participants to express themselves more freely.⁵ We know counterpublics want to influence mainstream publics. But given that prisoners have been effectively sidelined from public life by their incarceration, how are we to hear their voices—that sound of their citizen-selves becoming?

When I walked toward Redemption Chapel in the heat of July for my first class, I carried with me that hope of helping ordinary people participate in public life. I even considered the possibility that my whiteness, class privilege, and ignorance about crime and jail might be strengths if I could use them to catalyze dialogue—a process Linda Flower calls an "intercultural inquiry," in which everyone taps their diverse experiences and modes of expressing themselves to negotiate meaning about a shared social problem.⁶ Crime and the revolving door of incarceration would become our shared social problem.

Cornel West's concept of "prophetic pragmatism" is an important touchstone here. As West explains it, prophetic pragmatism authorizes "an all-embracing

---

3 John Dewey, *The Public and its Problems* (Athens, OH: Swallow Press, 1927); Jurgen Habermas, *The Structural Transformation of the Public Sphere* (Cambridge, MA: MIT Press, 1991); Craig Calhoun, *Habermas and the Public Sphere* (Cambridge, MA: MIT Press, 1993).

4 John Sloop, *The Cultural Prison: Discourse, Prisoners, and Punishment* (Tuscaloosa, AL: University of Alabama Press, 2006.); Bill Yousman, "Challenging the Media Incarceration Complex through Media Education" in *Working for Justice: A Handbook of Prison Education and Activism*, ed. Stephen Hartnett, Eleanor Novek, Jennifer Wood (Urbana, IL: University of Illinois Press, 2013), 141–159.

5 Gerard Hauser, *Vernacular Voices* (Columbia SC: University of South Carolina Press, 2008); Michael Warner, *Publics and Counterpublics* (Cambridge, MA: Zone Books, 2005).

6 Linda Flower, *Community Literacy and the Rhetoric of Public Engagement* (Carbondale, IL: Southern Illinois Press, 2008).

democratic and libertarian moral vision" of social change. It channels "moral outrage and human desperation in the face of prevailing forms of evil in [individuals and institutions]" into the zeal of conversion.[7] In layman's terms, he's arguing that *people need to be converted to the cause of their own development.* Teaching writing would be my way of inviting prisoners to join that cause. We would not dwell on craft, in other words, but on the person *becoming* with each draft. We would imagine those scenes in our lives when we became what we are today, and we would ask how and why. As the rhetorical theorist Michael McGee explains:

> The entire socialization process is nothing but intensive and continual exercises in persuasion. Individuals must be seduced into abandoning their individuality, convinced of their sociality, not only when their mothers attempt to housebreak them, but also later in life when governors ask them to obey a law or to die in war for God and country.[8]

Within the safe space of our writing workshop, we would inquire about those moments when we had abandoned our individuality and been convinced of our sociality. And we would venture a judgment or two about the ethics of the socialization process. We would write hopefully, and with the intent of steering the ongoing process of becoming who we are, not only for ourselves, but for the greater good.

Writing like this is hard enough under normal circumstances; for prisoners, writing toward a solution is made harder by the inherent instability and indifference of the system. Nevertheless, we wrote. In contrast to the romantic image of a writer writing alone, originating thought, breaking the eternal silence, we wrote together for years. I was like a skipper of a small boat, defending the hull of our idea, this workshop, from waves of delays and dead ends in the system. More than a few men whose work does not appear here wasted my time and tested my resolve, sending me drafts and letters up until the moment I asked one too many hard questions or they finally laid their real cards on the table—when a motive other than writing honorably emerged. A few broke my teacher's heart. But I kept it moving. With each letter sent back unopened, each time I was denied sending my guys a book, each unexpected transfer or other mysterious gap in communication, with each phase of the workshop, I was learning to appreciate both my insignificance and significance in the system.

The book ends with each man released from prison, freed to feel his way toward

---

7 Cornel West, *The American Evasion of Philosophy* (Madison, WI: University of Wisconsin Press, 1989), 229–232.

8 Michael McGee, "In Search of the People: A Rhetorical Alternative," *Contemporary Rhetorical Theory* (New York, NY: Guilford Press, 1998), 345.

a new life. My ending, like theirs, led to a new beginning: Open Minds, a program I founded in 2010 as a way to continue the spirit of this workshop. Open Minds enables college students from VCU and prisoners at the Richmond City Jail to take courses in the arts and humanities—to journey toward a new understanding of their shared humanity. What we pursue in this book is what we pursue today in Open Minds: that exhilarating experience of inquiry and discovery. It is "the artistry of agency," as long-time activist, scholar, and prison educator Stephen Hartnett describes it: a feeling of becoming intensely human and creative through the act of creating and connecting. It is a feeling especially treasured in jails and prisons, where anything can be taken from you at any time. Or you can lose your grip. Even in freedom, you can lose your grip.

PROLOGUE

OVERLOOK

"Dave, what do I always try to tell you?"

I say nothing, the cellphone pressed to my ear as I wait for Kelvin to lead me to the answer. From somewhere deep within, he sighs.

I'm walking fast, bearing down in my thoughts as I approach the picnic tables in the part of Libby Hill Park that overlooks the James River. It was here, in the summer of 2004, that four teenage boys raped a young woman, beat her boyfriend, robbed them both, and fled. It was here—the day after a crime I had not seen—that I first envisioned criminals, the kind of people I had never known, becoming writers, taking control of their stories, and plotting their futures away from crime.

And it's here that Kelvin tries explaining crime to me now.

"Guys like us always take the easy way out."

"But after you've written to understand why that doesn't work, why would you go *on* taking the easy way out?"

"I know you don't want to hear this, Dave, but there *is* no *why*. No answering that." The cell signal chokes in and out along with my memories of Andre writing his memoir at the jail and in prison and then coming to see me in my office at Virginia Commonwealth University years later, after prison—his memoir complete along with Kelvin's and the others. I stare into the fog, past the streetlights and stars.

"He could have been high right then," Kelvin offers.

"But he wrote against that," I protest. "He'd been down that path before, more than once. It's in his story!"

"He could have needed money for something else, a woman maybe."

"But he had a job!"

"It could have been he had no one to talk with about whatever he was going through." I walk down the hill toward the parking lot of the Fas Mart. There, for the second time in four years, I imagine a crime I did not see: Andre pushing his way out of the store with his carton of Newports and a few hundred dollars, the police across the street watching the whole thing before chasing him and his driver around the sudden turns and horrendous dips of the road until the truck hit something hard enough to bring it to a sudden stop.

"I know I get depressed like that sometimes. No one to talk to," I hear Kelvin concluding. People are pumping gas at the Fas Mart, lost in their routines. I listen to the traffic and finally let go. I have to let go of what I can't know.

"Hey, Kelvin?"

"Yeah, Doc!" He brightens.

"Do you remember when I asked you in the jail to pinpoint the moment when you *chose* to go down this path in life? And after a long while, you finally said I was the first person who'd ever asked you that?"

"Shit, Dave. Now you're the *second* person who's ever asked me that. I keep telling you! You're the only one asking questions like that."

1

A World You Used to Live In

Between the sliding steel door and the first set of bars, Shakelia hands me the roster. She doesn't wait for me to read it.

"Look at this," she says, passing me a paperback. An image of a caramel-complexioned woman fills the cover—her expression the keeper of some dark secret, her tight V-neck exposing all secrets.

"Where'd you get it?"

"From Andre. You'll meet him. He says he knows the author. He wants me to contact her about publishing." A buzz triggers a click that releases the lock. She pulls the door wide.

"Are you going to do it?"

"Nah! I told him, 'You already signed up for Dr. Coogan's class—what do you think you're going to learn in there?'" Shakelia must have mentioned my idea of self-publishing a book about the transition from incarceration to reentry for Offender Aid and Restoration (OAR), the nonprofit that got me to this point, walking the halls of the Richmond City Jail with Shakelia.

"Do you think he understands I'm not here to teach him how to publish urban lit?"

"They'll get it once you describe it," she consoles me. "I told them it's a positive program." She clanks through a ring of skeleton keys. A small line of men passes. For a second, I think they might be my students. I don't know what to expect: what they'll look like, their charges, ages, criminal histories, levels of schooling, or personal stories. Shakelia offered this kind of information up previously, but I declined it. I didn't want to know anything that would color my perceptions or enable me to start shaping their stories for them.

"Take it down, gentlemen!" the deputy striding alongside the line commands. A few men at the end have started clumping, sharing. One man spins to face me and cups a hand to his mouth.

"E.T.! Phone home!" His grin, already wide, grows wider as he falls out with his buddy. Baffled by the joke, sheepish about somehow crossing a line, violating some unspoken norm in the first ten minutes of my first-ever visit to a jail, I study the linoleum. I want to resist this casting of me as the alien—scared, hungry, wide-eyed, and lost. I don't feel lost at all.

Shakelia connects with the key, but as soon as the door opens, I hear her sigh. The deputies have not stowed the men in the jail chapel like she asked them to an hour ago. She rolls her eyes, egging me to roll along. Faintly I do, as I fumble through her ideal scenario of strangers locked up, waiting on me.

"I'll be right back," she says. "Just take a seat in here." I follow her into the cinder-block chapel. The walls are painted sky blue. The altar is piled high with Bibles. I glance at the roster.

"Wait, where's the poster?" I ask before she can slip away. I can't find the write-up I e-mailed her that described myself and the goals of the class, a chunky paragraph I had agonized over for the better part of a morning.

"Didn't I give it to you?" She moves closer and shuffles my pages. "Yeah! There it is." I see my name, the day and time, the class location, and the words "creative writing." I can't understand why my paragraph on the virtues of writing memoir and the challenges of changing your life has been streamlined into this Rorschach test of a phrase, but I just shrug. Maybe "creative writing" isn't so far off from what we'll be doing. If our lives are like stories—ourselves the main characters, our actions the plot—won't these men want to write a new chapter? Develop their character? Redirect their plots?

To distract myself as I wait for Shakelia, I start reading the paperback. Instantly, I'm pulled into an orbit of clothes and guns and drugs and clubs and cars, and sex on drugs in clubs and in cars. Forty minutes later, Shakelia returns with a half-dozen men in jumpsuits, socks, and sandals. I close the book without marking my place and rise.

The men fan out slowly, a color wheel of tan and brown and black, closer to middle age than college age. For the first time in my career, I will be teaching men and only men—men who are mostly my age, or so it seems—and our subject, more or less, is how we became men.

I don't know them yet; but I soon will, and in my mind's eye, looking back, they're more distinct than strangers ever could be: Naji, Larry, Kelvin, Stan, Ronald, Andre, Anton. In this moment, I can't know which of these men will last the course, or what will become of them and their stories. I can only watch as they size up the situation.

Naji slips past me with a brief nod. He walks without seeming to move his upper body, strangely conserving energy. Larry accepts the handout from Shakelia and sits somewhere in the middle of the chapel, studying the thing ferociously. Kelvin sits down in the last row, leans against the cinder-block wall, and exhales. Stan takes the handout in his left hand, then reaches over to shake my right hand like he's receiving a diploma.

"Thanks for coming!" Stan says.

Ronald smiles and doesn't seem capable of stopping. He's slim and shorter than me, about five feet.

"Smurf!" someone shouts over to Ronald.

"Yo, Smurf!" Stan echoes. Ronald does nothing to prevent them from likening him to the old cartoon character.

"I see you got the book from Ms. Shakelia," Andre says, grinning. He points to the paperback I'm still holding. "You know, Dr. Coogan, my story's a drama just like that book, and I can tell it. You watch!" I try handing the book back to him, but notice Larry's eyes following the woman on the cover and his hands reaching to intercept her.

"I'ma check out this joint," he tells Andre. "Get it back to you." Shakelia shakes her head as the two of them conspire.

"Good," I say. "And when you finish it, could one of you show me the parts where the characters reflect on their lifestyles?" Their grins thin to wait-and-see stares. "I mean, I only read a few chapters while I was waiting, but mostly what I got was the lifestyle." Shakelia chuckles, then excuses herself. She promises she'll be right back.

"Just leave the door open," she suggests. "There'll be guards going by all the time."

I consider my students. Larry, who is blocking my view of his lap with his arm, is either reading the handout or staring at the woman on the paperback. Kelvin, eyes closed, is either listening with Zen-like discipline or napping. Anton is tittering quietly but uncontrollably into Andre's ear.

"All right, everyone have the handout?" I begin, as if I am standing before any other group of students I've known, and this is any other classroom, and my handout is any other syllabus, and this is any other course with grades and credits. When I start reading from the handout, Kelvin opens his eyes, strokes his cornrows, and stares.

Writing and Rehabilitation
Dr. David Coogan
Department of English
Virginia Commonwealth University

The purpose of this project is to help you write your way into a new life without crime: to honestly address where you've come from and where you're going through the art of memoir. I believe your life is unique, even though you share a lot in common with other people who have also gotten into crime and been locked up. Your challenge here, should you choose to accept it, is to make sense of your experience, to pick and choose what readers will see, to teach readers how to see your struggle to change.

I will work with each one of you individually to shape your story and will encourage you to work with each other. Because writing a memoir is hard work and not at all a confession or Statement of the Truth, we'll have to work hard to make sure that your words convey meaning; that the people you write about, including yourself, become believable characters; that your scenes are vivid and engrossing; that your message comes through, primarily through the action and dialogue and description; that the plot keeps us moving, wanting to learn; that we are learning not only about your life but about Life; that you are reflecting enough to make sure that we readers get insights from your story at each and every turn.

The following four categories are the basic areas for you to address in your memoir. Together they'll make up your "narrative arc"—that slow-curving line that takes us from somewhere to somewhere else. You can hit these points in any order while you're drafting. Each category has a lot of questions, but feel free to run with the ones you like best and ignore the others.

The Past

- Describe the people from your childhood who really made a difference in your life, who really affected you somehow.
- What do you remember most about your neighborhood, your home, your room?
- What did you do with your friends?
- What about school—what was that like?
- What were your dreams for yourself at this time?
- What were your parents' dreams for you?

The Problem

- When did you start to get in trouble?
- What sort of trouble was it?
- Did you think of it as trouble then?
- In your mind, how did you THINK about what you were doing?
- At some point, did you want to stop but couldn't?
- Describe some of the people you knew during this time and how they fit into your world.
- What was this world you had created for yourself? Define it. Describe it. What were the rules there? How did that world make you feel?
- What links this world to the childhood place you came from?

The Punishment

+ What are the facts of your crime or crimes?
+ How did you get caught?
+ What happened to you after you got caught?
+ What happened to you emotionally?
+ Did you do anything wrong?
+ Have you learned anything from the experience of being punished?

The Possibilities

+ What sort of things do you struggle with now?
+ If you are trying to change, how are you *really* changing? From what to what?
+ Describe something from your life that gives you hope that things COULD be different.
+ What's your ambition for the future and how do you think you'll get there?
+ What's your vision of yourself in relation to other people?
+ What do you think you can offer others, and what would you like in return?

I explain that we will spend six weeks writing in the chapel, and six more after they're released writing at OAR's office downtown. Everyone is invited, but not required, to publish his story, as a fund-raiser for OAR and as a much-needed infusion of understanding and empathy into public discourse about the challenges facing ex-offenders. I share that I have recently been through the process with another nonprofit, the East End Teen Center. Middle-school kids in my writing workshop wrote stories of their struggles to make it out of the negativity of their inner-city communities and into positive lifestyles and careers. Their work was self-published as a book and later featured in the *Richmond Times-Dispatch*. It was very warmly received. That whole experience gave me hope that workshops emerging from the ground up could, with publication, rise like beanstalks into the hard-to-reach public spheres of empathy, insight, and inclusiveness that were typically obscured by all of the rants, ignorance, and stale air below.

"I want this class to help you. And if it's at all possible, I want our work to help people understand what you've been through and how you're trying to change. We're writing for people who want to believe in second chances."

I pause for questions. The men's bodies are solid, still, with only a few mouths and eyes opening like windows. Some light and air is getting through. "I can promise you this," I conclude. "You'll get as much out of the process as you give. And you can stop whenever you want. No hard feelings."

"What's the *quid pro quo?*" Stan asks. With his reading glasses halfway down his nose and his hair neat and trim, Stan looks more like a businessman ready to close a deal than a prisoner stuck in a cinder-block chapel. "I mean, that's what OAR would get out of it—the little book. I can see how that would help them. And I can see how writing about our lives would help us—or me. I'll speak just for myself. It'd help me. But what about you?" He throws a leg up on the pew. I'm not sure what he's asking, really, but figure I must have explained the project too quickly. I shift back to drive my story again.

When I was volunteering at OAR downtown with my students, we were supposed to be helping them create a calendar to be used as a fund-raiser: "The Faces of Reentry," a project that folded after a few semesters because we had trouble enlisting ex-offenders to help us tell stories of reentry on a consistent basis. Once they got a piece of their lives in their hands and could carry it safely out the door without breaking it—the job, bus ticket, or free class—they were no longer interested in OAR or us. I could understand that, but I couldn't admit defeat. I was in deep—frustrated at not being able to finish. Seeing my frustration, the volunteer coordinator suggested I take the project to the jail. Start there and follow the transition to freedom.

"I want to get it right this time," I conclude. Stan raises a hand to stop me.

"No, man, *personally*. What's in it for you *personally?*"

I stare into the headlights. How could I explain that I wanted to enter more deeply, more personally, than I had before into an inquiry about writing and social change? How could I explain that this desire of mine was not entirely mine, even, but was a principle I'd been studying in my discipline, rhetoric and composition?

"Are you a family man, Dave?" Stan asks. I nod. He cracks a joint in his neck. "So right there, personally. Why leave your family on a beautiful Saturday afternoon to spend time with us?" I put my notes down on the altar and take a few steps in.

"Do you remember the gang rape in Libby Hill Park last summer?" I ask.

"Was that the one with the four young dudes?" Larry asks, making eye contact for the first time.

"They were teenagers, man." Kelvin shakes his head, disgusted. "They beat the boyfriend with a gun and made him sit there with his head down on the picnic table. Then they robbed 'em both. White couple."

"Shiiit," Larry sneers.

I interject, "Well, I live by that park. My daughter plays in that park. And I'd never—"

"Whoa," Anton interrupts with one hand up, seeming to tune in suddenly. "They did that shit in *Libby?*"

I nod and wait as they register the geography of my gentrified, inner-city neighborhood, connecting the name with the place: a scenic spot overlooking the

James River and downtown Richmond, lined by well-renovated old brick homes. Until that incident in the park, I had never really thought much about crime. I hadn't had any experience with it. To me, criminals were like oncoming traffic late at night: blurry shapes with glaring eyes, barreling somewhere. I didn't know where. I didn't wonder where. I just stayed in my lane and assumed they'd stay in theirs. But something had crossed the yellow line that night. And something else was compelling me to do more than swerve out of the way.

"Now, you're looking at a guy who grew up in an upper-middle-class, white suburb in Connecticut. In *Connecticut!*" I repeat, spreading my arms wide.

"Go on, now!" Stan cheers. Kelvin smiles with a lot of teeth.

"The only crime I saw growing up was on the TV news coming from New York City, OK? So this is my first time *living* right near a crime scene. I'm shocked like everyone else, but I'm a writing teacher and a scholar of rhetoric, and that part of me is more annoyed than anything." With their eyes they ask why, and I recount the way the newspaper characterized one of the rapists as someone who read at a third-grade level and the other as someone with a learning disability, and all of them kids who had either been suspended from school, or just stopped going and drifted down from their public housing community into the park.

"And what they're really saying is 'ignorant black teens from the projects rape white woman in safe part of city.' I can read between the lines."

"You're an *English* professor," Stan says in a fussy accent.

"You know what really surprised me about the whole thing, though?" I continue. "It wasn't so much the code words about race and class, but what the victim said when they interviewed her. It was amazing!" I look out the barred window toward the yard. "She asked the best question."

"What?" Kelvin says.

"It was 'Why would they ruin their lives?'"

"Yeah, 'cause you know they goin' give 'em some *time*," Larry blurts.

"They did. Tried them as adults," I explain before skidding sideways unexpectedly into a speech. "Like a long prison term is going to stop more rapes from happening! Like there aren't more rapes going on that don't get reported because they don't happen in gentrified parts of the city!"

"I know *that's* right," Andre mumbles.

"Crime affects all of us," I assert. "But I don't know that jail and prison is solving the crime problem." I look at them looking at me. "Has it solved yours?"

"Hold up," Andre says. "That's some nasty shit, Dr. Coogan!" He shakes his head. "If I lived around there, I'd be angry." Somebody murmurs agreement.

"But then what? What comes after the anger? We punish people and nothing really changes. The crime is thoughtless. The punishment is thoughtless. Society becomes thoughtless." Around the room I see heads nodding, the harder stares softening. "Is this answering your question, Stan?" I don't let him answer. "I mean, if the *victim* could ask why, shouldn't the rest of us? Why don't we do that?"

"Because it's *rape*, Dr. Coogan," Anton says, spitting the sour taste of the word across the room.

"Rapists are the worst," Larry agrees. A small wave of hatred for rapists begins moving down the aisle. I watch it bounce from man to man. Then Stan rises slowly and stands next to me by the altar. Instinctively, I step aside.

"Those boys in Libby?" he starts, pausing to collect everyone into his baritone. "We *are* those boys!" Larry shoots a quick glance up without moving his head. Naji's eyes grow wide in amazement. I sit down in the front pew.

"We may not have raped," Stan continues. "People get too focused on that. 'Hey, I don't *do* that.' But if we stole, we violated someone's property. If we sold drugs, we violated someone's health. Look! You know what it is?" he starts preaching, his voice stretching higher and tighter into a rasp. "Everyone laughs when a new man come through quartermaster here. 'Oh, shit, he tore up! Man, look at him, all dehydrated. Can't walk straight!' Whatever. We forget. *We* were those guys." He points to them one by one. "*You* were that guy. *You* were but three months ago. You *healed* now, but you were tore up just like him! *I* was that guy. We *all* were. You just forgot!" He stares down the room, daring anyone to contradict him or say much of anything. Nobody moves. I slide out of the pew and join Stan by the altar. I am impressed, inspired. He has accomplished more in that short speech than I've sputtered over the last twenty minutes. And I remain ignorant.

"What does the quartermaster do?"

"You know, receiving. Takes your property. Processes you." Stan returns to his front-row pew, off to the side, where he can watch everyone.

"All right," I pick up, "let me try something, then. The heart of what I'm proposing is that you write about your past, the problems you ran into, the punishments you received, and the possibilities you see without any more crime or jail. I'm assuming, of course, that you don't want to come back here." Ron closes his eyes as if lost in prayer. Kelvin is nodding his long, serpentine head. I continue, "You're going to write, share what you've written, and write some more. You'll reflect back honestly what you heard. I'll guide everyone in the process. I'll keep us focused. That's my role. And really, that's it. I can't tell you what to write, just like I can't tell you what to do. Ultimately, you've got to make your own choices." I catch Andre's eye as he looks up, nodding. "Everyone's got emotional property. In this class, you're going to be each other's quartermasters. You're going to process each others' lives."

"That's clever, Dave!" Stan says. I turn to see him smiling. Then I gauge the room. Naji, who's been using the pew as a desk, stops writing and rests his pen on his paper. He looks like a cat about to leap.

"Did you start already?" I ask.

"I was just thinking that this will be published, right? And I was listening to what you said about why the city needs a book like this. So I started writing what we're doing as a group, you know, like what you'd see on the back of the book."

"A synopsis. Good! Let's hear it."

Naji stands to face everyone, clears his throat, and checks to make sure all eyes are on him before reading. "These men pour their hearts out. They allow you to enter the most intimate and painful moments of their lives in the hopes of shedding a new light on the causes of crime."

"I like that!" Stan interjects.

"I got more," Naji says quietly. I signal for him to continue with a small nod. Stan waves him through like a traffic cop. Naji finds his place in the text with his finger, then begins. "But the reader is cautioned not to interpret the stories as selfish pleas for pity by individuals seeking to blame their circumstances for their own bad decisions. The opposite is true. Some of these men have served or are still serving hard time for crimes that they have committed. They have accepted responsibility for their actions and are now sharing their stories, seeking answers, solutions, and a means to curb the cycle of dysfunction not only in their lives, but in their communities and ideally in society at large. Their concern is for the millions of children who are trapped in the very same circumstances in which they found themselves, and who are about to take their first steps down the dark roads of incarceration and recidivism. Their concern is for the indifference to this tragedy." He folds the paper and sits.

I'm stunned. "That's incredible, Naji! You really captured the essence of it!" He allows a little smile, his first of the afternoon. I press on: "You've got some skill. You know that, right?" To my surprise, he blushes.

"I've never really written before." That can't be possible.

"Dr. Coogan?" Kelvin asks. "So if that there what Naji just wrote is what we'd be doing in the book, what about you?" He points his chin at me, narrowing his eyes.

"We're the stew," Ronald says, turning toward him. "Dave's just stirring the pot." He looks back at me, smiling.

"OK," Kelvin says, "but you know, the best chefs on them shows always tell you what it is they're doing up there in the kitchen."

"How they *season* it!" Stan booms from the center of his chest. "But check it out: That's not how those shows start." He clears a space in the air with his hands. "It starts with nothing on the counter. He's got to take out all the ingredients. We got to see what we're making first."

"Which is what we're going to do now," I interject. "You're going to make something with these pads and pens." Andre presses the pen to the page and puts the cap in his mouth. He looks up like I'm about to signal the start of a race.

"Tell me about a world you used to live in."

15

Immediately, Andre starts writing. For the first time, I notice the noise in the hall and want to close the door.

"Did you make this world, or did it make you?"

Stan gazes through the barred window just past my head.

"Are you still living there? Or have you moved on?"

Larry starts writing, using a Bible as a flat surface.

"Tell me about some of the people in that world."

Naji grins, hatching something.

"And don't worry about which world you choose. You'll eventually write about more than one."

Ronald leans forward and to the left, spreading his chest across the pew, his face close to the page like a child drawing.

"Doc!" Kelvin scrunches his nose. He lifts his paper with one hand and points to it with the other as if it were defective somehow. "I don't know what to p-p-put down right now." I lean in to hear. Larry turns around to listen.

"Yeah, I've got a stutter," Kelvin says to the room. "Most guys in here know about it. It's when I can't get air up from my lungs in time. I can hear what I want to say but have to wait. Worse when I read aloud or when I'm pressured and c-c-conversation going too quick."

By now Anton and Ron are looking back, too. I'm willing the room to slow down with him, to hear each word more intently, the texture of this thinking. He notices the guys watching. "Look, man, if y'all got a Snickers or something, you might want to get it now, 'cause this g-g-gonna take awhile." They laugh and turn back to their writing.

"Maybe you could start with the world you knew as a kid," I suggest. His lips part in slow motion. "The world your mother showed you?" His eyes widen.

"See, right there!" He beams. "That's what I mean 'bout them TV chefs focusing your mind on what it is they're doing up there in the kitchen. Right there, what you just said!"

KELVIN

In 1977, I was living in a set of grey, brick apartments between houses that had no name. As a child, I didn't need anything, so the fact that my father wasn't around didn't really matter. My mother, she used to boost, and for those that don't know, that's stealing clothes and any other items she felt were worth it. I had all the clothes I cared about back then. There was no such thing as name-brand clothes for kids. But if there was, my Moms would have gotten them for her boys.

Around the street from our apartment there was a small store where a kid could get a bottle of soda, a couple of lemon cookies from the jar, or a big handful of penny candy for just twenty-five cents. But if I got caught crossing the street to go to that store, I risked getting my ass whipped.

To walk that block and a half to Idlewood Avenue and see the hustle and bustle of the people up there was like entering a whole new world to me. I never knew then what guys were doing dropping money on the ground, rolling dice, snapping their fingers. I marveled at the big Cadillacs and Lincoln Continentals and fur coats, but I never said to myself, "Yeah, I gots to live like that and have those things."

It wasn't until a couple of years later, when I was introduced to life on Second Street, that I started to get ideas. Second Street was where the pimps, prostitutes, hustlers, and users hung out. There was also a lot of bars and restaurants where you could hang out and listen to the jukebox. I used to be amazed at how the small box on the table could control the big box in the middle of the room. My mom used to take us with her, and the reason for this was there was no such thing as a babysitter. I clearly remember being watched by everyone from dope fiends to prostitutes while sitting there, waiting for my mom to come back from boosting.

I never looked up to anyone back then because my mom never raised me to look up to anyone but God. I was told quite a few things by Moms, and one of those things was to follow my own path and not the things I seen in hers. Moms was very well respected amongst everyone I'd ever seen come in her presence. This was very different for a woman back then. And after seeing her fight and split heads, I understood why.

I remember one night my Mom had us stoop beside a bush for a long time while she waited to bust this guy up the side of the head with a baseball bat. That's when I learned to handle my problems discreetly.

You see, being raised by Brenda—BAMBS, as we would call her later on—was different from your normal situation, right down to our meals. "Come and get it!" was the way my neighbor used to call to his pit bulls when it was time to come eat. This was also the way some dudes' moms would call them to come get their lunch or dinner. But not me. Not my Moms. My favorite girl didn't do much notifying, or should I say warning, as to when it was time to go eat. Don't get me wrong. She cooked. No, let me rephrase that. BAMBS could BURN! For those of you that don't know, that means she could cook her ass off!

My grandmother has never been no more than a boiler, and I preferred perfectly fried chicken over boiled any day. Now for some odd reason my Moms hated baking cakes and pies, but Ma-stine—that's Grams—oh, she was a wizard with the oven. See how my two favorite girls worked things out for the betterment of me? All this started me on my pattern of being spoiled, real choosy. You see, I was—and still am—very picky about what I put into my mouth and body. If it didn't look, smell, or especially taste like my Moms', I wouldn't eat it. So when it was about that time that we knew to be back for lunch, we were there. I'm not going to lie: lunch wasn't a given; there were no guarantees about nothing. Grams would be at work and Moms wasn't guaranteed to be there. But when she was, MMM-mmm, good! Now I'm almost to my point: I'm talking about what was good to my taste and what wasn't. I'm also speaking on having and not having.

I first smoked puff when I was very young in the West End. I would take the roaches out of the ashtray that my Moms or uncle or their friends would leave. No roaches were bigger than the ones these people would leave during Moms' socials. Remember, this was the '70s. Drugs were everywhere and accepted. I would sneak out of my room like a ninja, just past your eyesight in a puff of smoke. The added bonus was the half-empty—or half-full if you're an optimist—glass of wine or beer. The wine was always Thunderbird, or maybe Night Train. I wasn't much of a beer lover, at least not at a young age. When I got older, as I was introduced to the real world, I could get beer real easy. By the time I was eleven, I consciously started smoking weed and never looked back. I don't even know if I felt anything when I was that young, but once that sticky green became a permanent part of my life, there was no doubt how it made me feel. My world may have made me, but being the kind of person I am, I quickly shaped it to what I "thought" I wanted it to be.

* * *

I've got on baggy burgundy pants, suspenders, a white shirt, white gloves, and all-white Jack Purcell sneakers. I glide forward, flat-footed, then come up on the tips of my toes. I wave my body all the way down to my legs and lay down on my back, inching my way forward like a worm. When I'm done, but before I go back in line, I turn around and scan the crowd for my one-person fan club, Moms, who, by the way, has been hollering, "That's my baby!" the whole time.

This is the first time people in Richmond have seen anything like this, and the crowd is silent at Henderson Middle School—all except for my favorite girl! This new move that's so special to everyone else is nothing to her. I'm already special. After the show, I'm hanging out in my new, reversible, full-length goose-feather coat. I'm the man, at least for a little while. That whole week, all of the girls that heard about the show were on my jock, but none of them were there for me like my mom.

Stan

My story starts in Egypt, before my birth, with a child named Moses, whose mother placed him in a papyrus basket and, ever so gently, sent that beautiful boy down the Nile River of adoption. Little Moses was one of the first adoptions known to Man, drawn from the Nile by Pharaoh's daughter.

Like Moses, I was drawn from the current by a woman who had to learn how to love me. We were complete strangers. Her eyes were not like mine. Mine were not like hers. Love did not come naturally. It never does when two people just meet.

Why did I feel lost looking into this woman's eyes? The one who sent me down the Nile, I was close to her. For nine months I lay listening and feeling in her womb. Some days she laughed, and I not only heard it, I felt the vibration. I was happy because she was happy.

Hey, Dad! Remember when she said put your hands on her stomach to feel me kicking? Well, I was listening. That's why I kicked, because she told me to. She loved me, and I kicked harder and harder.

I remember the night I heard another voice. It was deep, and I trembled every time I heard it. I didn't like it, because it made my mother cry. Her heart would beat faster and so would mine.

People say he's an infant. He doesn't understand. But they're wrong. I realized the difference between my mother and this woman who drew me from the Nile. I remember all that I'm not supposed to remember.

"Take it down! Let's go!" the voice blares outside the chapel door. I check the faces of the writers.

"Yeah, Dave, we've got to go or we'll miss chow," Ron says. As they make moves to pack up and head for the door, I ask them to turn in their drafts, explaining that I'll type them up and return them the next week with some comments. Seeing all of their writings on my screen, I go on to explain, will also give me a better sense of how they'll complement each other in the book. The closer we get to actually making the book, the more we can focus on editing. Readily, all but a few men hold up their papers for me to collect. I move down the aisle toward Kelvin, who's been sitting quietly since he finished reading his piece to the class. He looks up.

"I realize I'm not supposed to ask a black guy about his mama . . ." I begin.

"Nah!" He runs a hand over his cornrows, grinning.

"I mean unless I want get my ass kicked, right?"

"Go 'head. Just say it."

"I'm trying to understand why you let her off the hook like that."

"Whatcha mean?" He wrinkles his forehead.

"She told you to do as I say, not as I do. Then she went on boosting and leaving the weed around the house. How did she expect you to ignore that? That's a hard contradiction for a kid."

"It ain't like that," he says in a quiet voice.

"There's a lot of love in what you wrote," I concede.

"That's why I call her my favorite girl." He spreads his memories over him like a blanket, sighs.

"But don't you think her advice to basically ignore her example was kind of impossible?" I ask. He raises his eyebrows and points over my shoulder.

I turn around to see Ronald standing right next to me. Again, he's smiling, pleased to have the right answer: "It may be broken love, but it's still love." Kelvin nods his approval, savoring something only they can taste.

"You know what you should do?" Andre asks. Like everyone else, he's standing now. "You should check out this Tupac joint 'bout his mama! I think it's called 'You Are Appreciated.'"

"'Dear Mama.' It's called 'Dear Mama,'" Larry corrects. Immediately, Ronald starts tapping the beat on the back of the pew. Anton starts mouthing the words to the chorus.

"Oh, aiight," Andre concedes. "'Dear Mama.' Listen to that, Dr. Coogan. It'll tell you why guys like us will say we love our mamas."

"Despite the dysfunctional homes they raised us in!" Kelvin tacks on. Ronald stops the beat. Andre looks like someone about to lose his place in line.

"Somebody had to say it," Kelvin adds and stands up. I step back to give him room to get out of the pew and into the aisle. My head comes up to about his rib cage. "Aiight, Doc," he says, extending a hand. We shake and he turns to go. Soon the others follow him out the door, each shaking my hand as he leaves.

"Listen, man," Stan says after everyone else has left. "You're asking us to write about our lives, who we've been and who we want to be. Right?"

"That's the idea."

We move to the hall. The guards shout in our general direction to keep it moving. Slowly, Stan shuffles, giving the appearance of walking. I mimic the stride but have a hard time not gaining speed.

"Well what if we don't know?" he asks, pulling my arm and tugging me back into the shuffle-pace. "I've never really known who Stanley Craddock is." We stop and face each other. His eyes are two brown marbles.

"OK, I was adopted, right? That's in my story." I nod. "So I don't know my birth mother. I don't even know my real name. I don't *have* an identity!"

I don't know how to address someone without an identity. I look down the hall, then at the wall—anywhere but at Stan. We resume the shuffle and eventually reach the second set of bars leading to the tiers. I can't go any farther.

Stan seems unfazed that I have no answer for him. "Hey man, this is a great class, a great project! I'ma *stick* with this! Just come here consistent. Don't let up!" He slaps me heartily on the back. When I stumble from the force of it, he reaches to catch me. "Whoa! You're just a little guy, aren't you?" He chuckles under his breath.

I nod, hunch my shoulders, and promise I'll see him next week. He leaves for his tier, shouting good-byes as he goes, and I move toward the lobby, their drafts in my bag, feeling like a Sherpa with other guys' mothers on my back. At the other end of the hall I see Shakelia looking into the chapel, annoyed again that no one's inside.

2

What Really Happened

The next week I go through the metal detector, get my visitor's badge, take the roster past the sliding steel door, hand it to the deputy at the second set of bars, escort myself to Redemption Chapel, and wait for the deputy to return with the men. Shakelia had offered to meet me in the lobby again to help me do all this, but I saw no reason to make her come to work on a Saturday. She's already walked me through the process once. And she's still involved: in fact, she's added a few names to the roster, assuring me over the phone that the new guys—Dean and George, who goes by "G"—have been given the prompts and asked to start writing.

I pass ten minutes leaning against the wall, my eyes tracing the pattern in the linoleum, before the deputy arrives to unlock the door. In the chapel, I take the drum stool from behind the kit, place it in front of the altar, and sit. Twenty minutes later, the men begin to arrive. Andre and Anton are the first in.

"How's it going?" I ask, rising to shake their hands.

"I had court last week," Andre reports in a flat voice. I open my bag and poke through my papers. "They say I was the driver in a whole bunch of armed robberies." I freeze. "But I was sitting in the *back* of the car," he corrects. "And the only reason I was in the car was to get a ride home. I really had no idea that car'd been in all them robberies. You know they chased us over the Manchester Bridge and we crashed?"

"Actually, no. I don't know anything about anyone's cases."

"I told you!" Anton says to Andre.

"Oh, OK. Well they chased us. And I mean *chased*. We were flying 'cross that bridge, Dr. Coogan. Then the guy next to me throws a gun out the window. When we crashed, all the people in the car flee. And I don't know nothing, so I just put my hands up, say my name, and that I don't know nothing. That's when they came at me and beat me down." He pauses to gauge my reaction. I stare, unblinking. "At the station, they beat me again and I passed out." He rolls up his pant leg, stops talking, and I realize he's calling me over to inspect. I lean in for a look at the lacerations. They look fresh. "They took my clothes and did an illegal cavity search when I was passed out. I woke up bleeding but they wouldn't let me see a doctor."

I am repulsed now and show it. But since I don't really know how he got these lacerations or how he got arrested, beyond what he's told me, I'm also a little reserved. Do I need to know what really happened in order to be his writing teacher?

"Can you write it?" I ask, watching him carefully and keeping my mission in my mind's eye. As he gets to work, I feel a clarifying breeze come between us—the familiar charge of the writing teacher to know the boundary between the person and the page.

Stan, Kelvin, and the others from last week walk in, followed by the new guys. Dean walks down the center aisle, bumping fists with everyone who'll let him and smiling his way to a seat by the window-mounted air conditioner. He leans against the wall, puts his feet up, and drapes one arm leisurely over the back of the pew. I walk over to shake his hand and ask if he has any questions about the class.

"None so far," he says, then adds, "I've actually already done some writing." I'm pleased to hear this, and begin making a mental note to tell Shakelia. Then I scratch that as he goes on to tell me about the whole book he's written, the first in a two-volume autobiography titled *A Major Struggle*. He asks if I'd take a look at it and maybe help him get it published. Curious to see what he's able to do as a writer, I tell him I'll read it and treat it as a starting point in our work here. He agrees and tells me his mother can send it to me if I give him my e-mail address. I give him my business card. Stan, who's been observing us this whole time, asks for one, too.

G lumbers up to me, a little bored, shakes my hand, then turns back to take the center left pew. He's got the girth and height of a bouncer—broad shoulders, heavy arms, and a disarming baby-face. I begin handing back drafts.

"Was it hard writing like this?" I ask them as I make way my back to the front of the room. I want to know how they're feeling about this mental stretching we're doing in sentences. With great care, I step around G's leg. It's taking up half the aisle.

"I know for me," Stan jumps in. "'Cause I go real slow, right? I mean, it may take me an *hour* just to get one little half page, you know? There are some words I can't even spell!" I grin and shake my head. "I'm telling you, Dave!" Stan persists. "I'll be *staring* at the page wondering what the hell word I wrote! You know?" He leans back against the cinder block and lowers his voice to a hoarse whisper. "So when you go to polish mines up for the book, you're going to need an extra clean rag!" He seals it with a grin.

"And more polish," Ron adds, bouncing a bit in his seat.

"You all right, Smurf!" Stan allows.

"But it's more than just the spelling that's hard, right? What's the hardest part?" I ask.

"Telling our stories," Ron says right away.

"Telling the truth," Kelvin adds. Except Andre and Anton, I notice no one sits next to anyone else. Each man has made a territory out of his place in the chapel.

"Right. But you know this class is not about telling the whole truth—every single thing that's ever happened. It's about crafting a *plausible* truth. You're writing the *story* of how you got here."

"I know how I got here," Andre mumbles. "Got the scars from the po-po to prove it."

"Not here in this jail," I add quickly. "Here in this life. Your story is bigger than any one crime or alleged crime." A little lull settles in as they consider the proposition.

"Excuse me, Dr. Coogan," Kelvin says quietly from under his cornrows. "Whatcha mean, not telling the truth? I mean, speaking just for me here, the reason I came to this class was to get *at* the truth, how I-I-I got stuck in this revolving door of incarceration."

"But you can't *not* have a point of view, right? The facts don't speak for themselves. Do they?" I raise my eyebrows.

"Oh, I see where you goin.'" He nods and starts marking up the handout.

"And to figure out your own point of view, you have to spend time with yourself. You have to care enough about yourself to *challenge* yourself. And that can be confusing, because it's not always clear what you're challenging yourself to do. But when you figure that out—"

"I love writing!" Naji interrupts. "It's like you're the star, the director, and the producer of your own movie! You're controlling everything from who says what to how the scene looks to what it all means. Honestly, I never thought I'd love it so much." He lowers his voice. "I even love it, you know, when it's hard. Because what I wrote about—my mother passing and all—you know that was a hard time for me. Recreating that made me relive it all over again." He softens as the memory of what he wrote comes into focus.

"With mines," Ronald begins, matching Naji's tone, "I was writing to figure out how my mom and Debbie and the rest of the family figured out their plan for me, what they were going to do with this baby. I never really thought about that. I was piecing together stuff my mom told me with stuff I remember feeling, and then I had to see if I liked the way I was telling it. I had to ask if that was me." He trails off.

"Yes!" I say. "Writing takes you away from yourself." I push the air to one side with my hand. "Then it forces you back into yourself. Arguably, it raises the *question* of self."

I touch my heart. Though I'm looking right at Ronald, strangely, he raises his hand, leg bouncing.

"Yes, Ronald?"

"I just wanted to know if I can read."

RONALD

Today, my feelings are often uncontrollable because of personal choices made by my grandmother, mother, and father. While I am piecing my life back together, I'm overwhelmed by my earliest struggles just to exist.

It's late in the evening on a hot summer night when Deborah enters Maryland General Hospital. Through the confusion she shouts, "I'm not due until August!" The doctors rush around to stabilize her. The nurses urge her not to go to sleep. At 6:50 in the morning, after hours of pain, she hears the nurse shout, "It's time!" That's when Deborah pushes out a four-pound, eight-ounce premature boy.

The doctors give her a sedative and tell her to get some sleep. Three days later, without telling anyone, Deborah walks out of the hospital in search of alcohol. My grandmother, Fannie, comes and stays at the hospital, begging the doctors to let her take me home. When my weight reaches five pounds, the doctors agree.

After many days of searching, Fannie finds her daughter at the end of a binge. She is brought home and sobered up to help take care of her responsibility. My father agrees to slow down on the drugs. Debbie agrees to help her mother by watching the baby and not drinking. But for three and a half weeks, after working long hours, Fannie finds me starving with drinking pals inside of bars or crying alone in Debbie's car.

"You are going to kill yourself and your child, but before I allow you to do that, I'll put you out of my house!" A big argument ensues, and Debbie runs out. The next years are strange and mysterious, as Fannie takes on the role of my mother. I'm told that Debbie is my sister. I call Fannie "Mom." I still do.

My days are spent with Debbie and her father, Grandpa Reese. My evenings are with Fannie. Grandpa's house is always full. Picture a house that never sleeps, with an endless drinking fountain. Each day I go from the chaotic and untouchable, back to the calm and collected. Debbie is well into her drinking these days, and most times I am with her, she is drunk.

"Do you know how to write your name?" she slurs one day after school. Even though I can do it, for some reason I say no. This sends Debbie into a rage. Immediately, she pulls out a sheet of paper and a pencil and tells me to write my name until there is no room left. I start writing and crying, and don't finish until late that evening.

I know today that because of this incident, I became determined to never say the words "I don't know." It became a part of my personality—the "I can handle it" or "I know!" attitude that would later push me to the breaking point. I learned something else from being around Debbie: how to be a loner in the crowd. I only recognize it now that I am older.

NAJI

My mother is sleeping peacefully on her back with her head turned slightly to the side. She's beautiful—thin, with smooth, ebony skin. To me, her eyes are her most endearing trait. They're large and bright and have this magical sparkle. One glance and I know exactly where she is, emotionally. She makes me feel like I am the only thing that matters.

She doesn't wake up right away, but I know she's playing. I can't remember ever seeing her mad. Even when she does get upset with my brother and me, her demeanor is more like a person who has experienced a great loss.

She has this old record player, a cabinet combination made of veneer wood grain with twin speakers built into the sides. It's filled with old records—33s and 45s. Her favorite artist is Sam Cooke. Every day it seems I hear him crooning that the girl was "only sixteen, she was too young to fall in love," and he was too young to know. The melody is slow. The rhythm is contemplative.

I climb into the bed, jump down on my knees, and begin tickling her. She doesn't move, so I begin shaking her. When that doesn't work, I start to get worried. Finally, I call my brother, and we both shake her and shake her until my brother explains to me that something is terribly wrong.

Of the few memories I have of home, the one of my mother dying is the most vivid. I internalized my pain because I didn't know how to express it. I really thought that was the worst thing anybody would ever have to go through. But I was about to find out that life hadn't even *begun* to get rough for me and my brother. Hell was on the way.

ANDRE

I placed my shaky hand on the silvery doorknob, then turned it slowly to peek in. This room was forever forbidden to me when my daddy and his friends were in there. But I possessed pluck and courage that day that I slipped into the small, yellow-brick bedroom. There was only a half-made bed, a TV playing a football game, and a dresser with the white powdery substance on it. I think it was a Dallas vs. Washington game, because my daddy had his Danny White #11 Dallas Jersey on. He loved his Cowboys, especially head coach Tom Landry. And when my daddy cheered on his team, his voice always sounded a level up. I asked him about this, and he said his tongue touches a place just behind his front teeth. I always wanted to make that sound, but my two front teeth was missing.

I scanned the room in search of Daddy. When I saw him, I smiled. Then my eyes were on the white powdery substance. I had never stayed this long in the room. Why didn't he tell me to leave? Was his team winning the game? Or was he trying to make me a man too early? Either way, I asked for it, and before I knew it, I was sitting on his knee, eagerly anticipating whatever was going to happen next. He took a playing card that was cut in half and put some of the white substance on it. Then he placed the card under my nose. "Now inhale it in," he said. So I closed my eyes and took it inside. It burned a little, and he did it again on the other side of my nose. Then everyone inside the room was making gestures and watching me, because it was my first time. What was I becoming? I felt different, older than twelve.

The effects of the drugs finally took over, and I laid on the bed and fell asleep. When I awoke, I was back in my bed. As I played back the events of that night, I wondered if my mind was playing tricks on me. Was it all a mirage? Surprisingly, my father came into the room. This was strange because he never spent the night at our house. So now this tall, dark-skinned, skinny frame of a man, my father, was standing beside me at my bedside. He said good morning and asked me if I was all right. Then he took a seat on the bed. My little mind was still trying to take it all in. But before I could say anything, he took out what appeared to be a folded-up dollar bill with that same white powdery substance as I just seen before.

Instead of him showing me how to read, ride a bike, or the million other things I missed in my childhood, Dad graduated me to the hard knocks of life as a dope-fiend junkie. Before that, you couldn't tell me I was going to be using or selling drugs. My childhood dream was to be a fireman. I had a positive expectation of achieving success and would take all setbacks as temporary. But I was addicted to heroin and needed it daily to even walk to the store.

> "Our plans miscarry because they have no aim. When a man does not know what harbor he is making for, no wind is the right wind."
> —Lucius Annaeus Seneca

———————————

The hallway noise seeps into the chapel and Kelvin reaches back to close the door. The guys let some air out of their mouths. I feel them looking my way but can't see. I can't speak. There's a lump in my throat.

"Mr. Coogan, you know what it is?" Anton says, fleshing out the feelings I'm just too stunned to articulate. "It's like at a family party, when you just a little kid and you get a sip of beer from your uncle. And then he gives you a little more, because it's funny, you know, to see the kid get drunk." Andre shrugs and chuckles over to Anton, a linebacker joking with another player in the locker room.

"I guess so," I mumble, swallowing hard.

"Well, that's probably what they was thinking. That it was funny!"

"When your dad started feeding you heroin," I finally say, "did your mom know?"

"She had to have known," he says, shifting from one foot to the other. "But nah, she was always kind of quiet. She didn't say nothing."

"So you had no one to talk with about it," I suggest.

"Nah, I talked to people about it. But I just thought it was normal. Most of my friends did, too."

"OK, here's the difference." I close my eyes to gather my memory of myself at the same age. "I was about ten or twelve when I rolled a piece of paper into a pretend cigarette. Then I colored the tip red and orange and took little pretend puffs on the back porch." I open my eyes to see Kelvin hiding his grin in his hands. Dean chortles. "But then my mother discovered me and asked me—shrewdly, I realize now—if I thought smoking was cool. That simple question! 'Of course not!' I told her. But I remember turning *away* from her so she couldn't see my eyes when I said it. Then she closed the door and just let me think about it. I had to figure out if what I just said was what I really believed."

"Man, what was your nickname back then?" Stan demands, stifling a belly laugh. "Because you know in here it's *all* about the nickname." He grins with a twinkle.

"Coogs," I say softly.

"COOGS!" they cheer. "COOGS!"

"You know what I like about that story?" Stan asks.

"The intervention," Kelvin answers. "She was right there, to show him the right way."

"OK, but what did she show me?" I ask.

"You damn well better not smoke in her house!" Dean yells. I laugh along with everyone else, but also shake my head.

"When my mother found me on my back porch 'smoking,' she set me up to make a moral decision. I had to find the words. It's like a character coming to know his part in the script. You see what I mean? I had to find the words. Words are the heart of thought. When your dad gave you heroin, Andre, how did you explain that to yourself?"

"I thought I was becoming a man like my daddy."

"OK, but how did you know *that's* what makes a man a man? Didn't you see other men not getting high?"

Dean releases a dismissive grunt, a train unexpectedly hissing to a stop. "Damn, Dave! You have so many *questions*!"

"I know," I concede. "I ask a lot of questions."

"Yeeaah!" he groans.

"I'm just trying to figure it out."

"Uh-huh." He entertains this. "You want to figure it out."

"I'm trying to figure out how you came to think about what was happening in your life and how that led you here."

Dean raises his draft like he's got all the evidence I need.

DEAN

My Moms married a deadbeat, wannabe, player husband who didn't know the meaning of a being a father. Dean Sr. was addicted to heroin when I was a baby and before I was conceived. He was "the man" in our projects, the leader to his brothers. My uncles were deadbeat fathers like him who abused their women both mentally and physically. They were all abusing drugs and alcohol, too, trying to avoid life's challenging dilemmas.

My father had mad respect, and so did my family. All his lady friends used to pump me up because I was his son. Me and my father were crazy close, and most of my memories of him are good ones. But when I really sit back and analyze the relationship for what it's worth, it amounts to zero . . . nothing.

I would sometimes wait around in my projects for him to see if he wanted to go see a movie or have dinner, but he was too busy chasing skins—you know the rest of the story! I always kept a master plan in my back pocket for situations like that. I craved for my father to come to my basketball games, but he always let me down.

Most of my friends were better than me in basketball, but when it came to football, spelling, or checkers, I was at the top of my game. My main concern was football because I was in love with the Dallas Cowboys. I wanted to become a football star. I was quick and had good hands, so I was always one of the top picks. I played wide receiver and cornerback. I did a lot of the kick-offs. I would say I was an all-American, but I wasn't even in high school yet! But Pops missed it.

I overlooked those disappointments because he was into the number-running business. So I looked up to him for making the money. He *always* had money. Lots and lots of money. So I said, 'You ain't got to come to the games. Just give me some money.' To say I was young 'n' dumb, or maybe envious of my father because he was well known 'n' liked in our neighborhood, is an understatement. Maybe that made me blind to the fact that he didn't do a damn thing for me and he was really a piece of shit.

OK, fast forward! I had caught a case. A gun and weed charge. And while I was out on bond, I visited my mother in New York. I had the paper to pay for a lawyer, but she wanted to make a bet with me.

"I want you to see the *real* Dean Sr.," she said. "Because you're always thinking he's *this*, but I know he's *that*!"

"I said whatcha mean?!"

"We gonna put a test to him. You got the money for the lawyer, but we're going to ask him to help you with it."

"I bet he'll give it," I said. See, I thought I knew what my father thought of me, but I also wanted to prove my mom wrong, because I truly believed that she had it in for him. So we arranged to meet him outside his apartment building to discuss the situation.

"Your son needs money for a lawyer," she tells him.

"Oh, that's nothing," he says, looking at me. "How much you need?"

"Like a thousand dollars," I tell him. "I got the two, but the lawyer costs three."

"Aiight. Come by tomorrow. I'll give it to you," he says, looking at my mother.

"Why can't you give it to him now?" Moms asks.

"'Cause I don't have that kinda money on me right now. I'll give it to him tomorrow." Well, tomorrow never came. We called and called, and he *never* answered the phone or *nothing*! I was *crushed*. That situation never left my thoughts.

The fucked-up thing about the whole situation was that he didn't even call me to see how I made out in court. *Years* would pass by while I was incarcerated, and this cocksucker never wrote me or anything of that nature. After I was released from prison, I never contacted that motherfucker for nothing, because I didn't want to be disappointed again. I cut him off.

Then I got a call from my cousin, who tells me Pops is dying from cancer. He doesn't have that much time to live. Now, I'm *buggin'*! All that beefin' shit is put on the back burner. This is my father! The man who gave me life.

———

The room's stone silent. Everyone seems unwilling to let Dean break the spell he's cast on us.

"That's all I've got now, but I'm going to add on," he says, in a voice much less animated, much more vulnerable.

"So what happened?" Larry finally asks.

"Oh, OK, OK. I go to the hospital in New York, and it hits me like a bag of bricks. He was tore *up*! Still holding on, but he was on his deathbed. It was just me and him in the room. He had tubes coming out from his arm. His fingernails were all black, you know, from the lack of oxygen. And we talked. Or I talked. I told him, 'Even though you never came through for me, I'm here for you right now. I know you can hear me,'" Dean insists, a little louder, his voice all guttural, the gravel and grit of New York City grinding into an accusation. "'I still love you!'"

He stifles a tear with a tremendous sniff. The air conditioning hums. Down the hall, a lone walkie-talkie coughs into life, then goes dead.

"Man, you gonna make *me* cry," Stan says. Everyone looks like he is wrestling down something subterranean. "That piece in your book?" Stan asks, sniffing back his own tears now. Dean doesn't answer. No one says anything. "You write that, man? That'll be your best piece."

3

A Product of My Environment

I set my bag down on the table and unzip it to show the deputy. She paws through the men's drafts, and for a second I think she's beginning to read one. I start shaping a comment, a boastful father, but as soon as I make it through the metal detector, I realize she'd been looking for contraband.

"Raise your arms." She moves the wand around my body. Nothing beeps. "Why are you here today?" Her attitude tells me just how much detail she needs to hear about the strong drafts. I mumble "writing class" and am commanded to have a nice day.

Down the long hallway, at the second set of bars, I hand over my list to the man at the podium. Shakelia's added another name: Bill. When everyone arrives at the chapel, I realize I'm no longer the only white guy in the room.

"Did Shakelia tell you how the class works?" I ask him.

"Stanley did, actually." He runs his hand over his parted brown hair. He's clean-cut, broad-shouldered, in his late thirties, and cheerful. In a blazer and tie, he could be a TV weatherman.

"Do you have any questions?"

"Maybe just more of a comment," he begins. "I read the prompts and some of what Stan's written. And I see what you're asking us to do, to analyze our choices. But I got to wondering. Ultimately, aren't we more just products of our environment?"

"Yeeaah!" Dean growls before catching himself. "Oh! I didn't mean to cut you off," he says to Bill.

"No, go ahead."

"I wanted to know that too," Dean continues. "Because when I look back? Growing up in Harlem, surrounded by hustlers and pimps? All I see is me becoming a product of my environment."

"Could you define 'environment'?" I ask. Bill's lips part into a question. Dean chuckles and turns to G.

"Whatcha mean?" He leans forward with an elbow on his leg.

"I mean, break it down. What are the parts?" I watch and wait.

"OK, OK, OK." Dean clears his throat. "It's the streets. Peer pressure. That's a big one." Bill holds his chin in a Thinker pose. Stan cocks his head to the left, cracking the joint in his neck.

"Do those things exist on their own?"

Dean laughs. "Do the streets exist on their own? You crazy, Dave!" We stare at each other.

"Do you remember when Andre said his life is a drama?" I turn, asking the class.

"That's why they call me Nine Lives," Andre affirms. "I'm like that cat. I always survive."

"But everyone's life is a drama," I argue. "The real question is who wrote the script. You've been playing a role in the streets that's led you into jail. In order to play another role in life that keeps you out of jail, you need to write a new script. And to do that, you need to figure out how the old script got made, which means you need to question generalizations like 'the streets' and 'peer pressure.' You have to figure out what those things really are to you."

"That's what's up," G says with quiet authority, the bouncer lifting the rope for me so I can pass.

"Think about a little kid learning," I continue, encouraged by G's approval. "Your parents teach you how to deliver your first lines, right? And the people you came up with set the scenery." I lower my voice to a whisper. "Ah, but then you get a little older, bigger."

"A young buck!" Stan shouts.

"Watch him now," I continue. "Watch yourself from hindsight with that 20-20 vision. You're getting into costume. The music cues you. The scene starts. You go on stage and do your thing. Then it ends. Curtain!" I trail off on an imaginary darkened stage. "Will you go back the next night to play that part? Nobody's *forcing* you. At some point, you chose the role, right? You *became* the part!"

"Go on!" Stan commands.

"People get confused by this. They say *either* you're a product of some environment *or* you just choose it. But it's never just one or the other, is it? Right, Dean?" His eyes narrow. "I grew up in Connecticut, the other side of the tracks, so to speak, from Harlem. My choices were different because my environment was different."

"So what's the point?" Dean challenges.

"The point is that we don't need essays blaming abstractions like environments. We need the *story* about how you perceived the things in your environment."

"The story, huh." He smirks a little.

"Dean!" Stan shouts, unable to resist his impatience. "Let me share this with you, OK? Someone told me one day, 'Man, you can get a little money quick! All's you have to do is tell me which cars are coming in and which girls are going over and getting in. Just let me know which cars, which girls, and how long they gone.'"

Stan points at me now. "But someone else told *that* man to get a Ph.D.! He'd never be one of those dudes who'd even *see* what I was seeing on Grace Street."

"Right," I say. "But nothing's inevitable. Plenty of my friends growing up never went on to get PhDs. Just like I'm sure there are some people who came up in Harlem who didn't go toward the streets, right, Dean?" With his silence and a little sigh, he relents. "And really, I'm not saying you shouldn't tell the story of how the streets of Harlem shaped your life. I'm just saying, don't take anything for granted. Don't assume your audience will automatically agree that all environments produce the same things." I look around the room at the faces of the men. "And that applies to any issue. Not everyone thinks the same way about their color, right?"

"Honestly?" Dean begins. "Not to offend anyone raised down here, but I didn't really notice race coming up in New York. It wasn't until I came south that I noticed it."

"Right. Race may not be something you thought about growing up. Maybe you do now? Or maybe it's changed over time? But if race has something to do with the story of how you got here, maybe you should write about it."

Naji, who's been following this conversation carefully, raises his hand. "I've got stories to tell about the race piece, Mr. Coogan," he says in a quiet voice.

"Man, it ain't *about* that!" Stan interrupts, the lines in his forehead creased with frustration. Naji glares back, amazed, as the lighter-skinned Stan explodes in demonstration.

"Hey, Bill!" Stan bellows, on his feet, pointing his whole body at Dean. "Bill!" Dean stares, not comprehending. "Bill, I say, Bill!"

Baffled, Dean says, "I'm not Bill."

"That's it!" Stan flourishes. "You don't *answer* if it's not your name! You don't even acknowledge 'nigger' or any other name they say." A low chorus of groans and chatter begins. Dean and Bill start calling each other by the other's name, each time feigning surprise.

"It was a problem for me in the *past*," Naji says to Stan in a stage whisper, as if he and Stan could somehow get their lines straight without the audience hearing. "It's not a problem now." Stan shakes his head violently while Naji bears down. "Look! Didn't Mr. Coogan say to write on how we saw things in the past?"

"Did you write on it last week?" I ask. He nods.

"I did. I was trying to put it in the context of what I used to do." He looks past me, his eyes following a horizon only he can see. "I used to think a lot about my color, man."

Naji

Sliding up the sleeve of my black spandex muscle shirt, I glance at my Iron Man watch. The indigo light illuminates. It's three o'clock in the morning. The city is engulfed in a low-lying fog bank that limits visibility to twenty or thirty feet. Perfect! Dew blankets everything in a thin phosphorous film that glows in the moonlight. The smell of honeysuckle rides the early morning breeze, thick and sweet.

Creeping through this suburban neighborhood with its two-car garages and manicured lawns, I feel like I've stepped into some corny-ass fairy tale! Each home I pass, I notice curtains drawn back, advertising the intimacy of the dwellings, as if saying, "We have nothing to hide." Such a fucking façade! White people piss me off sometimes.

Knowing the evil history of European Americans, I trip off the blatant hypocrisy. Even though what I do is wrong, I don't attempt to cover it up under the façade of respectability. I immediately realize the incredible contradiction. My thoughts shift, and I wonder if the people who live in this neighborhood had some type of meeting with the criminal element of the city where it was agreed upon that their property was off-limits. If so, I never received the memo! Lucky for them, tonight they're not the target.

The absence of traffic and pedestrians makes this night perfect. Only the occasional acknowledgment from the dogs in the area marks my presence. The storefront of the yacht shop consists of a large, plain glass window sporting the name of the business in three-dimensional white and blue lettering. Previous recon has told me that there's no alarm system. I squat down beside a row of hedges. My mind races through the details of my escape plan in case things go astray. I search for the appropriate tool to enter the building. Finding it, I ready myself. My senses become keen. Every sound is accounted for. Everything moving is picked up on radar and meticulously tracked. The next minute and a half, I will be as efficient and stealthy as NORAD.

The wind shifts and my canine friends lose my scent. The sporadic barking stops completely. To them, I simply disappeared.

Standing up, I quickly throw the chrome ball bearing with considerable force. It strikes the middle of the glass with an almost imperceptible *thwack!* that blends in with the rustling of the trees. The sound even escapes the sensitive hearing of the nearby sentinels. They remain quiet.

The window shatters in a million pieces, but retains its shape and form. All that is needed is for me to pluck out a space large enough for me to enter. Flawless. High on adrenaline, I become the ghost.

Like so many childhood ambitions, my dreams of becoming a fighter pilot had long since been crushed under the oppressive weight of my warped reality. My core self—loving, kind, thoughtful, sincere, and compassionate—was buried deep beneath a legacy of cultural ignorance and social indifference. So here I am, the proficient illusionist. This is where I find mastery, constantly redefining myself, like a virus that seeks to be more, wanting that part of itself that is missing.

My self-perception is severely fractured, like the shattered window I'm climbing through. I can't be detected, defined, or circumscribed: I fit no multicultural niche. I have no political affiliation. I am the Black Ghost: cunning, illusive, deadly. I possess an insatiable appetite to prove to myself and to the world that I am more than the victim of the Judgments of Daylight. In blackness I am the master. I am whole, complete. I revel in the freedom of my destructive self-expression. Here, the possibilities of becoming are endless. I'm not judged but embraced by the comforting neutrality of night. The possibility of profiting from this insane misadventure is secondary to this momentary intoxication. I live for the transformation, the freedom of becoming, without doubt or contradiction. The repercussions will leave a bitter taste in my mouth if I'm discovered, but I gladly risk it to be alive in this moment, knowing who and what I am.

* * *

Being raised in Boston in a predominantly black neighborhood in the early seventies exposed me to the anger and resentment of those around me. While processing my own personal experience, I was privy to the social reality of blacks in general. It was a daily occurrence to hear statements like, "White people are shit. They just want to keep the black man down," etc. Being young and hearing this from adults gave it a sort of validity, even though it contradicted some of what I was experiencing. To the core, I was sensitive, compassionate, and inquisitive—perceptive and empathetic to the pain in others, while hiding my own pain. I was acutely aware of the soul and always sought to communicate that through my dealings. But I was learning to be self-conscious of my skin color.

I had a friend who was white and lived across the courtyard just outside the Bromley-Heath apartments in south Boston. We played together every day, collecting bottles to turn in for the ten-cent refund, and then stocking up on Boston Baked Beans, Lemon Heads, and Mike & Ikes. High on sugar, along with maybe ten of our other friends, we would spend the day running all over the neighborhood, playing game after game until our parents called us in or, in my case, until it started getting dark.

One day I went over to his house and he invited me in. We sat on his living room floor and played crash 'em up with his Tonka dump trucks. We were totally caught up in our fun when his mom walked in, her hands full of groceries.

"Get that Goddamn nigger out of my house this instant!" she screamed at the top of her lungs. I jerked my head around, paralyzed with what I was hearing and seeing. She appeared to be seven feet tall and over a thousand pounds. Her face was contorted into a gnarly mask of bright, pink flesh knotted up around her eyes, nose, and mouth. Her eyes were small, shiny marbles set back in her head, behind rolls of fat. They were black with rage.

Everything slowed down. I separated from myself and drifted to a dark corner of the room and watched as the big woman began gesticulating. Her mouth was moving, but I couldn't hear a word. All of a sudden I let out a wail, not realizing I had been holding my breath! This seemed to release me from the spell, and I took off through the still-open front door like I was on fire.

I learned to hate white people that day, and the more I began to learn about black history, the more I hated. I use the word "hate" very loosely. I was young. *Hatred* is probably too strong of an emotion to describe exactly what I was feeling. I think *reservation* is more suitable, because I did understand, through my interaction with classmates and teachers, some of whom were white, that all whites were not alike. This, I think, gave me an opportunity to understand racism before I had a working definition of the term. On a person-to-person basis, of course, racism is more complex—something I would discover much later.

The importance of having a father in my life was never lost on me. I noticed daily that the kids I hung around with, especially the white kids, had things and possessed knowledge that I envied greatly. I held so many fantasies about who my dad was, what he did for a living, and why he wasn't in my life. If the subject ever came up amongst my friends, I would say my father was a secret agent sent off on some mission. As I got older, I'd say he had an important job to do in another state, or that he couldn't come see us, we had to go to him. In my teen years, full of bitterness on the subject, I'd blurt out, "I never knew my dad, motherfuck the fag!" But to this day, I wish that I could find him to answer so many of my unanswered questions. Today, if anyone asks about my father, I reluctantly comment that I never knew him, and pray like hell that that ends it.

4

SORRY

"Pretend I'm in jail and these are the bars," my daughter says from her side of the sprinkler.

I poke my hand through the shimmering wall between us, disrupting the spray, then slump by the fence. The haze hugs me blind.

"What was the name of that guy from your class? You were talking about him yesterday." She pushes her matted blond hair out of her eyes.

"Stanley," I tell her.

"How do you spell it? What's the first letter?"

She picks up a stick. I begin spelling the name. Squatting, she pulls the puddle water like paint. After she's written the letter S, she asks why they are in jail. She wants to know what I do each Saturday when I leave our home. She nods quickly when I tell her I'm teaching guys how to write about their lives so they can learn how to live better lives.

"Did they put chemicals in their bodies?"

"Some of them."

"Are they robbers?" Her voice climbs high.

"Some are."

She puts down the stick and looks up and straight into me. Her eyes are green and oceanic.

"Did they say sorry?"

* * *

"Motherfucker!" Burt shouts, slamming down his pad of paper. He's perched in the front pew, sandals off, his white toes pointed toward the altar. "I don't want that punk-ass anywhere near me!" The other guys shift in their seats, eying me helplessly. The new guy is not working out.

"Look, you've got a right to be angry," I begin. "But in here, it's all about the writing. You need to get it down on paper so we can help you with it *as writing*."

I lean back against the altar and ask him to tell us a story about how things *first* went bad between him and his father. I'm searching for some logic, large or small, when his feet hit the ground and find their way to the sandals. He asks to go to the bathroom. Having never considered the idea they could leave the chapel, I nod, pretending I know the routine. A collective sigh cuts loose when the door closes behind him.

"That man's off the chain!" Kelvin says, jabbing his thumb toward the door where Burt left. "You think he'll stick with it?"

I shake my head. "He's thinking he needs to persuade us *before* he can write it. He's got it backward," I say. G squints at me, folding his arms across his chest, and I stare back. "He's got to write it for himself."

G shifts in his seat. "Why you staring at me?" He grins a little, embarrassed.

"He's got to make his own peace with whatever happened with his father," I conclude. "All we can do is help him craft the story of it." I turn to see Stan watching me with a steadiness, the air rising slowly in his chest.

STAN

"Hot dogs! Get your hot dogs!" the man at the baseball game sings out. "Hot dogs! Hot dogs! Anyone want a hot hot dog?" The man keeps on in a high-pitched voice, not knowing that his words are hypnotizing me, sending me deeper and deeper into a trance. For the next few moments, my life is frozen.

You see, hot dogs are my favorite meal. I'll eat hot dogs morning, noon, and night, and have many times. My fetish for hot dogs started when I was a child, around the age of five or six. My father and I would always share a hot dog meal together. Everywhere we went, we would get a few. Even at home on lazy days, my father would yell across the house, "Hey, Stan! Stan, you want two hot dogs?" And I would come running. "Yes, Dad, two!" So I grew up loving two things: my father and hot dogs.

Where I grew up, in the rich area near Byrd Park, everybody played sports. My father loved baseball. It's what he understood. But I excelled at football. Any stress in that game, I readily accepted. The press, third down, a yard to go? Give me the ball! Now, my father is not into sports where you sit in front of the TV and just watch a game. That's not his style. His character is more of a man who fixes things, outdoors, around the house. He was so involved in my playing baseball, he would drive the whole team to games. Now it's three balls, two strikes, a full count. I'm at the plate. But instead of focusing on the next pitch, I'm worried about what my father is thinking, watching me in the stands. My God! Here comes that last pitch! I'm going down swinging!

Our relationship was lost at three balls and two strikes.

* * *

The smiles and sounds of laughter are in the air. We see the "For Rent" sign. Hey look! There's a new Schwinn bike coming down the street! Though I am seventeen years old, I have the mentality of a twelve-year-old. Whatever you think is what you are.

I know more about bikes than anything. All my buddies want a Schwinn because they are the top of the line. But the world I was about to enter into on Grace Street was not about bikes, toys, and tag.

My father knocks on the door and I look up at him. With his eyes he smiles, reassuring me that everything is all right. Like a child, I trust what his expression tells me. His knuckles hit the wooden door again. It swings open to a big man wearing a white T-shirt with food stains all over it. His face needs a shave. His hair looks as though motor oil is his grease of choice. I'm not feeling this man.

My father chats with Sloppy Joe for a few moments. Then the man escorts us down the hall, where he pulls out a ring of keys and opens the door to a one-bedroom apartment.

The walls are painted the color of hopelessness. The windows are draped in sorrow. There are no pictures of loved ones hugging the walls, no sense of life in the air, just the stale smell of loneliness. I am used to the sweet smell of my mother's cooking, the warmth of her kitchen. But the floor of my new home has no carpet to warm it on the coldest of nights. It is my very first jail cell.

Like a ship sunk at sea, lost in the deepest of the deep—so were my father's thoughts to me that moment he drove off, leaving me naked in the cold world. At the time, I didn't understand. But I realize now that it didn't matter to my father what I was thinking or feeling, because he had already decided that morning that two of us would start our journey together, but only one of us would be returning to the place we called home.

According to my mother and father, I was the reason our home had no harmony. A lot of the issues around the household, I became the scapegoat. My father and mother were having problems in their relationship, but they made me feel like I was the culprit. Now, I'm no angel, not by far. But I don't think I'm the devil.

I don't recall how we said our good-byes. But our relationship would never be the same again.

We look to our fathers to give us a strong sense of who we are, to root us in love and form us as young men. All my life, I've searched for that. But I know what it is I'm missing. I know I don't have a true identity. When my father left me in that one-bedroom apartment, it was like he was sending me down the Nile River of adoption all over again.

I wonder, did *anyone* think about my safety, my emotional stability, or the long-term effects of placing a child out there unprepared? My father did take into consideration that I needed to eat. So he went to a place called Murray's Steak House that sold wholesale meat products and bought me a case of hot dogs each month. That's ninety-six hot dogs a month I ate.

"Hot dogs! Hot dogs!" the gentleman at the baseball game sings out, opening a place in my psyche where I would later become lost, not only to myself, but to all the dreams I'd ever had. Parts of my emotional system lie dormant, even today— undeveloped in that one-bedroom apartment on Grace Street. As a young boy on Grace Street, Wrong found me. Negative thinking came with him. I can still recall all the lonely days I spent there, in that room. Even today, as I write to you, my friend, I'm still living there in my mind. I just call it my prison cell.

"Hot dogs! Hot dogs!" again, the gent sings. As he draws near, I can smell them. I can't resist. So I shout in a very loud voice, "GIVE ME TWO!" One for me and one for that lost child. You see, the moment we came together as one, we were no longer alone.

Now, some things never change. I still love hot dogs. And I still love and care for my father, Mr. Stanley Craddock.

5

THE TRAP

"How's it going?" Shakelia asks over the phone the next week. We are reaching the end of the six weeks I had planned to spend teaching the workshop in the jail, but only two guys are close to being released. The rest are headed to prison but don't know when they'll be sent. I tell her about Burt's bathroom trip—he eventually came back some forty minutes later—and she scratches him off the list. Just like that.

"The ones who want to write are really digging deep. We're just now getting to their first crimes—when they got trapped in the lifestyle."

"Good!" she says. "Keep going!" But I'm starting to wonder where we're going, or maybe just who's coming along for the trip. Last week Ron was missing to go to court. Anton took a visit instead of coming to class. I couldn't blame him.

I have everyone's drafts typed up, with comments sketched in the margins. I'm ready to coach. But it's starting to occur to me that this is pickup ball, not a game in any league.

STAN

When I was a boy, I used to love watching the fish weaving about in my mother's aquarium. She had a beautiful one filled with so many colorful fish. So when I saw this tropical fish at the pet store one day after school, instantly, I could imagine it swimming in my mother's tank back home. The clerk scooped it out for me: one little fish, one little Glad bag. And I couldn't wait to get home and release him into his new environment. I wanted to see how he was going to function. Would he get along with all the rest of the fish? Would he be preyed upon? Or would he be the aggressor? Carefully, I lifted the lid. He hit the water with a gentle splash.

Years later, I'm the new member of the tank on Grace Street. Splash! I thought I was the coolest guy on earth to have my own place. There was no rule to live by! No curfew! I could stay outside all night long. And I did, all the time. It wasn't that I wanted to get wild and do wrong. I was just ready to explore my new environment, like any young boy would.

At this time in my life, I hadn't become hard yet. I was still a loving, carefree young child. But that's the type of meat sharks eat. The streets crave that diet. And the streets are very alluring. Each night when the sun found a place to rest, allowing the moon to fulfill its needs, I found myself becoming a creature of the night, in every sense and form. My life was no longer being controlled in a closed environment. My home was not a safe haven.

Grace Street had a lot of prostitution back then, so I would come out at night just to watch the women walking up and down the street, flaunting their bodies, laughing, smiling, luring men into traps to extract the money out of their pockets. To me it was like watching an X-rated movie.

When you see a woman's body, her eyes are seducing. Her smile is pursuing. Her breasts are conversing. Her hips are dangerous caves to explore. Her legs are two separate highways to travel. And her vagina is a place of rest. Women are beautiful. I bodily crave them, and I was at the age where my hormones were foaming and boiling. What I saw was what I wanted: women. But the reality was each night I craved more of what I did not understand.

I liken myself to an owl. I only came out at night to sit on my porch, head turning all the way around, watching women in and out of cars all night, working. Bottom line? I wanted to fuck one of those women. The only reason I hadn't yet was because I didn't have any money. I had to find another way to get these women's attention. I'm blessed with good facial features, a nice smile, and a lean, mean physique. These would become my currency on Grace Street. I would go on the offensive. I would make these women like me.

My trap was well placed, but I was the one who would fall into it.

The bait came in the form of a young lady named Carolyn. I met my dark angel early one Sunday morning. I had stayed up all night just walking around like a male dog marking his territory, memorizing every spot. I knew every woman that was prostituting. I knew every pimp and what kind of clothes he wore. I knew which people did not belong in the area and which ones did.

It was about 5:30 a.m. I was just coming home. The sunrise felt like a mother waking her children, greeting them with the sensation of love. A Ford truck caught my attention when it stopped in the middle of the street. The passenger door opened up, and I saw a woman's leg emerge. When she got to her feet and shut the truck door, our eyes locked.

I am pretty sure Carolyn knew what was in my gaze: that early morning, piss-hard lust. I needed her, and with the look in her eyes, I could tell she needed me, because on this particular morning, we were coming home together.

I can't remember exactly what words we shared that morning. But we would soon share many more. Carolyn was the first woman in my new world that I interacted with in a very personal way. She was the only guest in my one-bedroom apartment. She was wiser and far more advanced in life, and I learned from her with each blink of my eyes. I took in Carolyn's many points of wisdom, because my true desire was to look at her body.

Her skin was as creamy as caramel. She had a sunny smile that could warm any cold heart. Her body was gorgeous, banging, with a little soft Afro. She was a prostitute in every form and fashion: short skirts, low-cut shirts, and high heels. And I cannot forget her many wigs. Her age was unknown to me at the time. But if I was seventeen, Carolyn had to have been around twenty-seven.

She taught me street facts. Her number one rule was: use them before they use you. Steal from them before they steal from you. Kill them before they kill you. I'll never know the snake that polluted her mind and body, but someone had to have taught her how to use and abuse, herself as well as others. And she passed these lessons down to me.

As a young man with this beautiful dark angel by my side, I desired one day to share my ideal of intimacy with a gentle, passionate tongue kiss. But I found myself being rebuked. It hurt until she explained. I'm sure that the truth was hurting her more. Her mouth was polluted with the taste of many men's seed. She cared enough about me not to kiss me.

Carolyn was God-sent in my life. That's why I call her my dark angel. Like a mother, Carolyn protected and comforted me. She cared for all of my needs. That morning when our eyes met out in the street, I just wanted to wet her ass like every other man. But she did not offer me her body to use. She gave me her heart, her understanding of life. She gave me all that she really had. Our relationship was about the building of communication and the understanding of our mutual need to not be alone. We just wanted to survive to live another day. What can a prostitute teach you? You can only speak boldly about things you know.

Carolyn's office—the environment she felt most comfortable in—was the bedroom. All her tools fit that setting. Her power of persuasion was hidden between her beautiful brown legs, nestled under a well-manicured black Afro. And the more she allowed me to visit it, the more entangled I became. We had a conversation one night, naked in each other's arms, about how she could lure a man to a hotel room and set the stage for a relaxing time of sexual pleasure. What he and his pocket full of money wouldn't know was that he would actually be led to slaughter. This is how Carolyn and I got down.

"You know what's a trip, though?" Stan says once he's through reading. "That part where I tried to kiss her."

"Nah, they don't like that," Larry says right away.

"I thought, in my own way—I was seventeen—I thought this was romantic, something you do!"

"Nah, can't kiss 'em," Larry says again.

"She said, 'You don't *kiss* women like me! I suck *dick*! I suck *dick*! You don't *kiss* someone like me!'"

From where I'm standing in the front of the room, I can watch Stan and Larry like a tennis match.

"I went through the same thing," Larry says in a rasp. "I tried to turn this prostitute into my girlfriend."

"Everything was an exchange with her! Relationships were just like accounts, in and out. Use them before they use you! Do this? Get that!" Larry tries to get a word in, but gets blasted by Stan's conclusion: "A prostitute don't never see a *man* coming to her. She just sees his wallet!"

"Yeah," Larry says quickly, more congregation than conversation partner.

"You know, that's one of the most profound changes I need to make in my life," Stan continues, on his feet. "Carolyn's definition of a relationship doesn't have to be my definition."

"Great piece, Stan!" Bill says.

"What was your favorite part?" I ask.

"It'd have to be that opening image, the fish going into the tank." He pauses to scratch his chin.

"You know, there's nothing natural about a fish tank," I interject. "Environments are man-made."

"That's true," Ronald says. "Our aquarium was always changing. It started with just a jar of water. Then the five-gallon tank. Then the ten-gallon, the twenty-gallon. Each one was different. I could relate because that's how it was for me, too. Each time I got splashed into a new tank, it seemed bigger and more shocking." He stops talking to start writing.

"Is that how we grow up, just moving from tank to tank?" I ask. "If so, how do we get into these tanks?" I pause to look around the room. "Dean?"

"Who, me?"

"Yeah. Were you dropped in or did you jump?"

"Oh, OK, OK." He warms up to it. "See, I was fascinated with the streets. The hustling, the dark style, you know, the grimy! To me, the Catholic school my Moms sent me to was more or less the preppy. You know what I'm sayin'? You know how in school you got the prepsters? Then you got the so-called gangstas or ruffnecks? You see what I'm trying to tell you?"

"I feel you," G says sharply.

DEAN

It's summertime in Harlem. The year is 1978. Hip-hop is taking form, and the streets are filled with hustlers, pimps, and dope fiends. On this particular morning, the sun is shining bright, the morning air is fresh, and I can even hear the birds chirping. It must be a good morning because my Moms is up fixing breakfast. I can smell the bacon frying and the home fries cooking. Man, I can't wait until I sink my teeth into it!

While I'm in the bathroom getting myself together, I can taste the salt from the bacon and it's making my mouth water. But reality kicks in from the toothpaste, so it's time to make moves to the kitchen table. As I'm waiting for Moms to fix my plate, I dip over to the window to see if any of my buddies are outside. After I finish my meal, it's a must that I clean up my room before I ask the warden if I can go outside to play. My friends nicknamed my mother that because they thought she was mean. They didn't know the half of it!

Growing up in Harlem is a lot different than coming from the suburbs or the dirty south: there's a whole different atmosphere, a whole different mentality. Plus there's a lot more shit to get into, as far as trouble. You have peer pressure from friends and from older cats who want you to represent the block to the fullest. There's a toughness, an aura, regardless of the situation. If you aren't a tough guy, if you don't fight for respect, you can't be down. And if you ain't down, then you're considered a pussy, an outcast, and you get picked on.

My neighborhood and public school is where all my problems came about. P.S. 92 is a blue and grey building standing about three stories tall, with a fairly large playground. There's a hero shop at the corner of the block, which is off-limits to students during school hours. Lunchtime at Mr. Leroy's is busy. You have working-class people trying to snatch up sandwiches. Then you have the students from other schools trying to big-boy the shop or bully us. We, on the other hand, have to sneak out to get a hero. We aren't allowed to leave the schoolyard.

You take a chance going to get a sandwich because there are security guards who come through checking the shop to see if any of us are there. And there are disciplinary actions for getting caught off of school grounds: either the ruler, which is actually a bunch of rulers stacked five high, with a lot of rubber bands holding them together, or the pointer stick, which is long-n-solid but does the motherfucking job! Each time you get into trouble, the punishment is more severe: more lashings to those same hands we used to caress the girls or snatch up those heroes—the same ones that got me into this situation in the first place!

My friends and I are extremely tight. We don't allow anyone to come into our schoolyard or block. Outsiders never leave with a win or anything of that nature. During school, we turn it up a notch, beating niggas' asses. We start dragging them behind the school, the staircases, even the bathroom, because they're hatin' on us from the sidelines. We can't have that! We have our select few that aren't from around the way but chill with us because they can get dirty. They know the rules: if you backstab or betray us in any way, you get the same treatment those other kats are getting. I remember having a broken arm, and I still gave this kat an official beat down in the basement of our school for trying to feel my girlfriend's ass.

The older guys see that we're tough, and they make us fierce competitors. They tell us that we can't settle for less. As the next gang from 134th Street, we know we have to learn the game from all angles. The big dogs on the block are getting paid slinging that boy and that girl.[9] But first we have to hold down our own block before they'll pass the torch on to us. They go to different blocks in Harlem and talk shit about how that other lil' crew ain't fucking with us. They start betting big dough on whatever the case may be. So we go down to 42nd Street and steal football jerseys. We rock these on the block or at school to show toughness and togetherness. And it becomes a known fact that the crew on 134th Street is making a name for itself.

You must have some kind of knuckle game or at least a lot of heart, to run on our block. We witness motherfuckers getting robbed, kats getting pistol-whipped for coming up short, even people getting gunned down in broad daylight. On a daily basis, we see kats and bitches get they ass kicked for talking shit. I start getting into trouble for stupid shit, trying to impress my friends: spray-painting the trains, throwing rocks at moving cars, hopping the train. Catching us is very hard because we don't care about running on the train tracks or running through the tunnels to get to the next station.

One night we take the "2" train to 149th Street, go upstairs and catch the "4" train until we reach our destination. We're bugging out, taggin' our names up on the train. Then we find this bum asleep. Tone Rone has some firecrackers in his pockets so we decide to put some of those in the bum's mouth and light them. Shorty Black places the firecrackers in between his lips and Tone lights them. Quickly we bounce. A couple of seconds go by, then—BOOM! The bum jumps up, grabbing his lips with an ill expression. Me, I'm on the floor laughing my ass off, along with my crew. The bum—well, he just goes back to sleep.

***

I can't remember what I did, but I do remember being told to go to my room and prepare for a beating. When my Moms dished out a beating it was official! It came with extension cords, belts, shoes.

This time she's frustrated because I'm hiding under the bed. Knowing she can't get a good hit with the belt makes her even madder. So Moms leaves the room to

---

9 "Boy and girl" is slang for heroin and cocaine, respectively.

get reinforcement. Now, I'm thinking that she's going to get my stepdad, but she returns with scissors and begins stabbing me in different places. I can't believe it! My mommy is going to kill me! What have I done that is so bad that she wants to hurt me like this?

After my stepdad breaks it up, Moms packs up a few things and throws me out into the hall. Not only am I bleeding, but I'm homeless and confused about the situation: what to do, where to go, the whole nine yards. I'm embarrassed, humiliated, but I know that I have to get some help and get myself together before morning.

I walk down six flights of stairs before the brainstorm hits me. Go to my father's place! But after I explain to him what's happened, that motherfucker turns his back on me, saying he doesn't have enough room in his one-bedroom apartment and that I need to go to the police station so I can report the incident. My heart drops, but I suck it up like a man and keep it moving. Instead of going to the police station, though, I head back to the staircase in my building so I can finish crying and hiding out.

I stay there for quite a while before a good friend of my mother's discovers me. She asks me what I'm doing there, crying with bags in my hand. I tell her that my mother stabbed me with a pair of scissors and threw me out of the apartment. She asks to see my wounds. She gets so upset that *she* starts crying. Then she grabs my hand and rushes me to the police station. I'm reluctant to file a report because I know my Moms will get into trouble but I still want to protect her. Why? Because this is my Moms and I love her! Still, this incident changed my life forever. I just wouldn't understand the ramifications until later.

Back then I truly believed that inflicting pain on others was the thing to do. I thought fighting was cool because my mother beat the shit out of me. I thought that was the way of life. As I became an adult, I realized that wasn't normal thinking.

Back then, even getting caught, which didn't happen often, didn't scare me. The one time I did get caught, the police called my parents. You talk about scared to death! I knew that nobody in the bunch was getting their asses whipped like me, so I decided to postpone this for a few hours, thinking my Moms would cool off or forget about it. The craziest thing was she didn't forget about it, but I didn't get an ass-whipping either. So I knew right then that she was starting to ease up and let me learn from my mistakes like a man.

The more my Moms eased up, the more shit I got into. I really wanted to please my Moms and stay on the straight and narrow, but once I realized that she was all for self—her happiness and selfish ways—I began to pursue street dreams and kingpin fantasies. Me and my friends went from small-time criminals to doing bigger things.

* * *

A car pulls up with the music playing real loud. It's my man Charlie Bow. He turns down the music, beeps the horn, and calls me over.

"Yo! Whatcha doin?"

"Shit."

"Yo! Take a ride with me downtown so I can check on my new whip to see if they're finished hookin' me up."

"No doubt!" I shout and get in. He peels off and turns the music back up so I can feel the vibe. I can't front either. I'm open right now, wishing I could get money like he has so I can get me something like this. The car is a Datsun 260zx with BBS rims and a crazy set inside. And believe me, we were *racing* down the West Side Highway to get to this dealership called Formula One, which I later found out was owned by the mob. All the big-time drug dealers who were somebody in New York back in those days spent paper to get a whip from these dudes, just to say you got a car from Formula One.

When we get there, I'm going bananas because there are so many hot joints on the lot that it's hard to pick just one. Charlie Bow tells me to look around while he finds out what the deal is with his car. On the lot, there are BMWs, Benzes, the new ZXs and all that, but the joint that catches my eye is the BMW 635 CSi with the two-tone BBS rims on it. The stick shift even has an eagle's head on it in diamonds! This shit is crazy!

After a few minutes blow by, they bring Charlie Bow's car out: a new 280 ZX, T-top, champagne gold. I almost throw up, I am that determined to get me one. They tell him it will be ready in two more days, so we bounce. In the meantime, I'm hungry as a hostage. But I tell him straight up that my pockets are low and could he lend me a few dollars to get me something to eat? Instead of giving me the money, he treats me to some pizza.

We go to a joint on the east side of Manhattan called Ray's Pizza, which is a high-class jump off to all the other spots I was used to going to, but I'm not complaining. I'm searching for movie scenes and mob hits. It was an official Italian restaurant. We sit down, order a pie, and then start chit-chatting about the block, what I'm doing with my life, about our friends, and so on. Then comes the question I'm looking for. He asks me to work for him. He states that he likes my style and how he trusts me. I'm listening to every word that's coming out of his mouth, but the main thing that gets me in the door is him saying, "I'm going to teach you everything I know."

"It's all about Harlem, and Harlem is all about the paper chase," he says. "It goes down like this: if the block that you're representing isn't about money, fly-ass niggas, and chicks, well then there's no need to be screaming about ya hood, more or less. It's all or nothing. 'Go get that paper' means you're chasing that bread all night. If you're a fly guy that means you stay with the latest and hottest gear all the time. Then you have pussy falling at your feet, and bad bitches at that! The hustling game is all about the lifestyle, the money, the cars, the women, the whole shebang."

It didn't take long for me to fall in line. After a while, I recruited my own team, stayed up long hours and bagged up mad work. I terrorized the neighborhood inside and out because I wanted to be down with a certain gang. But peer pressure is a motherfucker. Brass knuckles, pipes, bats, the whole nine yards. Guns really didn't play a factor until later on down the line, when crack hit Harlem and hit it hard. Still, I became more violent, especially to those that tried to come between me and my money. I once watched a guy get his whole stomach blown out, and just looked at him like oh, that's how your stomach looks. I had no feelings.

Soon I realized I was out of my element, wearing a bulletproof vest, packing heat, defending a profession that's destroying my people and killing my dreams. In this game, you're forced into manhood because if you let people walk over you, then they'll think that you're weak and that's a no-no. They'll take full advantage of you until you step up to the plate. I wasn't prepared for the ups and downs of the drug game, mentally.

The more I look back on the whole situation, the more I realize I was easy prey. I seriously thought I was ready to be a man, to take on responsibilities, when I was far from that. The jealousy that came with the money was mind-boggling. I would have never thought in my wildest dreams that friends would backstab each other over a dollar or cross each other because one guy is getting more paper than the next.

Seeing who could shine the most—that's where the beefs came in. I witnessed motherfuckers lose everything, but the most disturbing thing that I experienced was the bloodshed, seeing friends leak in the streets all across Harlem. When you see one of your homeboys or homegirls in a casket and you see the pain, the heartache, on the faces of their family members, that's when reality kicks in. I cried many tears for my homies but still I couldn't shake the obsession of the streets. It's more addictive than any drug they could ever grow or make.

"You know what I'm sayin'? You understand now?" He's smiling now, expansive as his Harlem. "I wanted to be *down*. I thought that's what I had to *do*!"

"And your mother was trying to steer you away from that," I say.

"Big time!" he roars. "I mean, like I said, I don't know what I did that day, but when she came after me with the scissors, she was mad!" Strangely, he laughs. Whatever hurt then doesn't hurt now.

"You forgave her," I intuit. He nods, a little annoyed.

"I could see what she was going through."

"Dean," Stan cuts in, chiseling a finer point on the situation. "You had a mother telling you *how* to be down. Right?"

"Nah, hold up. Lemme finish, lemme finish."

I hold one hand up in Stan's direction, signaling Dean to continue. "Maybe we don't know the whole story?"

"OK." He edges up to it like a diver on the board. "One, my grandfather, he never had a job. He hustled. Ran numbers. My uncles, my aunts, and my father, they did the same thing. Hustled. Ran numbers. Ran the streets. That's all I really knew. So what really had my attention was the glamour. I didn't *know* about the other side of the streets. You know what I'm saying? The down side, the murders."

"But your mother did!" Stan blasts. "See, that's why I always talk about the trap."

"You know, I grew up in a small town in Virginia," Bill interrupts, his voice a strange country sound in this inner-city jail. "There weren't any streets like Dean's talking about right outside my door. But I found them when I started drinking and hanging out in clubs doing drugs. I was just looking for acceptance. I looked for it everywhere I went." Dean and Stan nod to these terms. It's as if Bill's become a diplomat in the dispute-to-be.

"That's why I asked if you jumped or got dropped into the tank," I say, taking advantage of the moment. I reach for my bag and pull out my notes. "Do you guys remember this?" I hold up the handout I gave them a few weeks ago from the psychologist Abraham Maslow, his triangle of the hierarchy of needs in life. At the bottom of the triangle are the more physical needs—safety, food—and at the top, self-actualization, your true purpose or higher calling. "Bill just said 'acceptance.'" I point to the middle of the triangle that says, "acceptance, love, and belonging." "But what was he really accepted by?"

"I don't know," Bill responds. "Before I got locked up for the second time, I was already in a relationship. I was going to college. But I was fascinated with prostitutes. And my first time going to one, I ended up smoking crack and getting addicted."

"OK, right there!" I say. "What made you let that change happen? I mean, it could have been a one-time thing, couldn't it? You weren't looking to get high that night. What made you want to go back and *keep* getting high? What were you really looking for?"

Kelvin straightens up in his pew, riveted.

"That's a great question, Dave, and I just don't know. I've thought about it." Bill rubs his chin, enmeshed in the mystery. Kelvin nods along with us. I look over to Stan. Uncharacteristically, he's got his hand raised. I point to him.

"What can a prostitute really teach you, Dave? She can't teach you Maslow! She don't *know* that." He turns in the pew to face the rest of the men. "That's why I always talk about the trap! The trap is always something that catches our eye. It ain't never what we actually *need*. It's what we *desire*!"

"I don't know," Bill says—three notes descending high to low. "I don't think we really see the trap. I think we just see the bait." Dean mumbles his agreement. Andre follows suit. Stan senses he's about to lose the point.

"OK, look at a mouse. Right?" The men rumble their own theories of the trap as Stan fights for control of the floor. "If he can smell the cheese up on the trap, right, then he *got* to be able to smell the *blood*. He got to be able to smell the blood, because the last mouse spilled some on that trap!"

"Nah, if he smelled the blood he wouldn't go to da cheese!" Dean reasons.

"He *smelled* the blood!" Stan shouts, standing by me in the front of the room. "Man, let me tell you about a *man*!"

"Uh-huh?" Dean says all breathy, almost bawdy. I take a seat near Bill as Stan pulls his shoulders back.

"A man understands, right?" He cracks a joint in his neck.

"Uh-huh. Right," Dean grunts, clearly humoring him. So Stan directs himself to the crowd instead.

"I'm a grown man, forty-three years old, right? I *smell* the blood!" The words blast from the center of his chest. "But in my *desire* to get what's up on the trap, I'm no different than the mouse. I think I can get it. And guess what? I *do* get it sometimes! That's how I get so comfortable to come closer and closer!" By now the room's gone still. And all eyes are on Stan. Even Dean's muffled his grunts. Satisfied by these signs of respect, Stan lowers his voice.

"You ever notice a mousetrap?" he asks, spreading his hand palm up. "It don't ever get your hand. It always gets your *neck*. And the only way that it can get your neck is you got to come all the way up on it to get the bait." He smacks his hand. Bill jumps a little. "Pops you like that," he finishes. Then he sits down, triumphant.

STAN

"Run, Stan, run! Here's a way out!"

Blood had been spilled. Another young black man lay in a puddle. But who pulled the trigger? It was like an award show question. The street Grammies were being held that night in Richmond. Don't you know you can receive a standing ovation from all your street peers if you're the one who pulled the trigger?

I found myself being nominated for this award, along with another person. So it was time to hit the road. But to where?

The classified ad read, "Young people between the ages of eighteen and twenty-five, no experience necessary, but must be free to travel immediately. Call for an interview." But did I do the crime? That's what you are asking yourself, right? I answered the ad "free to travel." I'm going to Fort Lauderdale now. Are you coming along? Or are you going to stay?

Florida opened my eyes to sunny days and an overflow of bikinis. I joined a sales team that sold magazines door-to-door. I was the youngest member of the group—seventeen. But I lied and said I was nineteen. Carolyn had developed my personality to the point where I thought I was smooth. I was 6'1", 185 pounds, and E-Z on the eyes. My clothes were up to date and sharp; my teeth were bleach-white, so I had a great smile to conceal my fangs. My shoes stayed shiny to walk in and out of your life, plus I had youth on my side. I was filled with raw energy, just waiting to be tapped. Oh, and before I forget: I had a .38 snub-nose revolver lying dormant in my suitcase.

Being on the sales team was awesome. Each day we had sales meetings to rehearse our game—the craft of conning people. My new instructor's name was Jimmy. This cat was the smoothest brother I have ever met in my whole life. He was from Harlem, very street-smart, a great con man, well over 6'2", with curly black hair. He was a sharp dresser and a downright ladies' man. He was a man's man, too. I looked up to Jimmy from day one. He took in young people like me and turned out masterpieces! We became what he needed us to be. I loved it. Someone was taking the time to teach me.

Up to this point, I thought I understood the pimp game. And I did somewhat—but only at a street level, where a woman sold her body in exchange for her needs. But each day in our sales meetings and out in the territory, my understanding of the sincere art of selling grew.

Our theme was that people don't want magazines. One of the phrases we used in our pitch was "people need a magazine like they need a hole in their head." But how do you feel about young people working? Do you think giving a young inner-city youth like me an opportunity to get out of a negative environment and a chance to meet positive and successful people like you and learn from them is a good idea? All of that was a part of my sales pitch.

We were encouraged by Jimmy to stand in front of the mirror for an hour and practice. He insisted we know everything about verbal *and* nonverbal communication. Our body language should match what we said. It was a lesson that didn't come easy. On the contrary, I spent hours practicing my new craft. Every lady, I sexed up. My dark angel would have been proud of me. I used people before they used me.

KELVIN

After years of observing from behind closed doors and around corners, it was easy to see the opportunity, my opportunity, to gain from the drug game. My Uncle Tweetybird never knew it, but I watched him. He was the weed man before me, and he never had to tell me. You see, I had a pair of eyes, two nostrils, and a brain that worked together. He didn't put any weed sales in front of me and say 'this is the thing to do,' but I paid attention to how the same people would come by for only a few minutes. Any child can figure out what's going on in their house over time.

My brother Ben, he was one of the ones who showed me how to pile up the money. I never saw his total bankroll, but I know he had two paper routes on Chamberlayne that kept him paid. I could see my brother's money every time he would count it in front of me. I was never the type of person to let you know I was learning from you, but if you watched me like I watched everybody else, you'd see I was always picking up things and using them in my life. By watching the alpha males of my group, I learned to seize every opportunity I could.

I had people in my family that worked and had their own homes, cars, and material things, but the only one I saw every day was Grandma. Maybe I should have paid more attention to how Grandma did it. Or maybe I should have followed my two aunts, who are now ordained as a minister and a deacon and are married with homes. I watched them, but only from a distance, and it was by their choice, not mines. I always thought that I could get the house, car, and money, and that it didn't matter how I went about it because none of my financial role models had gone to jail at that time. As a matter of fact, besides my Moms, who left every now and then for a few months for stealing, I was the first to go to jail.

***

My first year at John Marshall high school is my first year selling. Not only do I have the joints for you to smoke, I also have the candy bars to cure the munchies after smoking. I get the weed and the candy from my brother Ben, who gets the weed from my cousin and some white guy I don't know. The candy comes from a friend of ours, who steals it. Every day I go to school with a plastic bag with fifty to one hundred joints, and a backpack full of candy. Of course I'm not the only person in school with weed or candy, but I remain on top as the best seller.

Every morning before we went to School at John Marshall there was a small candy truck parked across the street, and the name of the truck was Crew's Quarter Snacks. On the side of this candy truck there was a picture of a pot of gold with one coin sticking out, and every morning the line behind it was so long you wouldn't believe. But regardless of that fact, I still sold out of product almost every day. I think all of this may have played a part in my wanting—and later getting—my own candy truck.

It makes me happy, this ability I have to get people to purchase things from me. I'm not going to go as far as to say that I can sell ice to an Eskimo or salt to a slug, but I guess by my saying those two things you get the picture. The thing about me is I always have to have good products. I'll sell any kind of candy bar, but the best seller is Snickers. As far as fruit candy goes, the best are Now & Laters and Blow Pops. The best sellers for Now & Laters are always pineapple, chocolate, and banana. As far as the Blow Pops are concerned, I never go wrong as long as I keep watermelon and sour apple. Most days all of my candy is gone before I go to lunch. On a typical day, I sell sixty or seventy jays. I sell so much weed and candy, the basketball coach asks me why I have my money on the spot every time we have to pay dues! I keep so many people looking for me that a couple of my teachers let me out of class to talk to people. Of course, they don't know what's going on. I'm thirteen years old and have John Marshall High School on lock.

Now here it is, the end of the year, and guess what? I pass! Not to the tenth grade—I fail in all my classes. I move on to cocaine. I quietly become the powder boy. But it isn't just powder. It's powder, baking soda, water, and fire: freebase. I put the powder in pieces of brown paper bag, carry it around with me, and rub the paper together to fluff it up. I come to realize that a person using drugs will accept anything I have, as long as I keep good shit. And if I give them *enough* good shit, they'll show a little patience and not go to anyone else. Ten dollars of base taped to the side of ten dollars of very good marijuana. How can you beat it? People love to smoke that base any way they can: by antenna, glass tube, drinking glass with foil on top, or bent-up beer can with holes punched in it. They have to have it.

I'm still the weed man in school and all my teachers love me. They plead with me to stop cutting, because when I am in class I make good grades. But I fuck up and get put out and stay out. So I move into the streets of Highland Park and frequent That's Nice restaurant before this new fat boy comes through with his weed. It's not that I can't compete. I am now, and always have been, a people person. The fact is I have three other places to sell at, and I'm more of an Ebony Island dude myself. All of the people that come into the club come to me and get their weed after going to the bar and getting their coffee brandy, Singapore sling, or blue motorcycle.

But that's not all. Not only am I fourteen years old and accepted as a drug seller in Highland Park—one of the hot and hard spots in Richmond—I'm also going door-to-door in Nottingham to all the peoples' houses, selling them powder coke. You see, none of my friends that still live in the Ham know that all of these people get high. But I know, because I let the old heads from Washington Park know that I have powder.

Carefree is my way of life. My days are spent sitting in my room in Brookfield Gardens, smoking the weed I am getting by the pounds, with my 15" speakers blasting RUN-D-MC and Public Enemy. I'm fourteen and living the life of a hustler, or so I think. People are knocking on the door all day to buy drugs, and when I don't hear their knocks, they start throwing acorns at the window.

I don't like to feel hyper—sniffing powder showed me that. So joining that crowd isn't for me. I've been a weed man since the age of twelve. Hmm. I wonder if they mix well? Yep! Before long, everyone in Brookfield is smoking jumbos, and all the people from Newtown, Jackson Ward, and North Side that were coming to see me for weed now come for the combo. Guess what they bring? Their friends. And the friends bring friends. Before you know it, there's no more sitting in the room. It's time to stand outside on the block and catch these people outside because the flow is too constant. The legend of Tall Slim is born!

———————

"Can I say something?" Anton asks. "I just wanted to say to Kelvin, I remember all that. I remember your old room and us throwing little pebbles against the window so you'd come out to get us that bomb." He's grinning, shoulders back.

"Yeah, the traffic got so heavy on the sidewalk, I h-h-had to get out there."

"What do you guys think he should write next?"

"It'd have to be him coming out the room," Stan says. "We're going to see him next in public." Kelvin nods quickly and starts writing.

"Before you do that scene, though, can I ask you a question?" I say.

He looks up and nods again. "Go ahead."

"When did you know that this was what you really wanted out of life? That selling was not something that you *could* do or *happened* to be doing but something you really *wanted* to do?" Kelvin lowers his head, gives it a side shake. The others turn in their pews. I move toward him.

"Kelvin?" I ask. He's deep in thought and makes us wait. I lean against one of the pews while he shakes his head one last time.

"Honestly, Dr. Coogan, you're the first person that ever asked me that," he says, almost to himself. Then he looks up, and it's like I'm seeing his face and everything that face has seen in an instant. In a flash I recall how many times I answered that question—what I *wanted* to do—from family and teachers when I was in high school. I then learned to ask it and answer it for myself, and then ask it again when I got the wrong answers during college and beyond. I became conscious of myself and my purpose by paying attention to that dialogue. In a daze, I turn back toward the altar, wondering what it's like to not hear that dialogue, never really knowing that voice inside.

"Man, this is like a game of strip poker!" Stan sputters, breaking the spell. He's wearing the standard two-piece uniform, the khaki offsetting his cinnamon skin.

"You ever notice what happens in a game of strip poker?" he goes on. Nobody responds. "People don't get naked all at once. That's not the point." As he talks, a line of men passes by the open door of the chapel. One shouts to Stan, who booms back, "How it BE!" turning the greeting into a command. Then his voice becomes a conspiratorial whisper. "But I'ma share this with you, right?" He leans into the center of the room, looks side to side. Then he raises both hands, pointing them back toward his shoulders. "If you gonna see mines? I'm gonna see yours!" All at once he drops his hands. The challenge hangs like fishing line.

STAN

I'm in my room, preparing to go to a sales meeting around 7:30 a.m. when I hear the knock at the door. "Maid service," I hear as she places her passkey in the lock. This is not alarming to me at all. It's more or less her daily routine to come in and change the towels and clean and make the bed. But this day is different. She isn't by herself. She's training a new girl, petite and very feminine. Her skin is a Halle Berry brown. She has soft, pure bedroom eyes. And her hair is a long, reddish, silky crown. She has that innocent, shy look about her, too. But hindsight is always 20-20.

As I sit on the bed, listening to the cleaning women carry on small talk, the one I know, Linda, keeps making direct eye contact, giving me less conversation than the other lady, but more body language and more smiling at every word that comes from my lips. We're feeling each other, but I have to go. Jimmy has made me very punctual and precise in all my affairs. We say our good-byes and "Have a nice day"s, and Linda makes mention that she'll see me again. I'm under the impression that I'm catching Linda, but actually, Linda has just caught me.

When she gets off work, she comes to my room and asks me to carry her home. Yes, I took Linda home that night. It was my idea, before I dropped her off, that we should stop and dine. And we did. We flirted with each other over a nice dinner. I guess I viewed myself as some kind of game show host back then. Everything was just a game. But actually, I was lost in other people's perceptions. I'm thinking I look great on the outside, so to Linda's eyes I'm a good catch. But if she could have seen the DVD of who I was on the inside, she would have run. And I would have run from her, too.

How do you spell cocaine? I spell it L-I-N-D-A. I'm sure everyone spells it differently.

"Try this," she said matter-of-factly. After meeting my drug of choice, my life became a huge roller coaster.

Clank-clank. Clank-clank. You hear the chains pulling the cars by force. You wait patiently for your car to reach the top.

Clank-clank. Clank-clank. Peer pressure is like that. Even the most gentle peer pressure is a force to reckon with. Linda is going to get high with me or without me. And I don't want to lose her. I want to be loved. It doesn't matter what kind of love: good, bad, I'm fine with it.

Clank-clank. Clank-clank. After I reach my highest point with Linda, what's next? A fall! My heart starts racing! My adrenaline is flowing! I'm falling *hard*! I have spent all my money to ride this lifestyle. But what's next? All my finances are going to Linda, who says I need to please or she is going to leave. I'm open to lying, stealing, cheating—maybe not robbery or killing yet, but I'm not off the roller coaster yet either. How many lies can I tell my loved ones before that river dries up? It won't take long for them to say, "Slow down, I don't have it to give." But Linda won't let me rest, not yet. So she suggests I sell my rings, my watches. It's simply, "Stan, just do what it takes to keep me in your life." So, after selling my goods, I steal your goods.

KELVIN

I can't pinpoint a specific moment when I actually made a conscious choice to follow this way of life. But I can clearly remember the public service message that should've caught my attention, the commercial that asked that question: "What do you want to be when you grow up?" In this two-minute spot, I saw a policeman, a doctor, and a nurse. I also saw a construction worker, a fireman, a businessman, and a football player, but the thing that caught my attention was that they showed the policeman at the end chasing and catching someone, with the announcer saying, "No one wants to be a drug addict when they grow up."

If I was told at a young age that I should make goals for myself, I sure don't remember. I never wanted—or should I say, I can't remember ever wanting—to be anything normal, like a policeman or a fireman. These are the first goals most kids think of, unless you're like me and reach too high and go for the *almost* unreachable. I never sat around thinking, "I want to grow up to sell drugs, have children out of wedlock, and become a career criminal." I wanted to be a basketball player. It was something about the way Magic Johnson would smile that big smile after every play. It just made me feel like that could be me. But I didn't have anyone—not one person in my life—with the knowledge of what it took to succeed in the sport. To be truthful, I don't think anyone expected me to live long enough to do much of anything in life.

Now, for every action, there will be a reaction, and it doesn't have to be immediate. In my case, I did know more or less right away what would happen.

When you piss into the wind, you know you're going to get a wet pant leg. I heard the warnings. But I didn't pay attention to the things Moms told me, or nobody else for that matter.

* * *

I was about to step my happy, skinny little butt out of the shower and who's right there? Ninja Mom! I didn't see a belt, so I was very confused. But once she raised that extension cord, all my confusion went down the drain. I guess the cord must have been fun for her, or maybe it was the small space of the bathroom, because this beating seemed to last just as long as my shower. I swear she switched hands in the middle, and this never happened with the belt. Needless to say, this ass-whipping here kept me straight for a while. But as I got older, the beatings slowed down and eventually stopped, as they do with all parents. I know for a fact that my brother and I wore my Moms down. So I guess after she got tired of fighting, she had to let us do us.

It's true that as I sat upstairs in my room in Brookfield with my drugs, she let people come and see me. Her accepting my ways early on may have played a major role in the way I felt about selling and smoking weed. I guess if she would've told me to stop, I would've, but the fact is she didn't. So there is no way I can go back and call it any other way than it happened.

I was an opportunist. Every time I saw an opportunity to get more, I jumped at it. And because of that, I have played a part in destroying the futures of many people, which makes me wonder why so many people love me even today. You see, being a people person, I really do care, and I often spoke against drugs while selling them. To sell a pregnant woman cocaine, whether it's powder, freebase, or crack, always made me feel bad. But to fill up a cup with crushed ice and see her smile when she got that sno-cone off of my candy truck just warmed my heart.

6

A TIME YOU TAUGHT SOMEONE

"This in the chapel?" the man at the podium asks. He straightens my roster with the flat of his hand, then adjusts the volume on his walkie-talkie and steals a moment to tuck in his white polo shirt.

"Every Saturday. It's through OAR," I explain over the voices coming from his walkie-talkie. "Been coming here since the summer," I add with a shrug. It's late autumn.

"Yeah." He turns down the walkie-talkie. "But we got a service in there today. How many guys you got?"

I hesitate. I never really know how many guys I've got. "I think there's ten on that list." He looks down to check.

"It'll be tight, but we'll set you up in room C. You can go ahead wait in there."

I scan the bank of cinder-block rooms down the long hall where the lawyers meet with their clients.

"Is C the one with the seminar table?" I ask.

"The what now?" he snorts.

"I'll be in C," I say under my breath. But he's already turned away.

Room C is a rectangle about the size of a single dorm room, with two tables shoved together. I try arranging the chairs around the perimeter, careful to leave enough space for each man. Then I wait with the door open, exposed to the comings and goings of the staff, lines of prisoners, and scattered visitors like me. Stan is the first to arrive.

"What happened with the chapel?" he demands. Then he drops his papers down in a spot where he can see the door and sits. He has an instant command of the situation.

"I guess Father Pruitt has a special service going on," I offer. Stan shakes his head.

"I'm going to share this with you, right?" He reaches over to clasp my shoulder. "This class is special."

"Thanks, Stan," I smile.

"No, man, I mean it! You got the hottest ticket in this jail. If OAR can't keep your room, man, you got to speak directly with the chaplain." He leans back and forms a temple of his fingers. "His office got the juice." I nod. Then suddenly, Stan sits up. He's decided. "Matter of fact, I'm a trusty now. I'll tell him for you."

"No!" I lunge with my voice. I realize he's trying to teach me how to get things done in jail, but the last thing I need is to be in the middle of what seems like office politics between OAR and the chaplain. "I'm just a volunteer, remember. It's their program. I'll talk with OAR about it."

"Man, you are *not* just a volunteer!" Stan barks. Once again I thank him.

"What's up with the new digs?" Kelvin asks, ducking his head reflexively as he crosses the threshold. Stan starts explaining how I'm being disrespected. Naji sits down, opens his folder, and starts reading. He seems more intensely focused than ever. Andre comes in right behind him, carrying a few more chairs from the room next door.

"Dr. Coogan," he asks, "did you ever find that Tupac rap I was telling you about?" He's talking about "Dear Mama."

"Oh, yeah. That was great!"

"Do you remember it?" Larry is standing next to Andre now. They exchange little glances, egging me on.

"Go ahead, kick it," Larry says. Ron pushes through their shoulders to hear. I look straight at Andre.

"*Even though I had to sell rock?*" I pause and glance about the room. "*It felt good putting money in your mail box!*" Larry smirks. He rolls his shoulder into Andre. "*Even though you were a crack fiend,*" I continue with one finger pointing, "*you were always my black queen.*" Then I drop the mock seriousness, raise my eyebrows, grin, and find Andre's face. "Did I get it?"

"Oh yeah, you got it!" Andre erupts, high-fiving Larry and rapping the rest of the verse. G laughs louder than I've ever heard him laugh. While they're rapping, some young guys in their twenties come to the door and ask if this is the writing class. These are Stan's new recruits, and he flatters the first one like he's his father.

"C'mon in! Dave, this here is Raymond. He's a young man who knows how to do time!" He begins introducing the others. I scramble to remember the names. "These guys know coming here is doing something positive!" Stan concludes. Then he looks over to me, signaling that the floor's all mine. I stare around Room C, trying to ignore the noise from the hallway and the growing noise in the room. The older men quiet down the younger ones.

"Go ahead, Dave," Kelvin commands.

"What do you guys know about the class?" I ask.

"The writing class," Stan answers for them, "is all about the internal! That's what I told him the other day, Dave. We're following the story *inside*, not the drama *outside*."

I start bantering with Stan. I feel like a talk show host with a sidekick. I talk to recreate the first days of summer, the original pitch, the core of the project. The other guys nod respectfully, with cool reserve.

"OK," I conclude, looking out at their faces. "Let's just jump right in then." I pass out some paper and pens. "Write a piece about a time when you taught someone or someone taught you. But you can't use the words 'taught' or 'teach.' You have to show the teaching and learning through the action and the characters and the reflection about it all. I'll give you about fifteen minutes."

As soon as I finish talking, a group of prisoners passes by the large window behind me. The new writers shoot grins and peace signs in return, tapping the blunt ends of their pens to their chests. Some carry on with hand signals longer, like baseball coaches and pitchers.

I call time after fifteen minutes and ask Raymond to read aloud. He lurches into it, eyes close to the page, and grips it tight with both hands:

"One time. A friend of mine. This dude. I knew. Was getting dissed so I. Told him go. Handle your business!" He lowers the page and looks up at me for the first time. The longer he stares, the smaller I feel. He seems to think he's finished the story and owes no further explanation.

"What did you do?" I ask.

He looks at me like I'm stupid. "I gave him my gun."

"And what did he do?" I persist.

"Shot the guy!"

I can't hide that I'm repulsed. The room goes silent. And at first I think everyone's just as shocked as me. Then I realize they're stirred by seeing my shock. I struggle to see his point of view. I open my mouth to speak but can't find the words.

"That's a tough piece, man," Stan says. He eyes me cautiously.

"And who taught you to handle your business like that?" I finally ask, incredulous.

"My cousin," the boy murmurs. I pause to chart the psychological distance I've just travelled from childhood to right now—I had never fired anything bigger than a BB gun and had never known anyone who owned a real gun, let alone pointed it at another person. I zero in on what I'm feeling as I look around the room. I realize what bothers me is not just the story, but the lurching movement of his writing and, in conversation, his incuriosity about the details. How hard it would be to teach him how to analyze his experience when he's struggling so hard just to express it! Sorting through this paralyzes me and makes me appreciate Dean, Kelvin, and the rest.

"You know, he said a bad word in there," Stan chimes in. "A four-letter word. D-U-D-E. See, around here, a 'dude' ain't nobody you can trust. A dude is . . ."

"Is it too late for me to go to college?" the boy interrupts. This pushes me off balance. I stumble out of my thoughts.

"Of course not." I search for his eyes, buy he's already gone, looking past me toward the window and tapping his chest to someone I can't see.

"Tough room," Stan mumbles to me under his breath.

"Mr. Coogan, I got a problem." I turn toward Naji. I can't imagine a problem much bigger than the Raymonds of the room. Why didn't I prepare myself for moments like these, when guys would hit my writing pitch with line-drives straight to my chest?

"I'm 'bout ready to get shipped. Three weeks," Naji explains.

"Shipped?" I ask.

"That's how we say it when we're getting transferred to prison." He lowers his voice and smiles, amused. "You never heard that?"

"I bet there's a whole *lot* of things Dave never heard before coming up in here!" Andre says. I smile wearily.

"My problem is that I really want to continue with the project." He implores more with his eyes than his voice. I want to reciprocate. I like Naji. And I want to continue, too. But I'm confused. I'm not sure what the project really is anymore, or what it's becoming. It seems bigger, more sprawling and chaotic than I imagined. Maybe too much pickup ball and not enough organized play. I need to spend more time with each writer just to understand how their thinking about drugs or guns— or anything else, for that matter—has emerged and, possibly, evolved. But to do this, wouldn't I have to follow them much longer through the system? Maybe the project is not so much about one group of men meeting at the jail, but about a collective of writers working toward the same goals no matter where they are?

"All right," I decide. "We'll do it in letters."

Slowly, he offers up a fist. Just as slowly, I realize that's my cue to raise mine.

"That's power," Stan explains, watching us bump fists. "It's like, 'I give you a little. You give me a little.' That's power, when you share."

"And if you ever decide you want to stop for whatever reason, no hard feelings. Right?"

"Nah, man," he says unsmiling. "I'm going to stick with this. In fact, when I get to wherever it is I'm going, I'll scout out some talent for you. People who can commit."

"That's a possibility," Stan says. "Prison's permanent. People get rooted there." He and Naji share a grim nod.

"Dr. Coogan," asks Kelvin, "let me have another one of them set of prompts."

I reach for my bag. "Did you lose yours?"

"Nope. But you know, like Naji's sayin' 'bout scoutin'. I'm 'bout to get sent up myself, and I know I'm bound to run into someone I know. I always do."

I hand him and Naji three packets each. It all feels weighty, ceremonial. We've just sealed a deal.

Andre

I always offer some to Stickem and Dom. "Nooo!" they say back in unison. But I just smile, grabbing the game controller.

"You know, one way or another I am going to make all of y'all try it!" And again, I hear their voices—"Nooo!"—as I concentrate on the screen.

The next day I come back with a couple of cheeseburgers. When Stickem leaves the room to go get us some Kool-Aid, I open up one of the cheeseburgers and put some heroin on top. When he gets back I'm sitting down with the dollar bill, taking massive hits up my nose. I offer him some and like usual he says "Nooo!" Then he bites into his cheeseburger with ketchup and a side of heroin. After he swallows I yell, "Ha! I finally got you!" He looks at me dumbfounded until I explain. I watch him like a hawk for the effects. I figure it's my turn to watch him make gestures and pass out. But nothing happens. He isn't even that mad at me.

The next week Dom sees me on the block trying to make some money. He tells me he's got a new video game and that I could come to his crib and play it. He has a lot of swagger, and I really like that about him. So while he starts getting the game ready, I go into my routine. Before I even finish the sentence, offering him a hit, I can see the look in his eyes. I imagine it's the same look that I had given my father. After a few hits up his nose, it's a wrap. I finally get to see the effects. He even vomits.

It's safe to say that we never got to play the game, but every day after that we did. Dom would come on the block and hang around all the time, and we would get high as kites daily. I took him to a shoe store on Broad Street called New Rich, and I bought him a pair of the brand-new Nike Air Jordan tennis shoes. He was surprised because he thought I was going to buy me some tennis shoes, but I just wanted to do something nice for him because he was chilling with me while I sold drugs and was making money. I wanted him to benefit as well.

Dom's brother Anton seen this and he started hanging around me as well. Anton was taller than me, about five-foot-ten, and very outspoken and spoiled, I might add. I soon got him hooked on heroin as well. He didn't vomit his first time, but he had other effects.

* * *

I'm chillin' on St. James Street, selling my heroin and sniffing my heroin. The New Balance Tennis 925 series had just come out, $120.99, so you know I'm rockin' my grey-on-grey joints, with my blue Guess jeans on. Earlier that day, I went to Foot Locker to get me a grey New Balance sweater. I'm looking sharp as a tack.

A white, four-door Grand Am comes slowly up the street. Someone yells, "Yo Dre, your girl is coming." Michelle is a redbone, five feet three inches, 140 pounds, with brown eyes, and I love the way she says so whenever she's mad at me. (To this day I can still imitate the way she would say my name.) She's a rich girl from the suburbs who wants a bad boy in her life. And I want a high-class broad to show off to the cats in the projects. Her parents are still married and live in a big house with three cars. Did I mention she's rich?

The movie *The Fugitive* has just come out, starring Tommy Lee Jones. I love his acting and Michelle loves her rap, so we have 2Pac blazing out the speaker with "I Get Around." Michelle knows the routine. She slides into the passenger side. And I grab my drugs out of the Super 8 trash can. Then I tell everyone to peace out and I drive off.

One of the things I like about Michelle's car is that the middle of the steering wheel is removable, so I always put my drugs in it. If I'm ever pulled by the po-po, they'd never know. At a red light, I go inside my little hideaway to pull out two eggs of heroin. I take out a bill, fold it in half, pour the white substance, and take my regular hits up my nose. It puts me at ease and relaxes me instantly. I ponder what my main man Tommy Lee Jones is going to show me next. Then my girl interrupts my thoughts with, "Can't I have some?" She knows it boosts my sex drive. And she loves that. So I immediately put some on the bill and put it under her virgin nose. She inhales and switches to the other nostril. As I drive, I look to my right and see that Michelle is silent as a kitten. I think, "What is she becoming? Does she feel different, older?"

At the movies, I buy us some Cokes and a big thing of buttered popcorn, and my favorite, Goobers. But when the movie begins, Michelle starts to nod off and slouch in her seat. The heroin takes over her little body. People start to pay more attention to us than to the movie.

Was I an overnight celebrity? No. So I get us the hell out of there. Back in Jackson Ward, I kiss my baby, get her back in the driver's seat, and send her home. I don't know how she's going to make it, but in twenty minutes I call her house and can't believe it. She's there! I tell myself it was the heroin that got her home. But when I can see again, I know it was God and no other.

That night I didn't get to finish watching the movie. What I did get to watch was me becoming Dr. Victor Frankenstein. I began to feed her heroin daily. We became twins at it, and her sex life grew instantly. She no longer desired to do right. She just became what I created: a monster.

At this point in my life, if you wasn't using heroin, I couldn't fully trust being around you, and I thought something had to be seriously wrong with you. It took a lot of time and soul-searching before I came to the realization that I shouldn't do to others what had been done to me. Being addicted to heroin had me perceiving things otherwise. I now recognize that I was totally wrong. When I went to prison, I left Michelle with a dope habit. She went through withdrawals, too, but no one ever knew, and we went our separate ways. Dominique and Stickem both died years later in drug deals gone wrong. Dominique's mother blames me and only me. To her, I stole her dreams for Dom and Anton. But what about my dreams?

* * *

Me, Weasel, Donnell, and Toad is on the back basketball court in Jackson Ward. But we isn't playing no basketball. This is where the drug dealers lay to earn their keep. Even if you do want to play ball, it's totally impossible. The asphalt on the court is all cracked and everything. There's no rim on one of the backboards. Instead there's a reddish milk crate with the bottom burned out, so a ball can go through. Weasel has his boom box with him. He's just came from Carrington's Music Store on Broad and stolen the new Too Short tape called "Player Years." You can't tell us we wasn't the shit!

We all have our burners on us, except Donnell. He's the toughest of the crew, taller and bigger than us, his voice heavy and scary. We always listen to him on everything, even down to how we should treat our girlfriends. Donnell is five feet seven inches, 195 pounds or so, dark skin, with a smile like the Joker. He tells me that whenever his burner's on him, he's going to use it, no deviation.

At fourteen and fifteen, we don't possess an arsenal of weapons, but we have guns. Mines is a silver .38-special. Weasel is really skinny and he has a complex about it, so he lets his gun be the bigger man. He has a .41 magnum. Its bullets are so big it only fits five in a round, so whatever body part it touches, it destroys. Toad is a light-skinned, fat-framed dude. He wears glasses, so we always pick on him about it. He has a .357 silver and he is never scared. Donnell tells us that if we stay and play as one, then we can defeat anybody.

We're selling our drugs and using our drugs on the court. The heroin is flowing through my veins, and I'm feeling pretty good. But then a customer pulls out a .38 snub-nosed silver gun on Donnell. That's when I realize he isn't a customer. It's a set-up from what we did to them niggas over Church Hill. I try to get over there, moving fast as I can. I pull out my .38 special just as I hear the shots being fired on my best friend. I watch him fall to the ground. I fire, but the heavy tears falling from my eyes impair my sight. I miss my target, but I vow to myself that I will connect later.

As I watch the "customer" run back to his green Cadillac Deville, I notice Donnell is bleeding everywhere. I take his nice grey-and-black jacket off and make it like a pillow to put under his head. His eyes are on me the whole time. I begin to say things like, "Don't panic" and "Where else are you hit?" and "You're going to make it, Donnell." While I'm holding his head he says, "We stay and play as one." I wait for him to finish it but he can't. He dies right there on the street.

The next thing I know the EMTs are there. I draw my gun on them to make them back away, but Weasel slaps me back to reality and reminds me that we have to go before the police arrive. I have to get more heroin in my system to be able to walk, talk, etc.

I don't know how to believe in anything without Donnell. I don't know what grieving means. I just want revenge.

The rest of my homies feel the same.

* * *

I got on my sheepskin coat and matching hat, black Calvin Klein jeans, black IZOD shirt, and black Bally boots. I also have my .32-shot Mack II on me. After I finish bagging my cocaine at my Aunt Tammy's in Creighton Court and sniffing me some heroin, I head to Jackson Ward and stash my coke in the green super-size trash can. I put my gun in there too, just in case the police are riding heavy.

I know Weasel and Toad are across the street, over in Tiny's crib. I'm the only morning person of the crew, just sitting on the bench, relaxing and enjoying the high from the heroin, when four guys approach me at a fast pace. I'm not worried. I'm familiar with them. They are dealing with Toad. But when they get to within an arm's length, my red light goes on.

Instead of greeting me they pat me down. Their guns are drawn. Then the interrogation begins. They want to know where Toad is. They claim he robbed them last night and that if I don't tell them where he is, they're going to kill me. "Do what you got to do," I say, raising my hands, "because I don't know where he's at."

The first shot strikes the left side of my face. The impact of the bullet flips me over the bench. I scoot up under it, but bullets are being fired by all four dudes, penetrating my clothes and entering my flesh. I can feel each burn, but I don't feel no pain. The way I'm positioned under the bench, I can see the faces of two of the shooters. I look into their eyes and can see only one thing: they want me dead.

I close my eyes and see my best friend Donnell, and I keep my eyes closed until the shooting stops. Then I open my eyes back up and I am surrounded by a lot of unfamiliar faces: police and EMTs. I am still alive and being rushed to MCV hospital. I remember lying on a bed with wheels and a lot of lights above me, before I am put under anesthesia. When I awake, the events of that morning flood my mind.

I need to warn Weasel and Toad! As I begin to dial, I notice that I have a patch covering the whole left side of my face, including my eye. I am hooked up with IVs and a shit bag. My right leg is in a sling. I don't even realize Toad is screaming on the phone. He's happy to hear my voice. "We're on our way and we got good news!" A crowd of hospital people come around me and talk amongst themselves like doctors do, then they tell me what procedures have been done, how lucky I am. I see the awe in their eyes, wondering how I survived or maybe even why.

Weasel and Toad give me a big hug, and even though it hurts, it feels good. They've even brought me a gift. Heroin. We get high right in the hospital room. Then they tell me the good news: they've killed three of the four dudes who shot me. Toad says he's sorry. He feels it was his fault that I got hit up, but I tell him, "Remember, if we stay and play as one, then we can defeat anybody." Silently, we all think of Donnell.

The next day, I get a visit from the Richmond Police. The detective asks if I am doing better, you know, trying to soften me up for something. Then he asks about the shooting and did I know who did it? I glimpse at my wounds. Then I look at him and give him the same line I gave the other policeman. He shows me Polaroid pictures of three men on gurneys, dead, telling me he knows that Toad and Weasel did it in retaliation. I tell him I don't know those guys in the picture. When he leaves, I get right on the phone.

After my operation, the doctor told me that if I had gone into shock I would have died. He said the heroin in my system helped me through it. That was the good news. But I had lost sight in my left eye, and I couldn't walk. I had an iron plate and rod put in both of my legs. They told me that I probably wasn't going to be able to walk again.

I spent several months in that hospital and then checked myself out to rehab myself. People thought I was crazy. When we pulled up in the projects, my mom had to get two guys to get me out the cab and carry me into the house because I couldn't walk. My grandmother was so happy when she saw me. I slept in her bed until I got better. But when I went to sleep that night, I had my first nightmare about when I was gunned down. In my dream, they got the job done. It felt so real! When I awoke I was sweating. My heart felt like it was coming out of my chest. I never told anybody about that nightmare, and for a long time I was haunted by it every time I went to sleep.

"Stop that wicked lifestyle, boy! I know what you're doing," my grandmother said when I was well enough to be about.

"I'm not doing anything but looking out for the police for the big drug dealers." But she and I both knew it was a lie as soon as the words rolled out of my mouth.

7

TRUTH

"Man, it's good to be back!" Stan says, stretching his legs out on the front pew.

It's been a long and flawed process getting back to the chapel. I placed calls to Shakelia's boss, who then placed calls to the chaplain. I didn't want to put up with the hassles of Room C, so I stayed home while no one called me back. Weeks went by before Father Pruitt himself surprised me by calling me at the university.

"I told you the chaplain's office got the juice, Dave!" Stan says. Then he explains. He gave Father Pruitt my number when he got tired of waiting on OAR. I marvel that Stan has managed to get more accomplished than I have, without a phone or a computer.

"So have you guys been writing while I've been gone?"

Ron is smiling so big he looks like he's about to burst. "I was *writing* these past weeks, Dave!"

"What about?"

"When you was away, I really got to thinking." He pauses to pinpoint the moment. "I had a mother who was giving me *truth!*" The word pings like a bell. "But I couldn't relate to it. It's like I was in a box. I didn't know what was outside the box, what I was feeling. My mother, she didn't know about the life I was experiencing." A gentle silence settles into the room, the distant sound of *"truth"* receding.

"Man, what the hell are you talking about?" Stan asks. Ron smiles sweetly, his eyelids at half-mast. He turns from me to face Stan.

"What I'm leading to is the problem. You know how the prompts ask about the past and then the problem?"

"I understand that. But what's that got to do with a box?"

"That was me before I came out of the closet, where my mother couldn't reach me. But that wasn't even the worst part!" Everyone settles back. They know a story is starting. "When we moved down here from Baltimore, I had to do it all over again. I had to pretend I liked girls. Then I was lured by older homosexuals." A strange wave of relief splashes pew to pew.

"He's trying to say how he's attracted to *men!*" Dean says eagerly.

"He likes to do it with *guys!*" G adds, looking up at me and grinning.

"I get it, G. Thanks."

"But he had to *fake* it with females!" Dean explains.

"Because he was *homosexual!*" Larry interrupts.

"Nah, he was with females, too. That's *bisexual!*" someone counters. Everyone chuckles.

"Smurf, you know it's all good," Stan says after everyone's exhausted themselves. Ron flashes his perma-grin. No doubt he's heard it all before.

"Ron? How did you feel about what happened when you were lured by older homosexuals?"

"Well, back then, I had not yet identified my preference, so I didn't really know what it was they was doing." His speech eases to a stop.

"And you didn't like it," I venture.

"It came about eventually, that desire. But you gotta remember, I was really young when it happened." He looks down at his paper. A convict walking the hall stops to press the meat of his face against the tiny window of the chapel door.

"I'm trying hard not to put words in your mouth, Ron. But it sounds to me like sexual abuse."

He searches my face, considering the phrase. "You could call it that. But at some point, the hunted became the hunter." He leans back and crosses his ankles.

"Right, right," I begin. "That's how we learn." Just then the chapel door opens and Father Pruitt walks in. The man who was watching me from the window follows him.

"Dr. Coogan," Pruitt says, smiling, striding up the aisle to shake my hand. He wears a black shirt with a white priest's collar. His smile is broad and warm, his voice resinous. "I'm sorry to interrupt. I just need to get to the back office for a minute. Hello, everyone!" He faces the men in their pews. After he disappears into the back office, Stan explains that the other man is the chaplain's assistant.

"Look out!" Dean shouts to everyone. Pruitt has emerged from the back office with the trusty. They're each carrying two large plastic boxes of glazed donuts.

"I hear such great things about this class, Dr. Coogan," Pruitt says, standing by me at the altar.

"It's them, not me," I demure. "These guys are *digging*. I'm just watching it pile up."

"Dave's like one of them men on road crew, standin' by while we work!" G jokes. The joke becomes a topic.

"Dave's the boss-man in that little tiny office off the side of the road. Whatcha call that?" Dean asks.

"You mean the trailer?" answers Ron.

"Yeah, Dave stays clean up in there!" Dean adds.

"Nah, man. Dave gets dirty with us!" Kelvin claims.

"So, you on a mission, Father Pruitt?" Stan interrupts.

"I do have to take this box over to Belief Tier, yes. But then I thought while I was back there that if I could appease you all with sweets, maybe you'd forget that I interrupted you?" He starts moving about the room with the donuts. The men thank him, warming themselves around the fire of this unexpected generosity.

RONALD

My days become shallow and more secluded as I wander about in my future. I take on the personality of curiosity. Debbie is with a new guy named Chuck, a hard-working, attractive, older gentleman whose only desire is to satisfy Debbie. When she and Chuck are not around—and Grandpa Reese is in a drunken coma—is when I sneak into Debbie's bedroom. That's where I find their porno books. I don't really know what it is I am seeing, but I know that I want to try it.

My sister, Rosa, lives next door. I wonder why she has a different guy in her bedroom every week. Whenever I hear doors close I listen hard for noise. When it's Debbie and Chuck in there, I often hear sounds like *ooh* and *ahh*. Rosa, I would hear heavy breathing and screams. Now I'm looking forward to seeing what is actually happening!

With a lot of knowledge and nothing to do with it, I practice being a kid again. Fannie registers me for school and gets me my supplies. But since she works, our neighbor, Charlotte, has to bring me home. One evening, she decides to take a bath. I'm looking at her body when she gets out of the tub. Then I begin to touch her.

"What are you doing?" she asks, a little surprised.

"I don't know, but it feels right," I reply. She shows me her sensitive spot, and I rub it. Then she takes my penis and rubs it. It tickles and feels strange, but, oddly, I enjoy it. Then Charlotte and I get dressed. And just like that, I close the door to that experience.

Fannie gets me a full-time babysitter who comes to live with us. She's a big-boned, young lady with long, kinky hair and a flirtatious personality. She loves to conversate with men and show off her brown-skinned body. Outside, I pretend to admire the reservoir while watching her play with the guys. Whenever she notices me listening, she laughs and says, "We're just talking about work and fun." She doesn't know that I've learned a new word from her: sex.

I don't understand all that's happening around me. Nobody else seems too concerned. My family's biggest concern is seeing me smile.

***

"Come here, Ron. Let's take a walk around back." I repeatedly try to excuse myself, but they aren't taking no for an answer. It feels suspicious, but the look on Jermaine's face makes me think it'll be all right. After a few minutes back and forth, I agree to follow the girls, and they carry my best friend Jermaine and me behind the bakery.

"What's in your bag?" they ask.

"Soda." I notice another boy there, also named Jermaine but older than my best friend. He's eying the soda, so I just give it to him. The alley smells like piss. The girls start talking, trying to persuade me and Jermaine to put each other's private parts in our mouths. I hesitate.

"If you don't do him, I'll make you do me!" says Big Jermaine. Boy, if I knew then what I know now, I would have said yes! But I had not yet identified my sexual preference. I went home confused, upset, and curious. I couldn't stop thinking that I'd done something nasty and wrong.

The events of that day weren't discussed by anyone, but inside I felt like people were talking about it. When I played hide-and-seek with Charley the next week, he hid by my steps and when I found him, he pulled out his pecker. He asked me to put it in my mouth and lick it. I did it and Charley attempted to pee in my mouth. Immediately, I stood up and went to the curb. Two older guys spotted us and began to interrogate us. I ran into the house and hid, hoping I wouldn't get into trouble. I don't remember ever talking with anyone about the situation, but I know I didn't go outside for a week.

Finally, wanting to play, I went to Charley's house and knocked on the door. His brother, Michael, answered and told me to come in. Charley isn't there, so I decide to hang with Michael. We start wrestling and he pins me to the floor. I reach for his penis.

"I want some," I say suddenly.

"What are you talking about?" he blurts.

"I want to feel it in me," I smile. Michael seems shocked and also pleased by my answer, and is more than willing to act on my request. He tells me to pull down my pants and lay on the floor. Then he pulls his pants down and lies on my back. Suddenly, I feel a sharp pain that causes me to squirm. Michael, obviously, is enjoying himself, but I am feeling a new discomfort. I tell him to stop but my request is ignored. With all the strength I can muster I raise myself up until I can see out of the window. People are sitting on their front steps.

"If you don't stop, I'm going to yell!"

Abruptly, he becomes very apologetic. He must have felt scared, like he'd done something wrong and wanted to make it right. He gets off me and starts apologizing from the front room to the back. Finally things return to normal. In fact, he feels so relaxed he shows me a pair of Charley's underwear with doo-doo stains in them.

Then the front door opens and his mother comes in. Michael lets me out the back. The screen door slams shut.

Because I was so young, I had no clue that any of this would ultimately affect my future. Fannie did not know what was happening, because of her work schedule. I don't blame her for anything. She was a loving mother who always wanted the best for me. She spoiled me and told me I'm unique. I knew she was attempting to get us back on our feet and into a place of our own. But, of course, like any kid, I was curious. Learning, I was experiencing life.

In middle school my appetite and desire for a man grew strong. I had already had sexual experiences with boys, but a man was on a different scale. It scared me because of all the values and the things I had been taught about God, which conflicted with my feelings about being happy. The kid inside of me was crying for help, needing release. I was failing at being a little boy attracted to girls. I needed identification to survive, the security of knowing I would not burn in hell.

A temporary escape came about when I joined a marching band called New Edition with members from all over the city, many of them from a gay lifestyle with an openness that intrigued me.

Troy was one of them. He had a round and blunt body with skin the color of a Snickers bar. He had many sexual skills and was already living his life out of the closet. I was in awe of his complete confidence. I was constantly feeling lost, hurt, afraid, corrupted, abandoned—basically a failure. Troy shared his experiences with me, and more than ever, I wanted to come out and express myself like him. We discussed our faith in God, and Troy assured me that he wasn't going to hell.

"Why not?" I asked. "Isn't it a sin against God, and morally wrong?" But he just smiled at me, shaking his head. Still, I struggled. We were called all those ugly names during marching season. At first I cried. Then I got some heart and cussed the ignorant and educated the knowledgeable to the best of my ability. Today, I know one thing for sure, and that's that God does not show favoritism over his children. But at the time, uncertainty consumed me.

To compensate, I hosted as many females as I could, attempting to project a strong image of manhood. The relationships were superficial, to say the least, and I was scared about someone finding me out. I started going to the club on a regular basis to meet females, but the guys were what I really wanted.

After leaving the club one night and waiting for the bus, I am approached by a transvestite who seduces me with his charm. I know it's a guy because of the telltale signs: big feet, deep voice, big hands, and height. But my curiosity gets the best of me, and I go along with him to an apartment down the street.

We go to the bedroom and get undressed. He begins to perform oral sex on me. It feels good, so I grab his penis. I'm wowed at the size. My mind drifts. How did he hide a penis this size? I get back with the program and he's trying to get me to let him put it in my ass, but this is making me uncomfortable.

All of a sudden someone starts banging on the bedroom door. I am told to get dressed quickly. Then I'm pushed out the front door as the other guy storms the bedroom. An argument ensues and I quickly proceed back to the bus stop. All I know is that I have no more desire to be with a drag queen.

I meet a female from around the way named Lisa. I fantasize about men when we have sex. And I find other women to date. I am now fooling around with three on a regular basis: Lisa, Nicole, and Tarsha.

In the band I perform as one of the junior high steppers. We do dance routines to the drums. It's total hype. The drummers have a party over at their house one day after the parade, and Troy has sex with a guy in front of everyone. A few of the other guys show off their dicks, and I'm thinking, damn, this is a great party!

Later that night, I get a shocking phone call from Lisa. I listen intently as she reveals that she has become pregnant with our child. I am disturbed but excited. I think a child will provide the stability I need to go forth in life. But when I think more about the reality of being a father, I go searching for places to find men.

I walk up the street from my house to Clifton Park, where I meet a guy cruising. We go behind the train tracks. He gets me to unwind in front of him and we suck each other's dicks, then jerk off until we come. After that experience we promise to stay in touch. He says he'll show me some more places to find men.

Caught up in all that's happening, I forget about Lisa and our child. Or maybe I block it out. Life has just become so difficult. I start acting up in school. I rarely stay a whole day. I don't want Fannie involved. But the school calls her out of concern. So she takes the time to sit me down and try to find out what's happening. I resist her love and concern.

I am the chameleon: a thirteen-year-old boy from Baltimore telling everyone I am a sixteen-year-old from a big family in New York City. I tell everyone that Fannie is my real mother (even though by now I know it's Debbie) and that all her kids are grown except me and my little brother. The lies become hard to escape. I know without a shadow of a doubt that I am truly homosexual. All I need now is a plan for coming out. I am consumed with trying to be someone or something I am not. Calgon, take me away!

I ignore Lisa for a great while, but then I grow concerned and call her. We begin our conversation with friendly words, but I am disturbed by the tension I feel in her voice. Suddenly, she breaks down and tells me she has had an abortion, and I feel reality sitting in my lap, heavy and suffocating. My hopes of being a father escape me and the hurt is slicing me so deep I start to cry. Lisa explains she didn't know what to do and not hearing from me prompted her to make a decision. After our phone call, I know more than ever I must exit this closet before the door shuts. But my anger toward Lisa drives me deeper into isolation.

I spend the first few weeks going out on a regular basis. I avoid having sex with anyone, though the temptation is great. I sink into a depression and find some pills. I don't know what I've taken, but it gives me a really upset stomach and I end up at the hospital. When I wake up, I sit on my bed and ask God if he loves me, because this is an unjust life. My first attempt at suicide has failed. I consult Troy. He tells me that I am feeling gay. That's cool and all, but I am only thirteen years old! I can't possibly know what I am. Or can I?

Fannie allows me more freedom. I'll leave the house on a Friday after arguing all week with her and find gay people to hang with. When I return home on a Monday or Tuesday, I start yelling and arguing with her again. On June 1st, 1988, I declare my school year over. I spend my days hanging out in the mall bathroom, cruising guys.

On my fourteenth birthday, I am initiated in my coming-out party. No more hiding. I am sincerely coming out into my sexual liberation. Finally, I can kill the womanizer within. Troy and I soar to new heights in this lifestyle. We discover a place called The Meat Rack. It's known to the gay community as a meet-and-greet spot. There are times we go together, but most of my discovery is done alone. Learning to con becomes my art. I am an actor who believes his role is real.

My first name is Duke. With his young, attractive face, he is sought out by many. He meets men and learns how to pleasure them outside in alleys, around corners, on park benches. They drive him to their fancy apartments and treat him as if he is the most important thing in life. Illusions that are self-deceiving keep him believing in the unreal. Many times, he finds himself in places where he's not quite sure how he got there. But in his mind you can't tell him that he's not in control.

8

ODD MAN OUT

It's windswept and still, except for a faint creaking that I can't place and don't care about. I'm reading Naji's draft, a wad of legal-sized yellow paper filled on both sides, that I've saved for the end of the day like a favorite treat. My plan is foiled, though, when a police car arrives and blocks the intersection in front of my house.

The officers leave their lights on. Leisurely, they approach a man who has been pushing a Weber grill up the middle of the street. I'm cautious but nosy. I crack the front door but can't make out much. Soon, he's handcuffed and seated curbside, a benched athlete. The officers chat slowly, ignoring the man's belligerence. Then a police van pulls up and the officers greet the driver. After twenty more minutes or so they confiscate the grill and uncuff the man, who lunges off the curb, swinging his arms, cursing, a glaze of sweat running down his dark neck. His white T-shirt glows neon but soon disappears as he retreats.

I want to laugh at this episode of *Cops* unfolding in my neighborhood late at night, but something inhibits me.

The next morning I write to Naji to let him know I've received his latest draft. But what I really want to tell him about is the black ghost.

NAJI

The only memory I have of my mother's funeral is of the day itself, and of holding someone's hand and standing on the curb in the rain. No feelings, nothing dramatic, just a grey, wet, miserable day. The next day I'm standing before two of the biggest doors I have ever seen. I'm fascinated with how shiny they are and all the intricate patterns carved in there.

I am holding my grandmother's hand. She leads me to these huge wooden benches that seem to stretch on forever. The floor has a smooth-textured rug with beautiful flower patterns. It spreads all the way into the shadows underneath the benches. The ceiling is so high I can hardly see the top through the wide streams of sunlight that cascade through the enormous windows, crisscrossing down at either side of the room. Dust particles dance in the sunlight like little fairies in some magical epic. This is the first time I can remember being cognizant of my size. I am in complete awe!

There aren't many people in the room, just a few scattered bodies here and there, sitting in complete silence. The only noise comes from a few men and women who keep walking up to this huge box and talking to this grey-faced man with glasses. I am struck dumb by how tall he is. The people addressing him have to reach way up, handing him pieces of paper. I notice that every eye is on him. He might be a king, like in the stories I hear or the cartoons I watch. I must have been staring, frozen in place, because all of a sudden my grandmother snatches me and slams me into a seat and tells me not to make a sound or I will be beaten. I look over at my brother beside me. We both have tears in our eyes.

My brother and I had been formally adopted, right down to our names. Once Perrys, we were now Canadys, but almost immediately we were made to feel anything but. My grandmother's way of dealing with the smallest of problems was to scream. If she was trying to do something, no matter what it was, and it didn't go the way she planned, her response was "Shit! Dog-footed!" and whatever she had in her hand would be chucked across the room in any direction, regardless of who might be in the way. She chucked everything—from knives to canned food items if they fell when she was stocking the shelves. Between the ages of five and nine, I was completely terrorized by my grandmother.

* * *

The rug stretches to about twelve feet on a hardwood floor. It slides from side to side or wrinkles depending on how you walk over it. I'm a six-year old boy and my brother is eight. We're hyperactive—at least I am—and like all boys at that age, we horseplay a lot.

Running from the small living room where we're playing, game pieces in hand, I crisscross my arms, simulating the flight maneuvers of jet fighters (my childhood dream occupation). I'm totally engrossed in the game. My brother screams that it isn't fair; that I'm cheating because cars and army men can't fly. But in my world, flying is the least they can do. Wait until they become invisible!

My grandmother, hearing the noise, steps from her bedroom into the hallway and notices the wrinkle in the rug. She asks who did it. I hear my brother yell from the living room, "I'm in here!" Then she screams, "Jimmy, get out here!" Hearing her voice, I begin to shake all over. My heart is pounding in my chest, tears forming in my eyes. I step out into the hallway.

"Didn't I tell you not to mess up this rug?" I'm too scared to even answer. I want for the life of me to say I'm sorry, that I was just playing, but my vocal cords fail me. That's when I notice the extension cord in her hand. And that's when the dam breaks: I begin to bawl!

Like a wild dog sensing weakness in its prey, she's on me, striking me on every part of my exposed body: head, neck, back, arms. She doesn't care. I'm dancing around, screaming at the top of my lungs, trying to fend off the cord with my hands, but Grandma catches them, too, sending a pain so intense up through my arms that I think that I'm going to black out.

"I'm sorry! I won't do it again. Please!"

"Shut up!" she yells. I cry uncontrollably. I'm unable to comprehend that she means it literally, even as she persists in beating me senseless. My disobeying her command sends her into a rage. She tucks my head between her legs in a vise-grip and begins hitting me even harder, one lash for every word, as she verbally chastises me.

"Didn't! I! Tell! You! To! Shut! Up! You! Don't! Know! How! To! Close! Your! Mouth! Do! You! Do! You!" I'm wiggling around between her legs, snot and spittle mixing with the stream of tears running down my face, moaning, trying my best to be quiet so that she won't hit me anymore. My back, legs, and behind are on fire.

"Answer me!" she demands. This is crazy! I'm in extreme pain, but being able to let it out gives me some comfort.

"Yes, Grandma! I can be quiet. Grandma, I can be quiet!"

"Shut up then!" Whack, whack, whack! The beating seems to last forever. When she finally lets me go, I realize that sometime during the beating, I have wet myself. A pool of urine has polluted the floor. My pants are soaking wet.

"Now get in that bathroom and clean your nasty ass up and get this piss off the floor!" All I can think is, in the future, how am I going to *not* make any noise as she beats me?

Something in me broke that day. I became a nervous wreck around my grandmother. I feared her more than anything in the world. I truly hated her. I used to think she was incapable of smiling, laughing, or even making a pleasant face. She had absolutely no patience and the least little thing would set her off. I grew anxious with anyone raising their voice at me or raising their voice in general.

"James! Turn around and pay attention!" the teacher screams at the top of her lungs. I have been warned, but I kept turning around in my seat. Before I know it, I am standing up, screaming back at her.

"Don't yell at me! You ain't my momma! Don't ever yell at me!" And I run out of the room. They find me curled in a ball in the corner of the boy's bathroom, crying my eyes out.

I didn't know at the time why I was so angry and had reacted that way. It scared me. Being the younger child in the house, I needed to be held, told that I was loved, and made to feel like I was special. I was very sensitive. But in that home, I began to die inside. I also watched a darkness slowly fill the light in my brother's eyes. We were both changing dramatically and no one seemed to care.

* * *

I climb out of bed and make my way down the hallway to the bathroom, careful even in my grogginess not to disturb the place rug. My brother and I never expect there to be a Christmas with a tree and presents and all that. We have even been told as much by my grandmother—that this was punishment for our "bad behavior" during the prior months. But looking down the hallway into the living room, I notice the area illuminated with a soft yellow light. Strange shadows glimmer and dance on the walls.

Curious, I creep down the hall to see what's up. To my astonishment, in the far corner of the living room sits a silver Christmas tree with a silver star! It is the most beautiful Christmas tree I have ever seen. Different-colored ornaments of all types shimmer from the limbs, giving the tree a magical appearance. A small assortment of presents in colored wrappings are arranged under the lowest limbs.

My heart catches in my throat. I can't believe my eyes.

It has snowed Christmas Eve day and most of the night. "A white Christmas!" I think to myself. If what I am seeing is truly there, it would be the perfect Christmas, aesthetically.

I become so excited! I run back to my room and wake my brother. "We got presents!"

"Nuh-uh," he grumbles before turning over.

"I'm serious!" I insist. Slowly, we creep into the living room. We quietly run to the tree to see which one of the colored boxes belong to us. Caught up in the excitement of our first Christmas in this house, it doesn't dawn on us that we have probably violated a rule of some type. We are kids, totally caught up in the moment.

"What are you doing out of bed in this living room!" In our excitement we must have made too much noise.

"We were just looking at the presents," my brother says, wide-eyed and terrified that we are about to be whipped. I begin crying because I know we are.

"Well you ain't getting 'em! You ain't getting nothing! And what makes you think there's anything under there for you anyway? Since you want to be nosy, get your asses outside and pick up trash in that courtyard until I tell you to come in!"

She walks over to the front door and opens it. A cold gust of wind blows through the living room, chilling me to the bone. We are barefoot in our pajamas! We both stand up, huddled together, crying our eyes out, too scared to move. Going outside is frightening, but getting past her without being hit scares us far worse.

"Don't make me tell you again!" We begin inching toward the door. I am bracing myself for the anticipated blow. I am so conditioned to her abuse that I freeze and accept the beating, scared that if I try to flee or in any way protect myself, it will get worse. My brother escapes her wrath and makes it outside unscathed. When her arms get tired of wailing on me, she pushes me outside and closes the door.

My feet freeze instantly, and with the wind gust the rest of my extremities soon follow. Still stinging from the beating, cold, confused, and afraid, I just stand there, shivering in a daze, looking to my brother for answers. He is already ankle-deep in snow, picking up trash. I begin helping him clear the courtyard of debris. Within minutes, the pain from the beating I've received is forgotten and replaced by the numbing pain of partially frozen hands and feet. I truly believe that my feet are going to break off at the ankle.

"Hurry up!" my grandmother yells from the top of the stairs. Judging by her demeanor, I get the impression that she doesn't want anyone to see us out here. I can't believe how cruel she is, and also how devious.

Later that day, a friend of my grandparents, probably from the church they attend, comes to the house. Before she arrives, we are told by my grandmother that we better act like we have some sense! This means that if we say anything about what happened, we will receive much worse. But when the friend sits down in the living room, we are told that we can open our presents. The shock of this excites and confuses me. I can't understand my grandmother's motives, but being a kid, I throw myself into the moment with complete abandon. As my grandparents and their friend sit around and talk, my brother and I tear into our few presents: a plastic motorcycle, some pajamas and socks, a board game, and some cards.

My grandparents' ability to slip into the roles of doting, loving guardians who have suffered much to take care of their deceased daughter's children in the presence of anyone outside the family is amazing! I witness these transformations on numerous occasions. They are always successful in deceiving people about their true nature, provided the people being deceived don't have the opportunity to witness our interactions with one another. But this woman sitting in our living room must have noticed the unusual tension and lack of family spirit hanging in the air like a black fog.

"Thank your grandmother, boys." This catches me completely off guard. Not that I am an ungrateful child, but when you're made to feel that your very existence is a burden, that your basic needs are provided with reluctance and bitter resentment, being asked to say "thank you" is like asking a POW to thank his captors after receiving a plate of food infested with maggots. You're saying thank you for just enough sustenance to keep you alive to continue the sadistic torture. I'm also scared to death because, in my experience, any verbal or physical show of affection has always been met with hostile rejection.

"Thank you, Grandma and Granddaddy," we say. With a grudging smirk, my grandmother says, "You're welcome." I think the interaction between us is making the lady very uncomfortable and curious as to what is wrong with this picture.

"Aren't you going to give them a hug?" she says, speaking to my grandmother. I wish this lady would shut up and leave well enough alone! I can't conceive of putting my arms around my grandmother. But looking into her eyes, it's apparent that she is just as uncomfortable as me, if not more so. With a forced smile that seems like it's killing her, she stretches out her arms to us. I am the closest. So, slowly, I move to her. As she encircles me, I can feel her reluctance. My skin is crawling with anxiety, fear, revulsion, confusion, and an out-of-body sense that I can't fully explain. She quickly releases me with an almost imperceptible shove that makes me flinch as if I am about to be hit.

I would relive these feelings again and again from the onset of any intimate relationship I would encounter. To this day, that hug of hers is still the most uncomfortable position I have ever been put in.

Not having a family that believed in family was really difficult for me. I felt strange and out of place growing up, because I always wanted to do what I understood families to do—basically, enjoy each other's company and do things together that bonded them stronger than just blood. But as I grew up, I became painfully aware that I was the odd man out as far as family was concerned. My self was getting buried under cultural ignorance and social indifference. This is how the terms of my life were defined.

* * *

There's a large gingerbread house on the table at the place we go to, For Little Wanderers, not far from the school. My brother and I sit on opposite sides of it and are immediately attended to by the receptionist. My brother does all the talking, because my mind is totally zoned trying to figure out if the gingerbread house is real. There's white icing covering the roof, with different-colored sprinkles scattered on top, bushes of multicolored gumdrops, candy cane columns placed at the corners connecting the sugar-clustered sheets of gingerbread on four sides. There's even a chimney made of M&Ms.

Through my distraction, I hear my brother telling the woman that we are scared to go home. She asks why and he tells her that we're going to get a whippin' for running away. After their discussion, she goes back to work and leaves us alone with the gingerbread house. I'm too embarrassed to tell anyone that I'm hungry, and I guess my brother is too. But looking at each other, the solution is clear.

The anticipation causes my stomach to cuss me out! Carefully, I reach out and break off a piece of the icing hanging from the roof like icicles. I quickly shove it in my mouth while my brother waits for the verdict. My eyes light up! I start wiggling around in my seat, savoring the taste. After making sure the coast is clear, my brother snatches up a gumdrop, and it's on. In a span of less than ten minutes, we have completely decimated the gingerbread house without being noticed. All that is left is a sad cardboard structure with bits and pieces of icing stuck to it.

When the receptionist comes back, she just smiles. We must have looked real comical with crumbs all over our faces, hair, and clothes, trying to look innocent with a freshly gutted gingerbread house abandoned on the table. But when the front door swings open, I feel like I'm going to throw up.

The look on her face says it all. My grandma walks quickly toward the table, barely giving us a single glance, and starts talking to the woman. I look to my brother, and he motions with a nod of his head toward the front door. I'm too scared to move, and he isn't leaving without me, so we sit there trembling.

My grandmother puts on her act, telling the woman that she doesn't know what to do with us—that she took us in when our mother died and that we have become so unmanageable. "The teacher says he's a smart boy, but he refuses to sit in his seat and do his work," she says, looking at me. Then she motions toward my brother. "And this one's too busy messing with the little girls." The story is always the same. Never "Well, I beat the hell out of them every chance I get and treat them like shit because I had to put my life on hold to take care of them."

"Kids can be a handful," the lady says, nodding.

"Let's go!" my grandmother shouts to us. Before I walk out the door, I turn around, pleading with my eyes for the lady to help us. But she just smiles and waves goodbye.

We barely make it down the block before my grandmother reaches into her pocketbook, pulls out the extension cord, grabs my brother by the back of his pants, hoists him up onto his toes, and begins beating the hell out of him, right there on the sidewalk of a main street! She couldn't care less. She beats him almost all the way home. All I can do is walk along and cry. I feel every lick she gives him and know I am next.

When we get in the house she yells, "Get your asses in that room!" Minutes later, she returns with the extension cord and some rope. She tells my brother to take off his clothes and get on the bed. Afterwards she puts him spread-eagled on his stomach and ties his hands and feet to the bedposts. As I watch, she beats the blood out of my brother, leaving welts across his back, buttocks, and legs. His screams had to have been heard all over the neighborhood. But the extension cord isn't enough. She throws it down and grabs one of our broken hockey sticks sitting in the corner of the room and begins hitting him with that.

"Don't kill my brother, Grandma! Please! Don't kill my brother!"

"Shut up! You're next!" And just as she promised, when she finishes with him, she strips me and beats me with the extension cord for what seems like fifteen minutes or more. My whole body becomes an open wound, throbbing with pain. When she's finished with me, she leaves my brother tied down. Both of us are still crying.

"Are you OK?" I ask my brother through the tears.

"Thirsty. I'm really thirsty." Crying, I tell him that I'm scared. He pleads with me to get him some water, but I am too terrified to move. She leaves him tied up for hours. Needless to say, we are never fed. All night, I listen to my brother moaning in pain, and feel guilty and ashamed that I can't find the courage to help him. I still deal with that guilt and shame today. It hits me like a sledgehammer to the chest whenever I think about it, which is pretty much all the time.

The next couple of years are a blur of run-away attempts, brief stays at different foster homes, and even trips to child psychologists ordered by the state. But we are always returned to the care of my grandparents and the truth about what is happening at home never surfaces.

I begin to live to get out of the house. I feel stifled, trapped, claustrophobic. We are seldom allowed to go out and play because we are always on punishment for some trivial violation of my grandmother's rules. But when I do get released, I literally run as fast as I can with my face to the sky, as if I could somehow gather up enough speed to take flight. I do this every time with no exception, and begin to be recognized in the "hood" for my speed. Everyone wants to race me, and I always win. I learn to like the attention and acceptance. I crave it like a drug.

Being poor with not much to do in the hood, we find distraction in whatever games we can come up with. Firebug is my favorite, because it separates the brave from the scared. Firebug is played by setting something on fire and seeing who can put it out with their feet. I learn this game by watching the older kids play it. I learn that fire is not really as scary as it seems. The other kids just haven't noticed that fire feeds off oxygen, and the more you fan it, the bigger and hotter it gets. Provided the fire is small enough, you can smother it with little or no pain or damage to your hand. When I do this, I make up elaborate stories about how I am magical or immune to fire and can't be burnt. My peers are impressed by my stories and skills. I love it and become well-known. I begin to develop a rep.

"Get back! I'll put it out with my hand!" Always looking to be the center of attention I push my way through the crowd to the fire's edge. Acting before anyone else has a chance to grab the spotlight, I drop to my knees, and bring my hand down into the hot mess. The paper wraps around my hand, clinging to me. It's hotter than normal. I quickly withdraw my hand only to notice that the fire is now on my hand! This isn't paper! This is plastic! I've made a painful mistake! The plastic melts into my hand. I try to shake it off, but it's no use. I receive first- and second-degree burns to my hand and learn a valuable lesson about the effects of fire on different material, but it never occurs to me that my need for attention and acceptance was the ultimate culprit.

* * *

Evette takes me into her bedroom. My brother goes with Wanda. She strips me naked and then strips herself. She has me climb up on the bed between her outstretched legs and tells me how to touch her. She makes me do it on my own. When she starts to wiggle and thrust her hips at my hand, making noises like I am hurting her, I get scared and begin to cry. She won't let me stop and becomes even more animated and vocal. Finally she stops and pushes me down on my back and sticks her head between my legs. When she is done, she puts my fingers in her mouth and keeps apologizing, begging me not to say anything.

She gets up and tells me to stay there. As soon as she goes to the bathroom, I run across the hallway to get my brother. Before I get to the door, I hear Wanda moaning like her sister had been. The door is cracked, so I look in. She has my brother lying on top of her. Her legs are outstretched and she has her hands on his butt, pulling him into her. They are both completely naked. I run back to the room, terrified! To this day I remember the smell, like rotted fish.

I never spoke of this to my grandparents or any other authority. But as my brother and I got older, it became a macho-type thing. We learned that getting it on with the babysitter was every little boy's fantasy, although at the time there was nothing enjoyable about it.

* * *

"I'm going to visit my girlfriend," I tell my grandmother.

"No you ain't. You're going to stay your black ass in the house." When she goes into the next room, I sneak out anyway, taking a bottle of her cheap perfume with me as a gift.

Of all the girls in my neighborhood that I played with on a daily basis, it was indeed strange that I found this particular girl to be the most beautiful I had ever seen. She came complete with blonde curly locks and blue eyes. Although they say love is color blind, I believe that if you are brought up in a culture preoccupied with the color of skin, love can suffer from irrational tunnel vision. Not that I take anything away from her: she really was a pretty girl and very nice. I just don't trust that my choice was a free conscious choice.

When I get to my girlfriend's house, she's waiting for me on the porch. She takes me down into the basement of her parent's beautiful, two-story home. There, we sit knee-to-knee in the dark, holding hands and giggling. After a while I lean in and we kiss, a beautiful moment that comes to an abrupt end.

"Why is your skin so black?" she asks. It seems like an innocent question. There is no sort of malice behind it. In fact it shows that she is as affected by race/color issues as I am. Maybe she's grown up with a superiority complex? Although I am ashamed and embarrassed, I quickly recover.

"Because I'm a superhero. I got caught in a fire trying to save a baby!" As ridiculous as that sounds, it goes over well. But through the laughter, I go from having low self-esteem to NO self-esteem.

9

Sealed in a Jar

In the lobby of the visitor's center, I do the paperwork. I pause over the box asking *Relationship to Prisoner* and find no box for *Teacher*. I check *Friend* instead—acknowledging this new reality—then wait in line. I'm told I can't bring any paper or pens into the visiting room. "No business," is what the woman says. I offer up Naji's work and fan the pages so she can see I'm not a businessman or lawyer. But since there is no box for teacher—it's actually forbidden for teachers and counselors in the Department of Corrections to visit their students and clients—I go back to the car to stash his draft, along with any hope of continuing the workshop one-on-one.

After the private frisking, the drug-sniffing dogs—unusual, I'm told by the usual-crowd-visitors—I get an invisible ink blot stamped onto my hand. Then I process through the metal detector to wait outdoors in a chain-linked square. Thirty minutes and three heavy prison doors later, I enter the visiting room and wait in a rubber-molded stackable chair for forty minutes. I left the house in Richmond at 9:30. It's now about lunchtime.

Naji snakes his way around the perimeter. His shoulders are slumped, but his eyes are alert. "Thanks for coming, Mr. Coogan," he says. "I know it's a long ride from Richmond." There's a constant crackle of chips and soda cans opening at the table next to ours, where two women sit with three kids. I notice most everyone has clear ziplock plastic bags stuffed with coins. Naji notices me noticing.

"I'm sorry I didn't bring any money. I didn't realize how much of a junk-food fest visiting day would be in prison." He shrugs it off.

"I'm diabetic. So, you know, I can't have most of the stuff they got here anyway."

We talk about his writing, the pieces he's working on and the black ghost I saw by my house that night. Then I ask him about the new writers he's recruited. I want to know all about these guys who wrote me asking to join the project.

"Tell me about Brad," I begin. "How'd you meet him?"

"It's a trip!" Naji says right away. "Brad's like the complete opposite of me, the way he grew up knowing his mother and father, that big house in the country. And he's white. But we were talking at chow one day and came to realize we went through the same thing because of our addictions." He lets out a little laugh.

"And Tony?"

He shakes his head, laughs even louder. "Oh, the staff hates him. He's like—every little thing, writing up a complaint. And they don't like that. But he's always right. Powerful guy, Tony. Black like me." He pauses to take in the room, nodding to someone he knows.

"Karl will send me these letters—" I begin. And we both start grinning. "—and I'm thinking it'll be the next scene in his life. And he'll do a little of that, but then something just sets him off and he starts debating if God exists, if drugs are really bad." All this tickles Naji into a giggle.

"Karl'll be in the dormitory and come *right up* into a circle and say stuff like that." He's clearly fascinated by the boldness of it. "It could be anything! Like he's going to teach us who Thomas Jefferson is or why rap is bad. White guy comes right into a circle of *black guys* and wants to tell us what's wrong with rap! He just wants to put that out there."

"I mean, he's intelligent," I concede.

"But I keep telling him—you know, when we're by ourselves—I say, you got to focus on what Mr. Coogan's asking you to write about. And you've got to take it down a notch in the circle. Them guys we're building with aren't going to tolerate that kind of arrogance." He leans back into a more recent memory. "He came by my bunk the other day to kick it, you know, between meetings—because this place is all about meetings, you know, we're a therapeutic—"

Thud! A low, rising moan pulls our attention away. A little boy has tripped and is facedown by the side of our table.

"Get up!" the woman sitting next to us commands. The boy sobs, pulling the bag of chips to his chest. "*Get* your ass off that floor!" she barks, before catching Naji's eyes. Briefly, they exchange tight smiles. "C'mon!" she repeats to the boy. "You're in the way!"

A slender man in prison clothes stands smiling at their table. "Say hi to your Daddy," a second woman says flatly. In one fluid motion, she pulls the boy up by his arm.

Naji sits with his elbows on his knees, covering his face with his hands. I hear the long beep of the microwave and the *thunk* of a can dropping down through the vending machine. "That was hard for me," he whispers, dropping his hands and shifting in his seat. "I always see myself in situations like that." His voice trails off.

"Because of your grandmother," I add cautiously.

"I just remember all of it like it was yesterday." Then he straightens up, pulls his shoulders back, and nods. "Really, that's the main thing I think I'm getting from this project now, just remembering what she put me through, physically and emotionally, figuring out what that *did* to me!"

"I always read your drafts at night, after everyone has gone to sleep. I just sit there in my favorite chair, looking out into the dark and then back at what you wrote." I look over to the boy munching his chips. He's in a brand-new moment, sitting near his dad. "Most times your drafts make me cry." Naji sniffs the stale air. "I try to put myself in your shoes."

"Your parents never hit you?" he asks, a little startled.

"No!" I nearly shout. Then I stop to think about it a while. "I do remember sucker-punching my dad once." I chuckle at the memory. Naji grins, shaking his head. "All I remember thinking was that it'd be funny, you know, to surprise him like that with a light tap in the gut. He'd laugh and chase me. Then he'd tickle me." I pause to smile at the boy as he pushes his fingers deep into the bag.

"So, what happened?"

"The exact opposite. By mistake I actually hit him hard."

"Whoa!"

"Oh, he chased me down. But that was it. After he grabbed me, he just shouted, 'There! Now you know how it feels to get ambushed!' He didn't hit me. That was the closest I ever came to getting beaten."

"What about your mother?"

"No, with both of them, it was always something they said, like, 'David, you've really disappointed me.' Something that made me feel guilty. Or they'd take away a privilege. But no, they didn't—" Naji offers a knowing smile that finishes the thought.

"Hey, how's your brother doing?" I ask, the memory of the two boys being beaten suddenly vivid. Naji explains that his brother is incarcerated in another prison for murder. Most of his time is spent in isolation. And it doesn't look like he'll be getting out any time soon. This is the end of the line, I'm hearing. "So he's never been through a writing class like this?"

"Noooo!"

That's when it hits me how far Naji's come from their shared history.

"What do you think he'd think of you sitting here, talking to some white guy about your life and his life?"

Naji shakes his head and makes a slicing motion with his hand by his neck. "No, no. He wouldn't approve. It's not about you. It's just that he's never had that opportunity to get beyond the way we came up, you know?"

The voice on the intercom ends visiting day. Naji looks away, sighing, and stands to face me. We shake hands. Then the prisoners take their places around the edge of the room, and I line up with the other visitors by the door. There, we stare at each other from across the room like boys and girls at a middle school dance, just now perceiving a chasm we cannot cross. The boy with the chips taps my arm.

"Are you a lawyer?" he asks.

"Just a friend," I tell him. And for the first time he smiles.

"I got a white friend, too," he says softly.

Naji

When the Massachusetts Department of Child Welfare came to visit our home and it finally began to look like we were going to be removed, my grandparents packed us up and fled to Virginia. We never heard from the Massachusetts Department of Child Welfare again.

Arriving in Hampton, Virginia, felt like arriving in another world. The neighborhood was clean and extremely quiet. I had never seen so much grass, and the trees seemed to tower over everything. There was a sweet smell riding the wind and even the sky seemed different than the sky in Boston. It was somehow brighter, and seemed to stretch on forever. But it could not wipe out the dark clouds in my life.

The beatings and the ridicule; the lack of love and trust; the lack of confidence in my ability to do anything by myself and do it well; the put-downs, always being told that I wasn't going to amount to anything; the looks of disdain every time I walked into the house; the lack of interest in anything that I thought was important in the world; and the complete censorship in the home, where I was never allowed to express myself in any way or show any type of dissatisfaction at the abuse I was receiving—all this taught me to be very juvenile in my thinking and pessimistic in my worldview.

* * *

Bored with nothing to do in my room, I go to my brother's dresser and pull out one of the drawers. It seems stuck, so I pull harder, and slowly, it begins to slide. I can't believe my eyes! The drawer is filled almost to the rim with quarters! I quickly shut the drawer and wait anxiously until my brother comes in.

"Where did you get all that money?" I ask, in what I think to be a whisper.

"Shut up! What are you doing in my stuff?"

I tell him I'm looking for a pen. He knows whatever I'm saying is a lie, but he also knows it is more important to keep my mouth shut. I would never tell on my brother, but I want to partake of "our" newfound riches. And he can't take a chance that I might tell. So he gives me a whole bunch of the quarters, explaining that he got them from the large Smokey the Bear penny bank that belongs to a kid who lives in the apartment building next door. We both consider this guy to be a close friend, and the realization of what my brother has done blows me away.

Before this, the most I'd done or seen my brother do was lift a pack of Bubble Yum or a candy bar. These acts were motivated by a desire to have what we saw all the other kids enjoying. Allowance was a foreign concept to my grandparents: they felt we should be grateful that they were taking care of us. Asking them for money was one of the most aggravating, humiliating, and degrading things I ever had to do as a kid. It was rare that they would give us anything, and if they did, we would first have to sit through a two-hour bartering session.

The next morning before school, I stuff my pant pockets full of quarters. At lunch, I buy ice-cream sandwiches for about thirty kids. I am *so* high from the attention I'm receiving! Kids tell their friends that I'm treating, and it spreads like wildfire! My need to be seen with money is stronger than my desire for anything that the money can buy. I want to impress my friends and also make new ones, because I believe that you can buy friends.

After lunch I'm called to the office and asked where I got all the money from. I tell them I found it. My grandparents are contacted and the shit hits the fan. I am brought home and whipped, along with my brother, and made to apologize. I feel so ashamed looking into the eyes of my friend and his mom and dad, who have treated us so well. They tell us that they can't believe that we would do something so cruel and hurtful.

At the time, neither could I. I had no idea how starved I truly was. I didn't even know what it was like to have a key to my own house and to be able to come and go as I pleased! If my grandparents weren't home, we were to sit outside until they came home. If they *were* home, we had to knock on the door to come in. It was the most embarrassing thing to have my friends with me and have to knock to get into my own house. My grandmother always—and I mean always—came to the door screaming at the top of her lungs, her face contorted by contempt, "Shit! Every time I get busy doing something, here you come! You come to this door again, I ain't opening it!" It made me feel like an outsider even more than I already did. The most damaging effect it had on me was that I never grew up. I never learned what it was like to be responsible for anything, because I was never given the chance to be.

* * *

In an attempt to hide his drinking, my grandfather takes me and my brother to local bars and shot houses. He buys us sodas and lets us sit at the bar, spinning on the stools, as he and his friends get drunk and pick up women. It never occurs to me, as I watch my grandfather kiss and fondle other women, that it's wrong. The atmosphere is joyous, the music loud, and everyone who comes in seems to be having a good time. What could be wrong with that?

He always brings strange women over to us and makes a big deal about us being the children of his deceased daughter. In turn, they hug us and tell us things like, "He's going to be a lady's man," or "He's going to be a heartbreaker." I enjoy the attention, as they squeeze me to their breasts, spilling out over their halter tops, their breath fetid and sour. They lavish me with wet kisses, smearing cheap lipstick all over my face. This inconvenience seems a small price to pay for the physical attention that I so desperately crave.

But soon, my grandfather becomes a very violent and abusive drunk. He falls into a pattern of leaving the house early in the day and coming back early in the morning, stumbling drunk. He wakes me and my brother up and has us stand in the kitchen as he babbles incoherently for hours, drifting in and out of consciousness.

"Jimmy! David! Where is my watch?" Each night it's something different—his watch, his wallet—that he's supposedly lost. "Get up out that damn bed before I beat your asses!" We scream, running around the house, searching in vain for something we know he probably has in one of his pockets. He starts smacking us around with his hand or the extension cord, tearing the house apart with us. My attempt to suggest that whatever he's looking for is in his pocket sends him off into another rage. Strangely, my grandmother comes to our rescue and sneaks us off to bed, leaving him in a drunken stupor by himself. When he passes out, she goes in his pocket and wakes him up to give it to him.

Eventually, he stops drinking and becomes religious all of a sudden. We are forced to church every Sunday. I suffer from asthma, a condition that was diagnosed a couple of years prior when I told my grandmother I couldn't breathe. She thought I was faking and gave me a paper bag to breathe into. My temperature went through the roof, the sweat pouring off my body from the exertion of trying to breathe and throwing up bile. Only then did my grandmother reluctantly carry me to the hospital. She was quickly told I had asthma and that if they had waited even a half an hour more, I would be dead. I would be told this by doctors three more times during my preteen years, with different increments of time until death.

"You're going to church!" my grandfather yells, fixing his shirt collar.

"But I . . ."

"You're going!" he insists. At the time, I can't take five steps without bending over. The church is twenty blocks away! By the time I arrive, I am a wet, sweaty mess. I collapse in the aisle and am taken to the back, where I lie down until the ambulance comes to take me to the hospital. No one ever questions my grandparents as to why I was being sent to church so sick.

* * *

"You want to hit this joint?"

It's a simple yes or no question with dire life repercussions should I choose unwisely. I'm in the woods with my friend, Chris, grateful to be out of the house. Curious and apprehensive at the same time, I tell him I have never been high before. Chris knows this, but due to the absence of his regular high partners, his own boredom, and the novelty of seeing me high for the first time, he is more than willing to seduce me into a world he himself doesn't truly understand. I'm looking for him to rescind his offer and keep me from having to make the decision. But he does his little skit instead—you know, the one about how it's not going to hurt me and how there's nothing wrong with him. The logic seems sound, even though my flight instincts are going off like crazy! But who listens to instincts at fourteen?

"Fuck it, why not?" What influences my decision more than anything is the complete turmoil in my home life. Anything would be better than what I am going through in that house. And today, getting high feels like a direct reaction to a weapon my grandfather has made because he feels my brother and I are becoming too "mannish" for extension cords. He took a hammer, removed the metal head, and cut two large fan belts into strips. Then he tacked them onto the handle and further secured it with black tape. It looks like a whip straight out of an old English torture chamber. With every lick, bloody welts rise off my flesh.

"Just suck the smoke in your mouth and then take a deep breath in." I watch as Chris demonstrates with the joint. Then he passes it to me, and I do exactly what I seen him do. My chest explodes! I begin coughing uncontrollably. It is my body's way of telling me, "Whatcha doing, stupid?!" I quickly pass it back to him while I recover. Before I know it, he's passing it back to me. This time the smoke goes down a little smoother. I keep asking him what to expect. He says it will take a second, but that I'll know when it hits me.

I begin looking around the woods to see if anything has changed, half expecting the environment to be somehow different. There's a wild sunflower growing in the brush, and I become fixated on this large black and yellow bee flying around the plant. It seems off somehow, almost animated. I notice that I can hear the buzzing of its wings. And is that "Smurfs" theme music I'm hearing? I know I am high when the bee turns its head, looks at me with droopy eyes, and smiles, showing off two rows of sparkling white teeth. I begin laughing and can't stop. It gets to the point where I think I am actually going to die laughing. I look at Chris for help, but he's too busy laughing at me. Then as suddenly as the laughing spell starts, it stops. Wide-eyed and out of breath, I look at Chris.

"Yo! I think I'm high! I'm going to be OK, right?"

"Yeah, man, just calm down!" The sound of his voice sparks another round of uncontrolled laughter. He sounds like a cartoon character!

I spend the next hour in and out of the silly giggles. For Chris, the novelty of seeing me high for the first time wears off. He decides to go, leaving me not knowing what to do.

"Look, man, go home and play it cool. Get some sleep!"

I am so afraid that when I get home my grandmother is going to open the door and I'll start laughing. To say that I would be busted would be like saying Michael Jackson is somewhat peculiar. But I make it home without incident and they never find out. I can't wait to try it again. I like who I am when I'm high. I'm more creative, funny, and outgoing. I can make a world where my personal problems don't exist, where I receive all the attention I crave. This is where I want to stay. My perception of myself, my confidence and self-esteem, is heightened exponentially. I feel like there is nothing I can't do, and no one I can't be.

I never notice any physical addiction to weed, but I am ignorant. It's clear that I have to have it to keep up the "cool" façade. And even on some conscious level I know that I am in dangerous waters, but for the first time in my life I have something that provides some semblance of acceptance. My teenage mind rationalizes this as normal. Weed becomes my way out.

Around this time I meet a girl named Sandy at school. She has a smile that can light up a room. She's from California. For a long time she rides the bus with me every day, but I never notice her. Then one day I look over at her and I'm lost! I go and sit beside her and make her laugh all the way home. I get off at her bus stop and walk her home. Everything is right with the world. I am fourteen and in love for the first time. She and I spend all our time together. Nothing seems to matter but us. I don't care about what's going on in school. At home nothing seems to bother me.

* * *

Our intention is to get "tore out the frame!" But none of us have, or are willing to part with, the associated cost of the venture. So the only obvious answer is to "bum-rush" every 7-Eleven store in walking distance. The target? The beer cooler. Our objective? To steal as many bottles of Mad Dog 20/20 as we can.

Like pirates celebrating with the booty of a fresh raid, we begin drinking right away by the football stadium. From there, things get a little sketchy. I drink so much I black out and can only remember fragments of the night: most notably, everyone standing around me and laughing, counting how many times I throw up in rapid succession. The count is at thirty-one when I black out for the last time.

It's about 3:00 a.m. Everyone is gone. The wind is whipping through the alley. I am freezing my ass off, sitting slumped up against the stadium wall, smoking a cigarette. Then I doze off.

I awaken to the acrid smell of burning. The smoke I smell is coming came from a large, smoldering hole that I have burned into the fur lining of my parka. I start beating at the hole but only manage to feed it oxygen. My coat bursts into flames! I quickly try to stand so that I can take the coat off. But in my drunken stupor, I fall flat on my face. Finally, I manage to squeeze out of it.

I can't *believe* my punk-ass, so-called friends have left me in an alley like this. I get myself together and stagger my way home. I try to sneak into the house but the door is locked. When my grandmother opens it, I fall in.

After being cussed out for about five minutes, I stumble to my room and fall on my bed. Next thing I know, my grandfather bursts through the door, screaming at the top of his lungs. I look up and the ceiling starts spinning, slowly at first, then faster and faster, until my stomach lurches, and I throw up all over my bedroom rug.

My life is becoming an utter chaos, and it's evident to everyone but me. I begin stealing on a regular basis. I tell myself that it's because I want to lavish my girlfriend with nice things, but it's more because I want to support my drug habit. Sandy never complains about my drug use. Her issue is always my lack of interest in her when I'm high. I never feel as if I am neglecting her, but of course, being high all the time, I'm not always cognizant of the repercussions of my actions.

I begin to lose interest in a lot of the things that I liked to do: gymnastics, track, swimming, weight lifting, martial arts. These are the casualties in a secret war, secret even to my own consciousness, that I am waging against myself. I begin to use all types of justifications as to why I don't want to be around old friends anymore. I continually bury my feelings with weed or alcohol so that I don't have to deal with my life. I love Sandy very much and don't want to lose her, but my need to be accepted by my so-called friends finally drives a wedge between us.

At this time in my life, I spent every waking moment trying to figure out how to get my peers to see past my skin color. I hated looking at myself in the mirror. I was called everything: smut, tar baby, ink spot, crispy, blue, black, blurple (a mixture of black and purple), African booty scratcher. You name it, I was called it, and it only served to solidify the inferiority complex that was so ingrained in my psyche. In an attempt to be strong and not appear overly sensitive, I never let anyone know how badly these jokes made me feel. I imagined that if I laughed with them and made fun of myself, it would take the sting out. I didn't realize I was giving their ignorance a legitimacy that I would internalize and carry like a yoke around my neck for years to come.

It's confusing because I was really treated no better, and often worse, by my black friends. The white kids may have held racist views, but I didn't hear them. I noticed different things that they did, and sometimes said, that let me know they were racist, but I figured as long as I didn't hear "nigger" come out their mouth, I could tolerate their company. In the end, all I knew for sure was that getting high turned me into the funniest, coolest, and bravest person in school. It seemed to be the key to being accepted, because suddenly everybody wanted to be around me.

* * *

After getting nice and roasted, I go in to my first-period class, art. Sitting across from me is a pretty white girl named Allisa. We are on speaking terms but don't really know each other that well. We are doing something with paints when I accidentally spill some on her blouse.

"You fucking nigger!" she screams. Hearing the word come out her mouth with the rage in her face takes me back to that little boy sitting on the floor in Boston and being screamed at by a grown woman.

Allisa has braces in her mouth and a red bandanna around her neck. In one fluid motion, I snatch the bandanna off her neck, wrap it around my right fist, and punch her dead in the mouth, as hard as I can. As I retract my fist, a few strands of the bandanna get caught in her braces and out they come tearing into her mouth. Blood shoots across the table, and she falls back out of the chair, unconscious. I am kicked out of school that day and made to pay for her braces.

I stop hanging around my white friends and begin to buy into the racist views that my black peers hold about them. I watch Alex Haley's *Roots* and fight tears back throughout the whole movie. I'm shocked beyond comprehension. Nothing could have prepared me for the rawness of that movie. I latch onto the hate at the edges of my heart like a pit bull! It seems to have affected most of the black kids in the same way, because the next day everyone is talking about it, white and black. The black kids are mad and the white kids know it.

Rumor spreads like wildfire that there is going to be a big fight after school: the whites against the blacks. You can see in the white kids' faces that they want no part of what's going to happen, and all you can see in the faces of the black kids is hate.

"You're not going to fight us, are ya, man?" a white guy named Tommy says to me the hallway. I don't know what to say. I really have no desire to hurt anyone. I am just mad and confused. But I am also caught up in the sense of unity with my brothers and sisters.

"Have your parents pick you up at fifth period," I tell him.

When the bell for sixth period rings, it's total chaos in the halls. Some brother sets it off right in the hallway, knocking out white boys and girls, catching them unaware. Out in front of the school, a few scuffles break out, nothing major, but white kids are getting "stole on," which means hitting someone when they don't expect it. It's like a feeding frenzy, and more and more brothers get involved, even those who seem reluctant to. I am one of those guys asking "How many did you hit?" laughing like it's a big game, high on adrenaline. I feel it's a sucker move to steal on someone, but I also feel it's a perfect opportunity to further my rep and stop the jokes. So I wait until I see the biggest white guy come out of the building and I creep up on him. I hit him in the side of the face with everything I've got. He falls to the ground, banging the back of his head on the pavement, unconscious. He never saw it coming.

He's one of the guys I drank beer with in the morning, and I broke his jaw. Things don't improve as far as the name-calling goes. They only get worse. I am given a new name: crazy motherfucker.

After that incident, I withdrew from everybody. I began spending my free time at the waterfront, swimming in the bay or just sitting on the rocks reflecting. I'd often bring Rex, my German shepherd, and we would spend the day roughhousing and playing in the water. I felt akin to nature, connected in a way that I couldn't understand. I just knew that when I was troubled, nothing would soothe me like the waterfront, the beach, or a trek through the woods. I even loved the turbulence and violence of storms, because inside, much of the time, that was how I felt.

I had long stopped aspiring to be anything in life because I knew it wasn't meant for me. My true "self" was buried under cultural ignorance and social indifference. I was born into a family suffering from a legacy of abuse that was kept secret within the family, which, from what I know about African American history, seems to be a not uncommon phenomenon. It goes without saying that society has never truly been interested in the dysfunctional family dynamic that's so widespread within the African-American community. Not until recently have efforts been made to address the problem effectively. But for a lot of black males—locked up, dead, or in mental institutions—who have suffered through this type of dysfunction, those efforts are a little too late.

BRAD

"I can smell it, Bradley; you guys have been drinking," Brian's mom says, rolling her eyes.

"Just two six-packs." I grin from the backseat.

"You're such a smart-ass, Brad!" she says, exasperated.

"I know, but you still love me," I insist, catching her eyes in the rearview mirror.

When we get home, Brian goes to his room and passes out. Me, I don't want the party to end. So I go to the fridge and pour myself a tall glass of wine. It's just past midnight on a Saturday. Dokken is hosting Headbangers Ball on MTV.

"You're a bad boy!" Rachel says when she sees the wine. She smacks me hard on the ass and disappears into her bedroom. When she comes back out, she has a glass of wine in her hand and sits down on the other end of the sofa. She's beautiful—fleshy and gorgeous, a Goldie Hawn type, with dirty-blonde hair and stunning blue eyes. Believe me when I say I had thought about her many times, but she was my best friend's mom and Brian was just like a brother to me!

"Bradley, why *are* you so bad?" she asks, fingering the edge of her glass.

"'Cause the women wouldn't want me any other way," I say, staring.

"Is that so?" She narrows her eyes. "Is Brian sleeping?" When I tell her yes, the smile on her face lights up the whole room. She leans over, grabs my leg, and asks me if I want to play.

I didn't even have to think. I knew without a doubt: I absolutely wanted this woman. And let me say here that I fully consented to everything we did and would have had it no other way.

After that night, we started pushing our lust for each other to a limit that became dangerously exciting.

She'd call and act as though she was looking for Brian, but when my parents hung up the other line, she'd beg for my cock and tell me how much she needed to taste me. I'd tell her to meet me somewhere and pick me up. If sex was to happen, we would usually go back to the trailer. But then there were those rare occasions in commuter parking lots or behind schools. The public display made it more intense and the release for the both of us was always out of this world. Rachel enjoyed being dominated, and my control became the soul of our bond. It thrust the pleasure to levels so high it was unbelievable. I was allowed to have her anytime, anywhere I chose. Actual intercourse was very hard because, a lot of times, we were in public. Her true lust was giving me head on command, and the riskier the spot, the more we enjoyed it.

Being in such a strong sexual relationship at such a young age gave me a false sense that I had arrived, that I was a man, even though I was far from it. One day you're building tree forts. The next day you're looking for a spot where you and your best friend's mom can get your rocks off! For a long time, I regretted all this rushing around that I did just to grow up. I looked and acted older than my age, and that always seemed to keep me extremely popular in school. But the reality was that I struggled at almost everything I did—except getting women—and the only person who knew it was me.

My mother being the way she was, I didn't feel like I could talk about it. I felt separate and distanced. I just couldn't make her happy to save my life: I had no control over her. Then, in a strange turn of events, I found an older woman who loved to be controlled, who gave me all the attention in the world, and basically gave me the message that everything I did was right! But this woman—I say woman because she was twenty-three years older than me—was no less than a nymphomaniac! Deep down, I believed most women were like Rachel, even if they were just keeping it hidden. That kept me second-guessing what my girlfriends and, later, my wife were doing when I wasn't around.

As far back as I can remember, my mother was great at mothering, but terrible at loving. Did I know she loved me? Yes. Was she good at showing me? In her own way, I'm sure she thought she was. But I always felt like I had to find most of my joy from outside sources.

When I was a kid, the campfire and the racetrack were the things I looked forward to the most, besides Sunday mornings, when Dad and I would drive to get donuts and sports cards. In the early 1980s, my father opened a construction company, which became one of the ten fastest-growing restoration companies in the Baltimore/DC metropolitan area. Weekends were family time, and we always did something together. I spent my free time riding bikes, feeding horses, building tree forts, and just doing whatever I wanted. I had no worries. But things weren't what they seemed.

Around the second grade I came to realize that school was not easy for me like it was for my sister. It was downright hard! I always tried my hardest, but it was never enough, and my parents couldn't understand why I wasn't getting it. I think this is where my self-esteem started to fall: my parents spent thousands of dollars on tutors so that I wouldn't have to stay back. Yet I always just slid by.

My life felt like a video game, and I was always running out of quarters. I wanted the replay, the chance to make it all right. But I was afraid to ask for help. To me that was a sign of weakness. It would be many years later that my parents would find out I had Attention Deficit Disorder. That was the reason I didn't absorb my studies like other children.

When I was in the fourth grade, my family moved to Stafford, Virginia—quite a small town when we got there. We had to wait for our house to be finished, and while we did, we lived in rental homes. My mother had a beautiful, custom English Tudor home built deep in the woods at the end of a court. No one else ever built there. So all that land around us—hundreds of acres of old logging trails—was my playground.

I made friends fast and became kind of a leader in the neighborhood gang. I got a brand-new four-wheeler so I could get around faster than my friends with bikes. Skateboarding was the cool thing at that time, and we built a half-pipe along with a hangout house a little ways back in the woods. I learned fast which trails would get me to where I needed to be. I found ones that would take me all the way to Aquia Creek, where there were rope swings.

I'd follow the main trail back into the woods where this black family lived. They had chickens, goats, dogs, and other animals, but no power or plumbing. Their house looked like a shack. One day while I was riding and my parents were working the yard, I saw my father and a black gentleman arguing about how I was tearing up the trail. They were going back and forth for ten minutes, really getting nowhere, when all of a sudden, my dad pulled out his money clip and handed the man a hundred-dollar bill. It was at that moment that I came to realize that money makes the world go round. The gentleman never bothered me or my father after that. In fact, he came by the house every three to four months and got more money. My father and him kind of started a little friendship. He would do odd jobs sometimes for us, like taking a tree down or removing a stump.

Around this time, I started to notice two sides to me. On one side there was the Boy Scout, soccer player, and all-around perfect son. On the other side was this kid who started smoking by the age of eleven and was addicted six months later. I remember waiting for my parents to go to bed and then sneaking out the garage door at one in the morning to have a smoke. I began to swipe a beer here and there, along with spirits. And let me add this while I'm on the subject: neither of my parents drank, did drugs, or smoked. The liquor, beer, and wine in my house were strictly for special events and holidays. I have no memories of my parents ever drinking, or anyone in my family, as a matter of fact.

The wonder years: I reached puberty at a real early age—right around ten. It came on fast! I liked that I looked older and was shaving. I was really tall, too, so it didn't take long for me to realize that I liked girls, and they liked me. I just loved the way Kayla's arms felt around me when we went four-wheeling. We'd ride for miles, following the trail by the power lines. After I dropped her off, I would go home and have a smoke.

Even though I was only eleven and a half, I looked older and could get away with buying smokes. Captain Bob's Bait and Tackle, which was right next to my middle school, became the spot. I would sneak off during lunch and cut through the backside of the baseball diamond to a trail in the woods that took me to Bob's. I'd buy a pack of Marlboro Reds for ninety-nine cents and be the big shot in school. Money was never a problem for me. I was getting twenty-five dollars allowance a week! And at that time, that was a lot of money. I was one of the coolest guys in the school and pulled much respect.

At school dances, I always had my pick of who to take. The seventh grade was the beginning of "let's see how many girlfriends I can have." Virginia was a year older than me. On the bus one day, I asked her if she wanted to go riding and she said yes. I went and picked her up, and after a little while we went down by the creek and parked. Eventually I talked her out of her shirt and into letting me suck on her breasts and finger her down her pants. She had the biggest set of breasts I had ever seen. Her nipples were like silver dollars. I could have gone further if I had chosen to, but I didn't.

I had a very full life around this time. I was into scouting and camping. I was playing select soccer, so there was practice and games every week. But I began hating school with a passion in seventh grade. I found many ingenious ways of cheating. I would get girlfriends to do my homework and give me answers to the tests and exams. I flirted with my teachers, telling them how much I loved them—in a way, becoming the teacher's pet. And it worked! Stafford Middle School became my playground, and I was the master of its domain. All I began to care about was music, girls, and upholding my reputation as being one crazy person. No one could tell me a thing. I was in control, and that's exactly how I wanted it.

Weekends were spent at school dances or at the mall, but most often over at Brian's. Brian couldn't get girls like I could, and I used to feel bad about it. But it didn't seem like it bothered him. When I was skipping school or ditching class to grab a smoke, he always stayed back and did the right thing. Today he is successful and happily married.

Brian lived in one of the biggest neighborhoods in Stafford: Aquia Harbor. The Harbor days, as we refer to them, were the best of the best. Brian's room was like a sanctuary for heavy metal. Every inch of his walls was covered with posters. It was like walking into Kemp Mill Records. I absolutely loved it. Whenever I came over, I would always bring some of my albums or tapes. I was a fanatic about having the latest albums. I wanted them first, so I always kept up with release dates. We spent countless nights headbanging and moshing around his room to Anthrax, Iron Maiden, Metallica, Overkill, Dio, Black Sabbath, Kiss, and Rush.

Brian was like a brother to me. I used to spend a lot of time over at his house—whole weekends, sometimes—because his parents were more laid-back than mine. I don't think my mother minded, because it kept me out of her hair and, most importantly, out of her house. She kept it looking like it was never lived in: a picture out of *Better Homes and Gardens*. You could never really be fully comfortable in it.

Karl

When I was five, I was molested by the babysitter. The sixteen-year-old boy who did it was the son of someone my grandparents knew. He watched me for a few hours when the adults went out. The Event, as I came to think of it, didn't seem to affect me in any profound way at first. But as I got older and began to grasp the meaning and significance of what had transpired, I felt ashamed. Then I got mad. I began distrusting people. Could they tell?

My mother did not find out about the Event until about a year later. I told her in the car as we headed towards the store, and she positively freaked out. We never talked about it as I got older, though, and it became a dark secret between us.

My mom had me at sixteen. But if memory serves me right, she did great. She allowed me to play in the mud, to go four-wheeling, to make bicycle ramps and crawl around parks and fences like a monkey. She'd set up playdates with my childhood friend, Laurel. We'd run through the sprinkler or make a pool out of an old barrel, cause mayhem in the house, that kind of thing.

One time Laurel painted a part of my arm with dandelions. Another time we saw a shooting star together. In the autumn, the front yard would be covered in an assortment of orange, red, and brown leaves. My mother and I would rake them into big piles. But before the actual bagging took place, I'd run and jump through those piles. We would playfully toss the leaves. Laughing, playing, and working the lawn—who would have thought work could be such fun?

I was always curious, wondering how things worked and why they are the way they are. I remember wondering, *What's the deal with makeup?* So I got my mom's stuff and put on so much I ended up looking like Bilbo the Clown. I had lipstick from numerous tubes all over my face, and a bunch of powders. When Mom saw me she couldn't decide if she wanted to scream or laugh!

I remember wondering if orange leaves tasted like oranges. So I marched outside, grabbed two and stuffed them in my mouth. It was quite disgusting, crunchy and tough. The leaves wouldn't break up in my mouth. I had to spit them out. Well, I asked, *Why are they orange?* My mother just said, *Because God made them that way.*

Religion and superstitions like palm reading and astrology ran rampant between us. I believed in God and his angels. I believed in miracles and the efficacy of prayer. I pictured God as the archetypal, bearded, white man sitting on a throne in heaven. He was the all-seeing father. I was especially fond of the miracles of the Old Testament. But when I asked questions about the world and how things worked, my mom would give these simplistic answers that never really satisfied me.

We were at this really cool dam once, so high up. It had all sorts of old wheels and levers. They were a bit rusty and hard to turn, but I could play with them. I remember wondering how dams work. But I never did get an answer. My parents did not have higher education. And while my mom could give me religious answers and my dad could get me to question things, neither one had the background to answer my questions more completely. Nor did they help me find the answers. They did not take me to the library.

My father actually played a negligible role during these years of my life. He and Lana[10] weren't even together then. Dad was in the Navy, overseas. He'd visit on occasion, tell me stories. His motto was "Life is a journey. Many adventures lie in wait." I'd dig through his wooden chest, fumble with foreign currencies. I'd ask about the old dried rose hidden in a box. And boy! Could he deliver a story!

He'd take me to the pool. We'd see who could hold their breath or swim the farthest underwater. He would usually let me win. I used to love grabbing his shoulders and hitching a ride, holding my breath as he traversed the length of the pool with what seemed like lightening speed. I missed him during his absence, but I didn't hold a grudge. To say more would transcend memory.

---

10 Karl's mother.

From my point of view, everything was good. I grew up in my grandparents' home with a loving mother, aunt, and uncle. I cannot honestly say who had the most impact. It's like they all stood together, each doing their respective parts to perfection. Grandma cooked the meals, did the laundry, kept me in line, took me shopping, and told me stories. When she'd go to the garden, I'd bring my Tonka trucks and haul the weeds away for her.

Gram and Gramp, Wanda and Bob—they were always there for me. Gramp could fix stuff; Gram could mend me. Their house was a medium-size ranch with a furnished basement. And that basement was like my second home. I once worked up my nerve to slide down the laundry chute. I made sure there was plenty of laundry down there to cushion my fall. One room had exposed water pipes, and I used to jump on the bed and leap to those pipes, hanging from them like monkey bars. That ended quickly the day I grabbed the hot water pipe.

My aunt Angie lived in the basement, and her boyfriend, Dave, was often there. He was really my father figure. And I loved spending time with him. He had the patience of ages. One time he held down my seat at the movies for the entire length of the movie. I was so small, I would have folded up into the seat! Dave used to take me four-wheeling. After what seemed like hours of riding, we would head home. Naturally I did not want to go back. I wanted to explore more. He used to try to trick me into thinking we were doing more exploring, but I knew the trails so well this did not work. (It was still a fun game, though.)

My dad had taught me to hide my emotions, to seal them in a jar, something I was never very good at. I always bottled them up, but he wanted me, at times, to be inexpressive. I learned how to do this by copying him, sucking in a little air and biting the inner part of my cheeks, so I wouldn't smile or sneer. If I was really upset I wasn't supposed to cry: I was supposed to suck it up. He didn't tolerate whining, which was good, I think, for whining accomplishes little, and the majority of things we whine about, we've brought on ourselves.

He was strict about table manners: chewing with your mouth shut, no talking with your mouth full, no elbows on the table. I remember one time struggling to eat my cheeseburger over my plate. I was so short, I couldn't reach the table! And he wanted me to sit straight up. I was more comfortable eating over my lap. But this was not acceptable. Over time, he made me very conscious of table manners, which I still have today. I feel manners are very important. They convey class and respect. Of course, when you're eight years old, you don't quite understand that.

Life went on after the Event. I loved being with my family. But then my mother was involved in a terrible car accident with her boyfriend, Mark[11], and hospitalized for months. At the time I was so confused. I did not understand what was wrong—why she was absent and why she could not see me. Adult explanations confused me more. To say that she was sick did not make a bit of sense: I'd been sick before and I didn't have to leave.

My visits to her were always traumatic, and the words adults used to explain everything left me feeling lost. When I went to the hospital to visit her, she was unresponsive. She was in a coma for a long time. My childish, egotistical mind could not comprehend the meaning of this. I felt ignored, abandoned, like she no longer loved me. Yet when I visited her and looked upon her, I was scared, sad, and confused. Why did she look so ill? Was it my fault? Why wouldn't she speak? Was it something I'd done?

I remember sitting in the hospital window, looking at the sky. I was lost. Mom lay in the bed, hooked up to all sorts of machines, and it scared me to look at her. I felt helpless and worthless. I remember Aunt Angie and Uncle Dave giving me a tape recorder to speak into. I would think of it as a one-way phone to communicate with my mother. I would say, "Mummy, I wuv you," hoping that would bring her back.

My mother survived her ordeal. She made it home to me, but this event had scarred me. I did not know how to deal with it. My grief, confusion, sadness, and anger were all turned inwards. I did not realize it at the time, but these pent-up emotions later polluted me.

Sometime after my mother recovered, we moved to Virginia, and the world I knew was shattered. Most of the activities I enjoyed were gone. No more playing with Gram and Gramp. No more four-wheeling, no more Uncle Dave and Aunt Angie, no more big family dinners. No more Laurel. It was horrible. Virginia seemed so desolate. The apartment was small. My room was small. The dinner table was small. People were missing. And I threw all that anger and sadness into my jar. I pretended to be happy.

My mother started selling time-shares, which was good for her. She liked the people and made better money. All was going pretty good. At least, that's how it seemed to me. My father was still fairly authoritarian, but that wasn't exactly new. He could really put the fear of God into me. Things as seemingly small as dragging my feet would warrant a quick reprimand. Once, I was supposed to be grounded and confined to my room: no outside, no computer, no phone. When he came home I was outside looking at the stars with a telescope he had bought me. He was so mad because I was breaking his rules, but he was also happy because I was doing something productive. If I remember this right, he grounded me an

---

11 Mark and Lana dated while Karl's father was overseas with the Navy.

extra day but gave me an extra hour on the telescope!

He was always like that. Another time he punished me by making me copy fifteen pages out of *Beowulf*, the fight scenes with Grendel and the escape from the thunder caves. It was torture! But it was educational. I remember wondering how these people became such great warriors and how such stories of great heroes spring up and survive through the generations.

He could really be inspiring. One time he brought me on one of the Navy ships. It was huge! And there were these giant vehicles all over the deck, being transported from one location to another. I learned some of the hand signals and helped guide the vehicles. This was tremendously fun: here I was, about ten years old, helping to guide these humongous trucks off the ship! That day, my father truly shined in my eyes.

Then a couple of years later, my parents got divorced. So much for things going good. They had been high school sweethearts, but after my father joined the Navy, their relationship was effectively over. Let's face it: how you are at sixteen and how you are in your twenties is totally different. They tried to forge a relationship on how they had been, not who they were becoming. But they had just grown apart. Of course, at the time, all I knew was that my family kept getting smaller! Deep down I was furious. Why was this happening to me? Was this, too, my fault? Did people not love me?

Now it was just my mother and me. And I became one pissed off, angry, combative child. Trouble, the committing of crimes, the disregard of authority, and the disrespect of myself and my family really started after my parents' divorce, sometime during late elementary school. The negativity that I had bottled up, coupled with the impact of my parents' separation, provided the extra stimulus for me to rebel.

Each side of the family, at times, would vilify the other. If I was at my dad's parents' house and my mother was a few minutes late picking me up, I would hear how irresponsible she was. My mom's parents would say something similar about my dad. It didn't bother me, all their bickering. What bothered me was that I felt I was constantly disappointing one of them. Do I spend the holiday with my mom's family or my dad's? What about the weekend? No matter what I decided, I knew it'd come out wrong for one of them. I often wished I could just rebel against them both. Instead, I tried to harden myself.

I proclaimed I didn't care and that it didn't matter. But it did matter. I did care. I had so much anger seething within me! It was an irrational anger, amplified beyond reason and so blinding that I did not care who I hurt. It is questionable that I even cared about hurting myself. My emotions were kept sealed in a jar. Who needed them! What I didn't know was that my jar leaked a poison that burned the sweet, loving, caring little boy right out of me—the same poor little boy who was raised so well by a loving family in a nice home, the one who had such a good support base.

My first steps over the edge consisted of vandalism and stealing, then smoking marijuana for the first time in the fifth grade. Three associates and I were in the "cool room," essentially a huge walk-in closet with Metallica posters, black lights, and drawings all over the wall. In that room was a small sofa, some chairs, and my surfboard propped up on two shelves. Mom had drawn an eye on the wall and written under it, "I'm watching you."

My buddy Tom and I used to buy cigarettes out of vending machines or steal them from the corner store. We used to try to hook up with all the girls in the neighborhood this way. Or we'd spend our time catching stuff on fire, smashing pumpkins during Halloween, throwing water balloons at passing cars. Tom and his girlfriend, Ashley, used to come over, and one time Ashley brought her friend. We talked, made out. It was my first time feeling up a girl. We listened to Cypress Hill's "Hits from the Bong" and made a bowl from tinfoil.

I did not think of this as particularly wrong at the time, other than the obvious risk of getting grounded if caught. To my adolescent mind, the law was a foreign concept. It was just something you heard about, not something you experienced. I did not even take parental law seriously. If my mother tried grounding me, I would run while she was using the bathroom, or catch her off guard and bolt. If something was taken from me, I'd go off on a tantrum, punching holes in the walls, breaking chairs, lights, glass tables, anything that was convenient. I once put a hammer through my surfboard. I broke my computer to demonstrate that it could not be used to control me, which of course it could. I was so mad at myself after that.

When my mother tried to ground me for smoking, I locked her out of the apartment. Then I proceeded to spray-paint my room, bash my stuff up, and smoke pack after pack of cigarettes. In my room I raved like a madman, pouted, then threw up. The noxious paint fumes and cigarette smoke made me ill.

I may have seemed like a diabolical mixture of Dennis the Menace and Bart Simpson, but really, I just wanted to curl up in a ball and cry. I felt betrayed as my family kept shrinking. And I felt like a traitor when I moved, forgot about old friends, or remembered them but ignored them.

In my hunt for a reputation, I sometimes abandoned good friends so that I could hang out with people I perceived were cooler. I used to handle betrayal roughly: act out, get loud, get angry, let people know I was mad. I would spread lies, deceive, and if I was betrayed badly enough by someone I thought was my friend, I would try to ruin that person's reputation. I would snatch his friend or find a way to one-up him so that his "friends" would rather hang out with me than with him.

My mom had the den loaded with sofas and chairs. It was *the* party room, and I'd have people over just about every night. My place was the place to be. So if I decided I didn't like you, I could effectively cut you off. I could be quite cold and calculating.

I didn't have a problem betraying people. I sometimes did not even think of people as people. They were forms of fun, desire, entertainment, etc., but not emotional beings. I did not recognize their feelings. I used them and they used me. Thinking of people in such a distant and uncaring manner was a defense mechanism. By thinking of people impersonally, I could avoid emotional attachment and be devoid of guilt and sadness as people entered and left my life. The problem was that once I stopped empathizing with people, crime became easier.

"C'mon man, Jim's a chump!" the one guy said to me. Jim had picked on me earlier that week and had made me look stupid.

"Don't be a wuss, let's go!" said the other. I was listening closely, ready to rationalize.

"Dude, you said you'd love to hurt him. Let's take his Nintendo! What? Are you scared?" I had so much misguided anger, I did not think twice about breaking and entering Jim's house with these two guys. If I was grounded, I would just disregard the punishment. If I was forbidden from going outside, I would go anyway. What could be done to stop me?

I grew to be so out of control that my mother could not handle me. She would call the cops on me. She didn't know what else to do. Then, eventually, she sent me to live with my father's parents in Hanover County, Virginia. This was a major blow. At the time I thought that my mother did not love me: she was getting rid of me. It was the ultimate betrayal. First I nearly lost my mother, then after getting her back, I lost my grandparents, aunt, and uncle. Then I lost my father. And now my mother was sending me off. I was losing her again!

Living with my dad's parents was a bore. I was quite peeved at being sent there. But admittedly it did do me some good. I not only developed computer skills that went beyond basic literacy, but I also greatly improved in school. In my mother's home, I had failing grades and a horrid disciplinary record. My grandparents helped turn this around.

My grandfather, Dennis, helped me study every day when he came home from work. He would sit in his big La-Z-Boy chair and subject me to a battery of tests while I sat on the couch. Grandma usually got home an hour or two after Gramps. By then most of my studies were done. When she got home she would relax for a bit—drink tea and watch the news—before making dinner. I used to drive her crazy with computer talk, dragging her upstairs to see my latest graphic or web design. She would always be encouraging, even if she had no idea what I was talking about.

While I was living with my grandparents, I wound up having to go to court over the breaking and entering and larceny. I was scared in the courtroom, but relieved that all I got was community service. The fear of the court, the knowledge that I could get into legal trouble for my deeds—none of these sanctions really seeped in.

And I'm not sure why.

I'd go visit my mom. We would be beach bums, hanging out in the sand with the salty breeze and sunrays. Or she would take me places and show me off like a prize, her baby boy. She'd introduce me to the owners of hotels, restaurants, and bars, like we were social networking. She used to take me on boat trips with her friends and I'd sip on fake piña coladas. It used to be fun meeting people, hanging out with her friends, getting a sneak peek into the social life of a woman.

I could not deny that I was doing better living with my grandparents. But it was hard to be away from my mother. And it wasn't long before I derailed. I would often get in trouble at school after I talked with my mother on the phone. Somehow these talks soured me. I never noticed the pattern, but my grandparents did. They used to question me about it, like my mom was inciting me to misbehave. I used to feel so angry that she had sent me away. I loved her and enjoyed talking to her, but the anger was so strong! It was like our talks reminded me, subconsciously, that she had betrayed me. I didn't realize that she had sent me there for my own good. And she didn't realize that it had backfired.

I tell myself that the Event didn't bother me, but the fact that I hid it for so long and that I desperately don't want to write about it now means that I'm lying. It's almost like admitting to the occurrence of it makes me less of a man, less strong, less friggin' me! But I can see now that the Event made me more wary and suspicious of people. I started questioning everyone's motives. Things were never what they appeared to be. I felt, in a sense, like I'd been robbed.

10

THIS IS JAIL

"How many guys you got coming?" the deputy asks as we walk toward the chapel. I hesitate. I never know how many are coming and why.

"The list I gave at the podium has six names."

"All right, then," he says, unlocking the door. "You go ahead on in, have a seat. I'm sure the men are in transit now."

Inside, I spread my notes and paper and pens on the altar and begin pacing around the blue chapel. As usual, Stan arrives first and on his own.

"How it BE?" he booms. I give him a nod and look over his shoulder.

"What happened to that young guy, Raymond? The one who wrote about handling his business? Isn't he on the same tier as you?"

"Man, that cat got into a fight over his tats," Stan says, pursing his lips.

"Tats?"

"Tattoos," Stan explains. "He joined a gang. It's a trip, man! He joined but a week after you met him. And as soon as he did, this other dude challenged him. And in here, you can't let that go unchecked. So he went straight to lockdown."

"Is he still there?" I ask.

"Yeah. I saw him real quick—you know, as trusty for Father Pruitt, handing out Bibles—and asked him if he'd done any writing, and he was like, 'Man, I'm on lock! I don't have no pen!' But I knew it was a lie even before he finished saying it. You know, I've done lots of time on lockdown. I *always* had me a pen! So I was like, 'Man, you ain't even trying.' And I just let it go." He tilts his head. "I don't understand gangs. For real! I don't understand a man wanting to barter his life like that. There's other ways to get what you want."

"Where's Ron?" I ask.

"Oh, they shipped him. He's gone to prison." He shrugs.

"What do you mean?" I nearly shout. "Did he say if he's going to keep writing?" When a man left the jail—it didn't matter the reason—I never knew if he was leaving the workshop. I never knew if he would finish writing. "I have his work here, all typed up!" I continue. "What am I supposed to do with it now?" I push Ron's folder back into my bag. "How am I supposed to teach when they keep taking my students away?"

A curious caution creeps into Stan's face. It's the analyst seeing a new side of his patient. Then I see him waving someone over. I didn't even hear Kelvin coming in with Larry and Marvin, the new guy Shakelia has added. Sizing up the situation immediately, Kelvin leans in to address me while I stare, defeated, out the tiny, barred window of the chapel.

"Dave, this is jail. Nothing stays the same. You got men here for a few weeks sobering up. Then there's guys like Stan here waiting months on their court day. If you did this class in prison, you know, it'd be more stable."

I spin around to face him. "If I did it in prison, I wouldn't have met you!"

He nods and shares a glance with Stan. They hold back somehow, giving me the wide berth I seem to be asking for. Nobody makes a move. Then I tell them about going to visit Naji in prison and about the letters I'm getting from Brad, Karl, and Tony. I keep talking, trying to convince myself that we're achieving what we set out to achieve.

Then Kelvin shows me his writing.

"I did mine, too." Stan fans out the pages. I smile.

"And I wrote more than any of these motherfuckers!" Larry says, holding up a thick wad of white paper. Marvin grins. His teeth are yellow and bent like a jack-o'-lantern.

"C'mon, Dave. Sit down," Stan implores. "I got that piece you asked me to write about doing time here." I relent. And I resolve to write Ron a letter when I get home.

"Marvin, whatcha got?" I ask.

"Aiight, lookee here, then," he intones. "Because, you know, we all start somewhere. And in our community, in our religious community, here in the jail, we honor that, how we all start. That's building time, where we bring what we have to the circle. It comes from somewhere. It goes somewhere. And that's an important tradition. Our Muslim tradition. OK, then, before I got here. I wanted to remember how I got here, way back, how that tradition came to me."

"So let's hear it," Stan says.

"Aiight. Dig this, then. I call it 'The Making of Evil.'" He reads about his uncle, a Black Muslim. "If he tripped stepping up onto the sidewalk, his first complaint would be that the white man built that particular sidewalk higher than the standard because he knew that the Black man was being encouraged to hold his head up, and therefore, he couldn't see what was at his feet. My uncle had a racial explanation for everything!"

"So you learned racism from your uncle? That's the evil?"

"Yeah, man. He was relentless with it."

"But this was the 1970s. The black power movement. Couldn't you say your uncle at least had a point? What makes it evil—what he was teaching you about racism?"

"Ah, man, it went way beyond racism with him. He had an answer to everything, and he was hustling, and I was a little boy looking for—"

"When did your anger break?" Larry interrupts.

"I can tell you that. I can tell you exactly when, man. It wasn't 'til I got here the first time. I started seeing white guys come in here, man, all tore up. And I heard their stories. That's when it hit me. Their lives no better."

"OK, help me understand that," I prompt. "If you learned that the first time, how come you came back a second time? If that race hatred wasn't in you anymore?"

"Well, you see, by then I had it figured out. I got into drugs."

"Oh," I say. "You got addicted."

"No. That wasn't it at all. I got into drugs to be a profiteer! A friend of mine on the inside here told me, 'Just call this guy when you get out. He'll set you up.' And it was on, man. It was *on* from there!"

"That's the real evil, right there," Stan says, narrowing his eyes. "I can see it! Because when you talk about crack, man? Your eyes light up. It's like somebody set a fire in you. I'm watching you come alive." Marvin stares at Stan, slack-jawed, and is so still I wonder if he's breathing.

Stan continues: "But that's not why I write. Writing to me is like a safari hunt. I write to kill the evil within."

A passerby peeps through the tiny window in the chapel door. Then, just as quickly, disappears.

"How do you know for sure you've killed it?" Marvin asks in a hoarse whisper.

For once, Stan is silent.

STAN

I am sitting on the floor on a plush, luxurious carpet, in the privacy of her living room, with only a coffee table and candles between us. Dinner is over, and I smell the sweet aroma of dessert, just gazing into her beautiful eyes. There is no need for music, because the vibe between us has its own pleasing arrangement of sounds. Smiles and sips of a fruitful drink. I carefully pour this prize-winning substance into the glasses of our lives, not allowing even a single precious drop to spill, because I understand how significant this fluid is to the life of the evening.

The evening ends and I drift off to sleep. A few hours later, I hear something so profound in my spirit that, immediately, I realize I am being summoned. But by whom?

The blood cries out. It's running down his chest. He's fighting a battle that he can't possibly win. There are pit bulls all around him, ferocious and brutal animals disguised like men. Their forceful blows hit their mark. But the real danger comes only from one man. Gripped in his hand is a homemade knife. With each blow comes a piercing wound, allowing the precious wine of life to be poured into that huge glass beneath our feet: the chilled, hard concrete floor.

Men are lapping it up with their eyes. His wine, the very essence of his life, is crying out for help, but who is in tune to such a frequency? Who can hear words that are not formulated in English, but in a language that only our hearts can decode? How many of us are in tune with the frequency of our *own* hearts, let alone someone else's? Life can be very selfish, as we go about caring about our own needs.

Why did I get up and help this young man, at the risk being beaten or stabbed? This wasn't a battle the best of the best could have won. But I was summoned by a force greater than my own understanding: a God of love; a God that heard the blood cry out. God used me that night, because God knew that if he summoned me, I would obey. Now, I am not known for being anyone's hero. But you can't have God's love and find only one person to share it with. That's selfish love, not God's love. For God so loved the world . . . there it is. He loves all of us. This is God pouring his spirit into us. We are just the vessels for his fruitful drink.

"Stop! This is wrong!" I yelled. "You gonna kill him right here? Then what?" And the whole situation changed. That night on the tier, I became a leader. You see, I understood that young man's worth. He passed out from the loss of so much blood and was taken to the hospital. As for those who committed the brutal act, the guy who had the weapon caught a new charge. As for me, I took hits from snipers afterwards.

Things subsided long enough for the next storm to brew, because when the administration removed those four men, they brought in ten new guys, with ten different personalities to add to the 150 of us already stuck on the tier. Every day all day, and every night all night, I hear the sounds of 150 men entangled. Some speak quietly. Others are constantly in an uproar. Some are playing cards; others tap hip-hop beats on steel tables with raps intertwined, homemade rhythms.

It's summer, and the temperature on the outside is easily 95 degrees. But where I'm living, it feels like 125. All day long, I'm consumed with sweat. And all day long, I hear men crying out about themselves; how this isn't right or that isn't right; how this person smells; or how "I killed that nigga. Fuck this! Fuck that! Fuck him!" What I'm sharing isn't just some days. It's every day, all day and all night long. There are signs of addiction everywhere. Some of us are so dehydrated our tear glands can't produce even one small drop to express pain. Others just lie with their mattresses on the floor, covers over their heads, hiding their identities while they toss and turn, the sounds of their low-pitched moans filling the air. They are withdrawing from heroin and they vomit freely. It seeps from their mattresses to the floor.

But I'm not complaining. You see, this time I'm doing now hurts more than any other time I've done, because I realize I've been hurting other people all my life. I couldn't be the son my adopted parents wanted. And I wasn't there for my own son.

The day my son was born, I found myself cheering like some fan at the Super Bowl. My feelings were at their highest peak. I'd never witnessed something so awesome. After the doctor cleaned out his nostrils, smacked his bottom, and cut the umbilical cord, I spoke out in a very demanding tone, "Give me my son!" The doctor followed my command. He handed me my beautiful baby boy. I looked into his eyes as he continued to cry out into the world. Then I said, "Don't cry. Your Daddy got you now. Everything going to be all right. You are safe." There was a staff of maybe three people who witnessed my vow. But my very first words to my son turned out to be a lie.

Sometimes we don't know we are telling a lie, but in due time it's always revealed. Yes, I did make a vow to my son on December 31, 1987, at 11:45 a.m. But before I made that vow, I was living my life recklessly, without much concern for other peoples' feelings. I was acting like a child and thinking like a child, but fucking like a man. My emotional system wasn't developed to the point where I could carry the weight of being a father. I lacked the substance. Having substance means making a commitment of responsibility: doing what is always best for your child and making his environment safe and nourishing. But I wasn't raised in an environment where love was defined by actions and words. I knew the words of fatherhood. But I didn't understand the definition of fatherhood.

Today, my peace is in carrying my cross and, when I can, helping you carry yours. If my son ever had his back up against a wall, I hope someone would stand with him. What I want for my son, I gave another man's son: love. Not only in words, but in action. I'm taking responsibility, but the wounds are deep and I am still in quite a bit of pain. My blood cries out, too. Can you hear it? Not with your ears, but can you feel it in your heart?

Naji

My first night in the Hampton City Jail, I felt like taking my life. I didn't know how I was going to do nineteen years. Anger and sorrow crept into my heart and settled like thick, black smoke in a house fire. I stood up on one of the tables in the twelve-man tier. Looking up through the bars at the world I was not to see again for a long time, I began reviewing my life. I began a silent prayer, in which I said, in essence, "God, you said in your words that if I knock, you will answer. Well I am banging! Please, reveal yourself to me."

The next morning I woke feeling anxious to the point of distraction. I started doing push-ups to relieve the anxiety. Nothing. I played cards and chess. I took a shower. But nothing I did seemed to help. I thought maybe I could sleep it off.

Before I go to sleep, it is my habit to read a book. The only book I had at the time was the Bible, so I picked it up and began reading from the first chapter of Genesis. All of a sudden, a question that in all my years of being a Christian I never thought to ask struck me like a bullet! What does "Bible" mean? So simple! It's the first word you see on the cover of the book. So why didn't I know what it meant? I then noticed that my anxiety was gone. It had been replaced by something stronger: an insatiable hunger to *know*. The answer to the question "How am I going to do nineteen years?" was miraculously answered. I was going to spend my time educating myself.

Outside of my studies, though, I found myself fighting a lot, proving my manhood though physical combat. I spent many months in the hole, only to return to the general population more hostile. Then in January 1991 I was introduced to the Nation of Islam. I was fascinated by the concept that black was not only beautiful, but that it was the color of the first man on earth and indeed God Himself! I began studying everything I could get my hands on about the Nation of Islam. It was very attractive to me because it provided the pride in my skin color and race that I lacked. But other questions bothered me.

Their teachings about the true nature of Christianity, its origins, and its psychological impact on Americans of African descent left me questioning everything I held true about myself and the world. Was I somehow a victim of a mass conspiracy to destroy my race mentally? Was it by accident or design that in this Christian culture, black males are disproportionately represented in prisons all over America?

A new understanding of the world was opening up to me. Although it frightened me in many ways, I labored on in my studies. Racist views put forth by the Nation of Islam fed my anger and gave it a face. White people would discover! They remained my sworn enemies. It was easy to blame that race for everything that happened to me. The teachings of the Nation quickly took me into a land of hate. And I found a definition of manhood.

I began changing the way I communicated. My vocabulary had been very limited: I was maybe operating at a seventh- or eighth-grade level. Now I wasn't just learning words for the sake of sounding educated: I wanted to know their meaning and origin. My reading comprehension improved tremendously as I read the writings of Hobbes, Rousseau, Rand, Locke, Voltaire, Hume, Kant, and other European philosophers. Because my enemy was white people, I felt I had to know their history and culture in order to defeat them. But I also read Woodoon, Akdar, Diop, King, X, Garvery, Hughes, Haley: black historians, social reformers, and political activists. Words like *propaganda, reactionism, Neo-colonialism,* and *white/black superiority/inferiority* began to enter into my everyday conversations.

The hate in my heart reached its apex in mid-1991. I overcame my fear of denouncing my faith by seeking another foundation to stand on. I chose the Five-Percent Nation. It provided a sense of exclusivity and belonging. In my acceptance of the Five Percent, "I became God." They argued that believing in an unseen God was like believing in fairy tales and silliness. The term they used for belief in the unseen was "spookism." The Five-Percent doctrine was a mix of fact and fiction: mythological, fantastic, and in most cases outrageous. I always maintained the ability to distinguish between the fact and the fiction, which I credited to my research ethic and my common sense. But more than anything else, there was a voice driving me to "search further." The drive I had was insatiable. I knew I had gotten myself into something that was more God-related than anything else.

I also knew that what I was learning was a bunch of garbage. I was running around calling myself "Zaquan, Supreme Understanding of God, Allah." Literally, this was the name I wanted to be recognized by. All Five Percenters give themselves these fantastic names, like wise men, intelligent, manifest, born from some derivative of Quan: Ta-quan, Za-quan, La-quan etc. You could actually start with A and finish the alphabet adding Quan. It's really silly. But I reasoned that running around calling myself a Christian, before I knew anything about it, just parroting what I was told by my grandparents and their preacher, had been ever sillier.

I was truly lost at this point but I was learning things that the average person didn't know, and I began to use it to make other people—inmates and staff—feel intellectually, morally, and culturally inferior. It made me feel good to bash Christians about the beliefs I had so recently relinquished. I was the center of conflict and controversy everywhere I went within the jail.

ANDRE

I'm standing on the strip, St. James, in Jackson Ward, getting my grind on and selling my dope to everyone with money, and even those that don't have money. Everybody benefits. My pockets are fat, and I'm chilling in my green Triple F.A.T. Goose coat, my blue Guess jeans, my blue and green Nike Air T-shirt, and my brand-new blue-and-green Nike Air Ones. I'm rocking a fresh eight-dollar, ball-fade haircut straight from Harvey's Progressive Barber Shop on 1st and Broad. Squeaky is my barber, and he can only cut when he's high off that heroin.

Then, all of a sudden, the police jump-out squad surrounds me, screaming and yelling, pointing their black-and-silver 9 mm pistols at my head. "Put your hands up and don't move!"

Is this a scene from one of my favorite movies, or is they really taking me? Now I'm face-first on the ground, dirt in my mouth, being handcuffed. The old saying in the drug game is that we have to be lucky every day and the police just has to be lucky one time. So knowing those undefeatable odds, why did I still continue in the game? All those thoughts and more are going through my mind. In the back of the police car, I put my head down because I don't want to face the crowd watching me being hauled away like some animal. I didn't kill nobody! I didn't shoot nobody! I was selling drugs and using drugs. Eighteen years old.

I get one phone call. Nervously, I pick up the black handle. It seems bigger than my head. I pray for one of my three favorite girls to answer the phone, because I don't want my daddy to be disappointed in me. But guess who answers and says "Hello?" Gregory Simpson. Cool, calm, and collected, just like Michael Jackson in the "Smooth Criminal" video, my dad asks three questions. The way he asks them, right in unison, doesn't give me a chance to answer until he's finished: "Do you have a bond? Did you give a statement to the pigs? Was you caught with anything on you?" I say yes, no, yes. He replies, "How much?" and when I tell him he says "Good!" then "Damn!"

Back in my cell, I start vomiting. I get a high fever. I'm not eating or sleeping, either. Not being able to get heroin in my system after all those years is a cruel killer for about a week.

At this time, all I knew about prison was what I gathered from the streets and taking in a few prison movies. I was led to believe that prison is a place where only the strong survive and the weak get killed. I remembered the infamous "Wall"[12] in Richmond. People said that when they tore down that prison, they found many dead bodies. I felt strong representing Jackson Ward, but deep down inside, I was nervous. I was not in my element anymore.

The street talk was true, but what surprised me was that prison offered a lot more. No one had told me about that. It's just that you had to want it. They offered school, a chance to earn your G.E.D., trade courses, self-help programs like Substance Abuse Education, Alcoholics Anonymous, Narcotics Anonymous, Anger Management, Self-Esteem, Breaking Barriers, Productive Citizenship, Bible Study, and Church Services. Did I possess the potential to tackle all of this education? Yes, because I loved school. I went in headfirst.

I got my G.E.D. on May 16, 1996. Then I took a trade course in Commercial Arts and Design and got certified as a graphic designer. I'd been bit by the educational bug. I got into Introduction to Computers and learned how to type and do spreadsheets and was certified as a data-entry clerk. I could type thirty-six

---

12 The Virginia State Penitentiary, named by the American Civil Liberties Union "the most shameful prison in America."

words per minute. I also took self-help programs. Some I took more than once. These educational opportunities were made available to me, but I had to make the decision to rekindle my education or run around 24-7 doing or thinking about drugs and crime. See, everything that exists on the streets exists in prison, except the borderline word "freedom."

I know that God was walking with me—and sometimes carrying me!—because I never had a life-or-death situation in prison. I had a few fights and arguments but nothing that went to the next level. I played sports: basketball, flag football, soccer, volleyball, and softball. It was really fun. We did it organized, with referees and everything. And when I wanted to be alone, I just went to my cell. But I missed being able to vent to my friends. In prison, you can't do that. You would be deemed soft. So I learned to pray to God.

I thought my favorite girl, Karen, would "mother-up." But I was wrong. My mother just continued to ignore me. She moved out of our Jackson Ward apartment and into a big house over on South Side. In jail, and later in prison, I never received a letter, visit, phone call, or money from her. And those are the things you need when you're doing time. She just forgot all about me. I agonized for a long time and just came to the conclusion that my mother didn't love me anymore, because I became what she hated so much—my father. I was just her son on paper.

When I got locked up, I left Michelle with a dope habit. She went through withdrawal, too, but no one ever knew, and we went our separate ways. I went through a flood of emotions—happy, sad, angry, hurt. The list goes on. I know the effects of what my using did to me and my family and loved ones. I was creating distance and not even knowing it. But to this day, Michelle and I are friends. She never had to commit any crimes, and she is now in the law enforcement field. We spend time together and our conversations are positive, because we both know what drugs did to our bodies and minds.

It took a lot of time and soul-searching before I came to the realization that I shouldn't do to others what has been done to me. Being addicted to heroin had me perceiving things otherwise. I now recognize that I was totally wrong. Dominique and Stickem both died years later in drug deals gone wrong. I've lost a lot of friends to this game.

11

No Woman

"Are you hungry?" I ask Stan. He creases his brow.

"Man, don't ever ask a prisoner if he's hungry. The answer's always yes! Whatcha got?"

"Banana bread. Homemade." He watches with hungry eyes as I take out two thick slices wrapped in plastic. "They check my bag when I come through security. The sign says no food."

"Yeah, but you in now."

"So where is Marvin?" I ask, handing Stan a piece. "He said he had all this writing last week and we didn't even get a chance to hear it."

"I don't think he wants you to see him. He was up late gambling. All tore up now."

"And Bill?"

"He's on school tier. But I don't know if they called him."

I'm too defeated to inquire about the new guys Shakelia's put on the list. Instead I think about the writers who aren't here. Ron is gone and has not yet written to me. Dean has been released and is working part-time at a steak house in downtown Richmond. I've seen him a few times, but he's tiring of writing. Andre is about an hour south of Richmond in a prison, writing me letters that, increasingly, are asking for help researching his court case. G is in another prison about six hours away, almost at the state line, and has not responded to my letter. Naji and Karl and Tony and Brad are still at Indian Creek Correctional Center in Chesapeake. I have told them I'm making plans to come see them in the summer.

"Let me ask you something, then, while we wait."

"Go 'head," Stan says, munching.

"What are you going to do when you're released?"

"I know for sure I can't go to no woman," Stan says right away.

"Why?" I ask.

"Because she wouldn't give me the guidance and structure I need." I stare, unblinking.

"What?" he says, smiling. "You looking at me like, 'Whoa!'"

"Structure and guidance is what a mother gives a child," I begin. "You can't expect a lover to be a mother." Then I pause to rephrase and rethink it. "You can't go to a woman, because you're looking for the wrong things." He chews the bread and swallows hard. Then he just stares at me.

"But what if I still need that *now*? How do I get that kind of love now?"

I lower my head. "I'm sorry, Stan. I really shouldn't be asking. It's none of my business what you want from women."

"No man, for real? This is good! No one's ever talked to me like this. No one's ever taken the time. Hey, are you going to eat that piece?"

I shake my head. At first I don't know what else to say. Then I think back to the beginning, the first day of class. It was the first thing he said to me.

"You know how you like to thank me for coming?" I ask.

"You share with us. That's why."

"But I get it back, don't I? You know I learn, too, right?"

Stan nods, breaking off another square. I hear a squeak of shoes in the hall and a deputy shouting commands.

"Maybe when you're free, if you spend as much time thinking about how you're going to *give* love as you do about how you're going to *get* it, you'll find it coming back to you."

He smiles. "Go on!"

"It could start small. Something simple through your church, maybe: helping somebody with something you know how to do. They'll want to do something nice for you, right? Most times, that's how it works."

"You're right! He's a God of love. He wants us to give it. That's deep, Dave!"

"What's deep?" Kelvin asks, suddenly appearing at the door and sitting down in his favorite back pew.

"God's love!" Stan grins. "Plus, Dave brought banana bread. You want some?"

A new guy follows right behind Kelvin. Quietly, they share the last few chunks.

The chat cranks up a notch. The new guy can't stop calling someone a bitch. When I look over to them, Kelvin interrupts him by introducing us.

"Dave, this here's Malik. He just now got off the phone with his girl." He turns back to Malik. "Look, I know you're upset. But I'm telling you, I know plenty girls go for guys just like you: dark, with that bald head and New York accent. C'mon, man. Tighten up on this one."

"I never met none!" Malik shoots back. "How do you think I got back *here*? I mean, shit, no one's going to give me that *ass* unless I have the *cash*! Excuse me, Dr. Coogan."

"No, go ahead," I say. "I want to know why you think that's true."

"It *is* true!" he says, raising his voice in this, our first conversation. "I can tell you why *exactly*. Because when I got out last time, I had nothing. No ride. No money. But when I did what I had to do and got me that joint with rims, they came calling!"

"Yeah, but you don't want none of *them* girls," Kelvin says, shaking his head, I can only assume, with his own memories of them girls.

"Are you going to write on any of this, Malik? It'd be compelling to figure out how you came to think like this about your color and about women. Because I bet not all dark-skinned guys feel the same way, or if they do, act to fix it like you did."

"And look, man," Stan interrupts. "Plenty of women down on red-bones."

"Redbones?" I ask.

"Yeah," Stan says under his breath, gesturing to his own light-brown skin. "Like me. My color."

"But this is bigger than color, isn't it?" I venture. "It's about the man behind the color. It's about your perceptions of color, the stories of how that came about. Why don't you try writing it?" Malik looks out the window.

"I could spit it to ya," he says suddenly, catching me off guard. "Who was it typed Malcolm X's autobiography?"

"Alex Haley," I say in a quiet voice.

"We could do it like that," he shouts, pleased with his idea. "Like Malcolm spitting to Alex."

"We could," I concede warily. Kelvin cracks a smile. "But this is really more about you writing." He's barely listening. Out in the hall, I hear someone call his name.

"Excuse me, Dr. Coogan." He moves to the hall. And while we're waiting, Kelvin tells me and Stan that he's getting shipped in a few days. He nods, trying to hasten my acceptance of the fact, but all I can see is our workshop ending. I'm tired of meeting guys like Malik.

I sigh and voice the conclusion I've been putting off. "Guys, I'm sorry. We're going to have to finish up in letters. This is going to be our last class."

Stan and Kelvin look at each other as if they'd foreseen this moment months ago. They nod briefly. Kelvin smiles from deep within. Stan gets up and looks down at me.

"Stand up," he commands. When I get up, he hugs me harder than I thought possible, finishing with a two-handed back slap. I lose a little wind.

"Kelvin!" Stan says, stepping back from me. "Hug your teacher!" Kelvin stands, rising endlessly, a beanstalk of a student stooping now to reach me. When our shoulders are about even, he grabs my hand in that bro-hug maneuver and pulls gently.

"Thanks, Dave—for everything." I smile and ready myself to say that this isn't goodbye, just a new phase.

But Kelvin isn't done: "It's been shocking."
I part my lips to ask why.
"You always knew the right questions to ask."

KELVIN

She wasn't one of those girls from school who knew me as the guy with the big-ass stack of ones and fives. Kelly didn't even know how funny I was. Nor had she ever jammed to any of my go-go beats that I played on the wooden shelves in school. These were our drums, and that hallway had more music coming from it than the band room right around the corner. We had a ball in that hall. But Kelly wasn't there for any of it. She only knew me as that tall, slim, shy young fella that she met on her way home.

I was drawn to her silhouette from across the street. I couldn't even see her face. To think back on it now, that was really a leap of faith. Or maybe it was a gambler's impulse on both of our parts. But I could feel her hurt that night. After a while, she knew about the weed, but it wasn't about that with her.

Kelly was the first female I really slowed down for. Before her, it was "get in where you fit in." So to be with someone and actually care about her was really new territory. I was a mama's boy. I had just stepped off the porch in the girl-relationship-game. And now I'm all messed up, because I actually liked the hell out of this female!

Like a lot of women who get pregnant, she was feeling insecure and doubted her looks and appearance. The whole time she was carrying Lil' Kelvin, I thought all the fussing and back-and-forthing—all the bickering we did—was normal, because she was pregnant. Boy, was I wrong!

Then she lied and told me that she'd gotten rid of our son. And that was the start of the end. That night in front of Thalhimers, on the corner of Seventh and Broad, is when I showed a sign of weakness that I never recovered from. I cried. I thought I had lost my first child! But that facial rain shower of mine pushed us down a steep and steady slope.

Every woman, though they are scared to admit it, wants a man that's rough and abrasive, like number-four sandpaper on stucco brick. I wasn't the take-charge type of guy when it came to women. Don't get me wrong: I wasn't as soft as you might think. But then again, let me come clean. We act too damn hard when it comes to this type of thing. I'm going to tell y'all the truth: I was soft! Now, on a scale of soft to hard, I wasn't cotton-ball soft. But everybody has felt a Nerf football as a little boy or girl. Well, that was me: hard enough to make a tight spiral pass, but I wouldn't break any fingers or knock the wind out of you or your child.

Well, the truth came out eventually, and she had our child. Being a new parent caused her to look and think differently, but I just seemed to stand still in one spot. She developed mentally, physically, and emotionally. The mental part of her growth was that she no longer got upset about everything. Then she started not caring when it came to us. The physical development could be noticed by all of the guys, it seemed. After having our son, that damn girl got compliments from every dude we saw! Kelly told me on a couple of occasions that all the attention made her feel good. Her emotional development was becoming more and more clear to me as each day passed. As her caring about us died, so did any emotion that I used to bring out of her.

So there we were, two young teenage parents. One had been reduced to a sperm donor, while the mother had her newborn son, and every man she saw was trying to holler. You want me to tell you what came next?

Rrrring! Rrrring! Rrrring!

"Kelly! It's for you," I heard her mother say from the other room. Now mind you, I was right there beside her like that good little boy-man I considered myself to be. And my girl, my baby, crushed me when she took that call from him.

STAN

He shows me the photograph on the prison rec yard: a beautiful woman sitting at a desk. Ellen. She's the sister of a woman my workout partner is seeing. But all I see is this beautiful woman seated on a throne. She wears black, thin-framed librarian glasses. She is conservative, professional. I'm loving what I'm seeing. But I can see more than what the lens of that 35 mm camera captured. At this moment, I know I've found my Eve.

Adam's first words recorded about Eve were, "Bones of my bone and flesh of my flesh." Adam knew Eve was a part of his own being. His first words were internal— "bones of my bones"—and external—"flesh of my flesh." My very first words after seeing her photo were, "This is me." I couldn't take my eyes off of the photograph, because it was like looking into the mirror. She reflected my spirit, and I knew it, like Adam knew it. But was Adam ready for the gift God brought him? Did God teach Adam how to love and care for Eve?

How many times have you gazed through the want ads of your local newspaper and come across the familiar words "Only Experienced Need Apply"? It's a phrase that is seldom spoken about our intimate relationships, but sometimes it's implied. There was a position available in Ellen's life, but I had to be experienced in order to apply.

At the early age of twelve, my father and mother enrolled me in a class at this company that makes landscaping equipment. There, I learned how to run my own little grass-cutting business, and I had great success in my neighborhood, around Dogwood Dell, in the West End of Richmond near Byrd Park. I must have had about twenty customers that I supplied a whole host of different services to, from grass cutting to snow removal. I also worked for the *Richmond Times Dispatch* as a paperboy. I had maybe 145 papers on my route and I delivered them daily—all this at the age of twelve.

As I grew older, my interest in landscaping only grew stronger. Do you remember Lawn Doctor? You've seen the trucks. They have the man with the green thumb on his hat. That was me. I wore that cap. But before I put it on, I had to obtain my pesticide, herbicide, and fungicide licenses. I'm a bona fide and certified master gardener, registered at Southern States Corporation. I have more than enough experience to apply for any landscaping job. I can run a crew well. What I couldn't run was my emotional life.

Meantime, I was still trying to land that position in Ellen's life. Each week Ellen came to interview me for an hour. We shared thoughts, dreams, kisses, touches, laughter; I scored high marks. In that controlled environment, I even sold myself with my words. Earlier I gave you a list of my professional qualifications. But this part of my life wasn't about gardening. It was about emotions, sharing, caring, loving, respect, accountability, stability, and responsibility. Those are just a few of the credentials and characteristics Ellen was looking for in a partnership—key ingredients in any successful, intimate relationship. She wasn't looking for perfection out of me. She was mature. She just wanted to plant the seeds of our relationship on fertile ground. That's why she only wanted experienced men to apply.

When I was released on parole on February 11, 2005, I had served twelve years of a twenty-five-year sentence. I must admit, I thought I was a mature man. I had brown eyes and curly brown hair, forty-eight inches of rock-hard chest, twenty-two inches of biceps, and could squat over five hundred pounds. I was 225 pounds of flesh, waiting to share it all with Ellen. To anyone's eyes, I appeared to be a complete package. But there was a wounded little boy hiding in a well-guarded place inside the walls of my emotional system. Ellen never had the opportunity to really meet him. And he's the one who's been controlling my life.

* * *

She answers the door and leads me in. The colors of her place are soft but strong. I am fascinated—overwhelmed, actually. King Solomon said, "There are many beautiful women in the world, but you excel them all." King Solomon must have met Ellen in a vision from God when he said those beautiful and powerful words 2,000 years ago. I'm seeing in Ellen what he saw, too: a beauty of the rarest kind. I can't describe what she's wearing, because to me her entire body is draped in the finest silhouette of brown, silky skin. I am drowning in the moment.

The spirit of that moment leads us upstairs. We are high above life but just short of God's heaven. Ellen knows that I am intoxicated with just the thought of intimacy. There are sweeping sounds of passion. Then Ellen's voice becomes clear: "Stan, don't flood me with your love." And in an even clearer voice, she commands, "I need for you to be responsible with me, as I am with myself." She looks into the pupils of my eyes, searching for a man she can trust and take comfort in. But deep inside of me, that responsible man does not exist.

I look into Ellen's heart by way of her eyes. I see all the casualties of wounded trust. But I march past these fallen bodies with the passwords of love, find a clear passage, and land a fatal blow of emptiness. What's inside of me, I transfer to her womb. I flood her with mistrust. I violate her body with 225 pounds of child.

My semen does not bring life, only the death to our relationship. Ellen reprimands me harshly for defiling her trust. She looks into my eyes but can't see me. I really don't comprehend. I speak as a child. I understand as a child. I think as a child.

Prisons are overflowing with men like me: forty-year-old boys. Age doesn't make you a man. We become men when we learn to put away childish things, childish thinking, childish emotions, and childish actions. I don't know about Adam, but I wasn't prepared for the woman God brought into my life. Everything Ellen wanted from me, I had no experience in. I was truly indigent. It hurts to say that. I know how to kiss a woman and touch a woman but not how to love her.

Ellen, please forgive me for my inexperience. I was lying to you and to myself, but I didn't realize it. To Ellen and to all who read my words: it's time to resubmit my application. I finally have the experience.

12

Best Intentions

Hey, everyone!

I've been meaning to write you for a while now. I miss having the chance to address all of you as a group. And some of you, I realize now, have never been a part of that group or heard me talk or met the others. Some of you might not even know the names of the other writers who will be in the book with you. I want to try to compensate for all of that as best I can with this letter.

The photos I'm sending, along with the names and addresses of all the group members and sample passages from their stories, will, I hope, help you see what I get to see from my vantage point as the teacher/coordinator. I'd encourage you to send me a photo, if it's not too much trouble to do so. I'd like to assemble it all into one collage and give each of you a copy.

The first picture is of me and Stanley Craddock in the Richmond City Jail chapel. It was taken toward the end of our year of classes. The second is of me and Dean Turner, taken in my office at Virginia Commonwealth University. Dean was also with us for most of that year. Both these guys used to play football, and clearly, I need them on my team, because I got nothing. Look at me! I didn't realize just how much smaller I was until I saw these pictures.

For those of you just joining, the workshop started in July of 2006. The group never got too big and usually hovered around seven or eight men, though there were always a lot of guys cycling in and out, testing the waters, I guess. The other originals from the City Jail days who have stuck with it are Andre Simpson, Naji Mujahid, Kelvin Belton, and Ron Fountain.

After Kelvin was shipped, he encouraged Terence Scruggs to start writing. Those guys grew up together. Terence is now released and, like Dean, meets with me in my office every few weeks. The first time we arranged to meet he told me not be alarmed—that he was over two hundred pounds and over six feet tall. You can imagine the looks on my neighbors' faces when I told them I had to go to work Saturday morning to meet a BIG ex-con! Of course, I was joking, and Terence and I had a pleasant meeting, just like when we talked on the phone. He wasn't anything like what I thought he'd look like. (And neither was I to him.)

Ron Fountain was also released over the summer, and I have met with him a few times too. Ron, Dean, and Terence are all working at restaurants or in catering, living with family, and doing well. They will visit the new class I've started on campus, Prison Literature, to discuss their stories with my students. I hope all of you will someday make it to this class as well.

After a long and much-needed rest from writing, Kelvin is back. Meanwhile, over the summer, Andre exploded with a burst of new material. I'd get at least a letter a week, sometimes two. And he's still going. Naji, too, kept up on his drafting, staying true to his word. And he also recruited Tony Martin, Bradley Greene, and Karl Black. I hope to meet them someday.

Our project is growing, guys, and our book is developing. We are most definitely on track. Stan, Naji, Dean, and Andre are mostly finished. Each is working on a final piece, perhaps two, mostly about their futures or filling in parts about the past. The rest of you are half-done or have only just begun, but are going strong.

Enclosed is a statement of intent[13] I'd like you to consider signing as we move forward. It helps, I think, to keep everything up-front and transparent. It always has. But it's especially important to do now as we make plans to actually make a book.

STATEMENT OF INTENT
Prepared by Dr. David Coogan
Virginia Commonwealth University
July 16, 2007

At the Richmond City Jail in 2006, I, _____ , began writing my autobiography under the direction of Dr. David Coogan of Virginia Commonwealth University. Or I joined the project through the mail. Either way, I signed a consent form that explained the nature of the project: a writing workshop culminating in a book. I understood from that form that I would be writing about my childhood, my first crimes, and my current efforts at rehabilitation; that Dr. Coogan's students in his prison literature class would eventually see my work; but that the consent form did not obligate me to publish my story in his book.

I hope to be paid if my work is published. But I understand that such arrangements must be made in accordance with the law and spelled out

---

13 When I mentioned to colleagues at Virginia Commonwealth University that I planned to publish the stories from this writing workshop, I was advised to seek permission from our Institutional Review Board. In the process of completing the application, I created a form for people to sign what would formally express their desire to participate in the project, to make clear their awareness of the emotional difficulties in life writing, and to acknowledge their rights to stop participating for any reason.

by a publisher in a contract. I believe Dr. Coogan will make every effort to find some way of compensating me for my work, but if I am unable to be paid, *(circle one)*

    a) I still want my story to be included in the book

    b) I do not want my story to be included in the book

If my story is included in the book, I want it to appear with *(circle one)*

    a) my full name

    b) my first name only

    c) a pseudonym

At this time, I believe that my story is *(circle one)*

    a) Finished.

    b) Unfinished. And I agree to finish writing my story by January 1, 2008.

In signing my name to this statement, I agree to correspond or (once released) meet in person with Dr. Coogan to further edit my story or respond to questions about its content (even if I am through writing new material). I understand that Dr. Coogan will continue to edit my story, write commentary about it and our interactions, compare my story to other inmates' stories, and in other ways analyze the meaning. I have seen the latest version of my story and some of Dr. Coogan's commentary and generally approve of both. I reserve the right to make changes to my story and suggest changes to Dr. Coogan's commentary all the way up until the January deadline, but I also understand that it is my responsibility to keep in contact with Dr. Coogan, especially when my address changes, either through prison transfer or release. I understand that Dr. Coogan needs to show my work to publishers, and authorize him to do so at this time.

    Signature: _____

    Current Mailing Address:

    Alternate Mailing Address:

* * *

Everyone returns his form, agreeing to use his full name and to finish writing and to let me share his writing with students and prospective publishers. Only Dean, sitting in my office with pen in hand, getting ready to sign the form, hesitates about going forward if he won't get paid.

"We didn't start this thing to make money," I remind him.

"Ah, but you have a job, Dave." He sucks some air through his teeth. Eventually he signs the form and rises to leave. I stand to shake hands goodbye. "All right, Dave. Just don't think you're getting one over on me!" He grins and rolls a shoulder into mine. I push right back.

But no form I could draw up, no plans I could arrange, could get me in to see Karl the following week at Indian Creek Correctional Center.

I have already been there to see Naji. But I have yet to meet Karl, Tony, and Brad. My plan was to visit each a few times over the summer. The rule I do not know about, the rule I drive an hour and a half to learn firsthand, is that people are not allowed to visit more than one inmate at the same prison at a time unless they are family. The deputy telling me this seems to realize that I can't comprehend it; I need time. And she provides that, lowering her eyes and allowing me to fume at her counter in silence. I carry that strange solace with me in the long car ride home through the Chesapeake Bay, seeing none of the vistas, tasting none of my lunch, and feeling stupid, angry, and bored all at once.

KARL

After I got shipped off to my grandparents' house, I turned into a recluse. All I did was play the computer and go to school. My computer experience began with simple gaming, which turned into multiplayer gaming on the Internet. My horizons expanded quickly, and I eventually formed my own clan, called Crypt Killers (CK), on Battle.net.

At first this was just a social outlet and a means to deal with my lack of popularity. But my investment in the activity became considerable. My reading and writing improved. From leading a CK clan, I not only learned advanced computing but the basics of diplomacy, which would later help me survive my first few years in prison. Most importantly I learned how to motivate, reward, punish, cut losses, divide resources, measure skills, and appoint tasks. Because of this I can honestly say that the five years I spent gaming were not a waste of time. Those games were all about strategy, Machiavellian tactics, and control. But I had few friends and fewer girlfriends.

I had so much frustration, anger, and sadness. I took it everywhere I went. At the time, I couldn't fathom the continued relevance of the Event. Even today, my calling it "the Event" is a way of depersonalizing it. It's out there, like a distant star, the horizon of a black hole, billions of light years away. I know it's a delusion to say that the Event doesn't bother me. It does. And yet I know life goes on and that's the past. So I don't dwell on it.

After I completed the eighth grade, my grandparents sent me off to live with my father in Connecticut. By now I was fed up. I was sick of being bounced around like a ping-pong ball with no control. So I decided that I was going to reinvent myself. I was sick of being viewed as a computer nerd. And though I remained a computer-science lover in secret, I became the party kid, the one who could party harder than everyone else and was not scared of anything. Translation: young punk with something to prove.

At the Muni, in Hartford, I tried special K, acid, mushrooms, ecstasy. Drugs were just something that were done, part of the social norms, an experience. It wasn't about addiction. And in this subculture, certain drugs—most notably, crack and heroin—were off-limits. We did not view ourselves as bad guys or lawbreakers; other people just did not understand the concept of a raver. We were about the moment, the party, getting lost in the music. PLUR: Peace, Love, Unity, and Respect. On the dance floor, high on psychotropics, I could explore worlds within worlds. Caught up in the constant motion and fun, I could forget about my fractured family, my frustrations. I was part of something foreign.

On Sundays, when I wasn't partying, I'd hang out with my dad. We'd watch a movie, listen to George Carlin, or talk about the craftiness of women. He used to tell me things like:

1. Men do what they think they should do and not what others think.
2. Men honor their prior agreements. They do what they say they are going to do.
3. Men don't have to do what they don't like to do, but sometimes they should.
4. A man should not subjugate himself to another.
5. If you see something wrong, act to fix it.

We'd talk about the troubles awaiting me in the party scene, including interesting anecdotes from his life. Hell, I was partying in some of the same places that he used to when he was a kid! My father's parenting emphasized my freedom, but he would teach me what lessons he could and let the natural consequences of my actions take their course, with him pointing out my mess-ups.

I did not recognize, nor did I care to see, that messing up in school had long-term consequences. I dropped out in the ninth grade. Then I lost my job at the grocery store. The consequence was that I now lacked income, which was necessary for me to do the things I enjoyed. A few days later I got a job roofing. It was much harder. I had to get up at 5:00 a.m. and do heavy work by 6:00 a.m. I soon realized I could not be dragging. But the bigger paycheck made it worth it. It enabled me to party more on the weekends. Once I started working construction, however, my smoking died down quite a bit. Weed, for me, had a natural consequence of laziness and fatigue. So I couldn't smoke and work. I also quit smoking cigarettes.

My father's emphasis on natural consequences, I think, was a very good thing. But it took longer than normal for me to develop a real sense of morality. By seventeen, I was largely Cyrenaic. By twenty-one, I was more Epicurean. Sure, I was told that smoking, fighting, stealing, and swearing at others was wrong, but I had also been told that eating junk food before dinner was wrong, and I still did it. For me, being told that something was "wrong" was absolutely meaningless. It just meant that the person didn't like what I was doing, so I would not commit the act in their presence. I resorted to being sneaky.

Over time I began to question myself. I questioned why I did things. I often found the answer to be that I did it because I thought it benefited me. I did a lot of things for purely selfish reasons. It was all about personal gain. I didn't realize my mental calculator was broken. What I thought was in my best interest was not. What I thought wasn't risky was. I did not properly weigh my actions. I consistently made the wrong decisions.

One night, I went for an introspective walk after clubbing and wound up lying on the roof of some tool shed, tripping off of LSD, just gazing up at the stars, entertaining thoughts of getting my life together. I remember thinking that I should cut certain "friends" off, stop partying, go back to school, and try to get— or perhaps even *get*—my GED. I even remember thinking about college. In that trip I thought about how fake my friends were and how destructive my life was. I dreamed of being a computer programmer or an astronomer, but what I really lacked was the ability and dedication to formulate long-term goals and plan for my future. I was largely stuck in the present. The moment was what was most relevant; my immediate situation and desires were all I really thought or cared about.

I moved in with some guys—it might as well have been a frat house, really. There was a party every night. A lot of people were gang-affiliated, others were prospects, and life was pure drama. All we did was drink, crash parties, and cause trouble. We rarely went anywhere without ten people. There was a rush, an adrenaline surge, and a near-constant state of excitement that came along with the risks we took. My anger was released in acts of crime, and these crimes aided me in the acquisition of "respect" and "status." It became a game for me. Crimes gained me points and these points got me to the parties, kept me in the know, and essentially kept me feeling important.

* * *

I'm walking down the street about a half a block from our place when my associate says something slick to these Hispanic guys driving by. They slam the brakes, pull onto the curb, jump out, and the brawl is on. I lose right away, but the fight is actually won on account of my associate, an accomplished boxer who has won many tournaments.

Two days later, about fifteen of us are at the house drinking when a bottle gets thrown through the front window. We all get up and run outside. Hispanic guys are everywhere—it seems like twenty people. Some have weapons, bats, brass knuckles; things aren't looking good. I freeze. Then I am abruptly brought to my senses with a punch to the jaw. I try to defeat my foe but am quickly stomped to the ground. The women in the house are getting beat up, too. Some of us end up at the hospital after the police break up the rumble.

Over the next few weeks, the streets grow increasingly hostile. We cannot even walk anywhere without getting jumped. Once people start talking about guns, I decide it's way past time to disappear, as do a few others. I'm not prepared to go that far. The risk and dangers are too great.

My strength, at this moment, comes from my father. Would I be a man if I continued to do what I do not want to, when I know I shouldn't be doing it? No. Would I be I subjugating myself to others by giving them the power to dictate what I do? Yes. Do I think I should continue to live the life I'm living? No. So, I call my dad and have him pick me up. I never look back.

* * *

I'm at a beach party, skinny-dipping with one of the girls, but it doesn't go as far as I want it to.

A stranger approaches our gathering with his girlfriend. "Whatcha y'all doin'?" I ask in a drunken and mocking drawl. He gives some good-hearted response, but I scream him down. I'm frustrated, insecure, and drunk. When my anger reaches a crescendo, I hit him in his jaw. He falls to the sand, and his girlfriend rushes to his side. The girl I've been swimming with comes to me. She steals my attention with her lovely green eyes, shapely legs, and fiery attitude. But she shouts and cusses at me before dragging me away.

It could have ended there. But then one of the guys I brought down to Virginia Beach comes up to me and points out that we have no money, and we need money to keep partying and to get back to Connecticut. He points to the guy I've hit, saying he probably has a wallet on him. The guy is slowly getting up to walk away.

I don't want to lose face by saying no. I want to show that I'm hard. We jog up to him like dogs smelling blood. Three of us punch him and kick him to the ground. When his will to fight is broken, we run through his pockets. We find ninety dollars in his wallet and a few pills. We leave him there, lying in the sand, his unscathed girlfriend crying next to him.

It's August 10, 2001. I am fifteen, and, though I don't know it, I have just landed myself in prison.

Naji

That first time that I was incarcerated really only introduced me to the game. I left healthy after serving one year and eight months on a three-year bid. I worked out and lifted weights daily. But mentally I was none the better. I immediately tried to rekindle my relationship with Sandy, but it was clear it was over. This hurt me because in my life at that time, she was one of three people in the world that cared about me.

Alcohol soon became my friend, but not for the taste. I couldn't stand it! I was only able to drink beer, but I drank to get drunk, my way of escaping the pain. I would force down straight alcohol if nothing else was available, but I would soon become sick. It was strange, my relationship with alcohol. I could drink beer all day and be OK, but two shots of hard liquor and I was guaranteed to go to jail for fighting or disruptive behavior. I couldn't hide the pain I felt when I was on hard liquor, and it would always surface as misdirected anger. After a couple of stints in a holding cell, I learned to stay far away from hard liquor.

Time was getting very short for me at home after my release. My grandmother had been telling my brother and me ever since I can remember, "I'll be glad when you turn eighteen, 'cause you're getting out this house!" My brother was already on his own, but not faring too well. He was known as a ladies' man. He always had a woman somewhere waiting in the wings to take care of him. Working wasn't his style. He once told me, "Why work when I got hoes to take care of me?" I was the opposite. I tried my best to keep a job. I watched how he would get kicked out every time a woman was upset with him, mainly for cheating on her, and I vowed that that would never happen to me. At nineteen going on twenty, I was still trying to hold on to my childhood. After being released from prison, instead of preparing myself for independence and trying to build a life for myself, I was trying to catch up on what I had missed.

I stayed in the streets, trying to find old acquaintances to impress upon them how "diesel" I was and how much cooler I had become as a convict. Of all my friends, I was the only one to graduate to the pen. Back then, that was a sign of being "hard" or "thorough," two of the highest titles to aspire to in the street. Although I had gained this reputation, it did nothing to fill the empty hole eating away at my soul. Still searching for self, identity, something to make me whole and accepted, I bounced around from bad situation to bad situation until I met a woman who introduced me to a girl that would forever change my life.

I was twenty years old and was basically living here and there. I left home and had no clue as to what I was going to do or where I was going to go. I wasn't working at the time, because I didn't have the maturity of a twenty-year-old man. I hadn't prepared myself financially for the day I would leave home, so I was just "out there." I dropped out of school upon my release from the pen because I couldn't stand being held back. I saw my failure reflected in the faces of my peers. I convinced myself that the best way to counter my shame was to enter the adult world before them and establish myself, even though I was ill-prepared.

* * *

She has a beautiful, small-featured face with Asian eyes, perfectly pouty lips, smooth, olive-tanned skin, and long, coal-black hair that falls like a waterfall midway down her back. She is 6'1", fully endowed with voluptuous breasts, a small waist, and a backside plump and apple-round. Her legs are statuesque and flawless. She's wearing a red, Asian-silk dress with a turquoise, dragon-print slit up the side. On her small feet are exquisite red stiletto pumps. One is propped up on the edge of the sink. Her dress is pulled back, exposing the neatly trimmed hair around her vagina. With the pinky finger of her left hand she has one of the lips of her sex stretched out. In the other hand, she has a syringe and is injecting a yellow liquid into the moist fold.

"Whoa, excuse me!" I say, quickly stepping out of the bathroom.

"No, it's OK, you can come in," she insists in a sexy, Southern drawl.

"Are you sure?"

"Yeah, baby. It's all good."

"What you doin'?" I've turned my back to her to urinate in the stall, swaying back and forth, intoxicated.

"Getting high, boy," she replies, as if it's the most natural thing in the world and I have to be an idiot to be asking the question.

"On what? And why are you doing it *there?*" I say as I flush the toilet and turn around to watch.

"I don't want to leave any visible marks," she says matter-of-factly. It's most disturbing—and as a male, quite intriguing—that she has no shame to her game. Standing there with her snatch wide open to a total stranger doesn't bother her. I can't get over how beautiful she is, and I feel special that she feels comfortable enough to do this around me. The way she looks at me hints attraction, but I know it has to be something else. When she finishes, she cleans herself up and begins cleaning her works.

"You're a handsome black motherfucker, you know it? I've always liked my men black and sexy." For the first time in my life, I'm glad to be so dark-skinned because I don't want her to see that I'm blushing like a virgin on her wedding night! She seems older than me by five or six years. I'm completely blown away, flattered, and dumbstruck that she is even talking to me.

"I'm alright," I say, instantly realizing that for the first time in my life I'm trying to appear conceited. This is new! I had always felt that I had nothing to be conceited about.

But now she has me under her spell. It doesn't occur to me the danger I'm about to get myself into when she offers me a "blast" and I accept. I start to panic, asking her what it is she's just given me. "It's *girl*—cocaine," she tells me.

"It's not going to hurt me, is it?" I ask nervously.

"Nah, baby, here, this will make it feel even better." She squats down on her knees in front of me, unzips my pants, pulls out my member, and begins to perform oral sex on me. When the drug hits me, my heart feels like it's about to jump out of my chest. Everything seems to brighten and become clearer. My sense of smell becomes keener: my sense of touch, sharper. I can even feel the individual buds on her tongue as she works her magic on me. I climax in less than a minute. I feel like I've just seen God! And in that instant, I'm hooked. I've found the cure to all the pain in my life. I imagine it's like the rush you'd get falling to earth at terminal velocity from fifty thousand feet with no parachute and then suddenly stopping inches before your body smashes into the ground! You're on the verge of death, literally. Every time.

But the fact that I've just let a complete stranger draw a yellow substance that I couldn't identify out of a dirty spoon and up into a syringe and inject it into my body demonstrates that at this point I have lost what little bit of dignity and common sense I had left.

She's a go-go dancer at a local club. Every night for the next two years, we get high together. I become a junkie so quick, it makes my head spin. I begin doing more and more B and Es[14] to support both my weed addiction and my much more powerful cocaine habit. My body goes through anticipatory tremors before my paycheck is even in my hand. Then I get that churning feeling in my stomach that most addicts know as "the shits" before I can score. I'm broke within a few hours of cashing the check.

On the weekends, I start sleeping during the day, staying up all night, plotting how to come up with enough money for the next hit, not willing to part with the drug on Monday morning. Then I'm too tired to work and have to call in sick. My employers learn to recognize my pattern of drug abuse and let me go. But I'm OK with this, because I'm beginning to look like a zombie, and I'm tired of the strange looks and questions from my coworkers. I just want to be left alone to get high.

Though I know I have a problem, I don't have the will to stop it or even the desire to try—until I meet a little girl named April at the park in downtown Hampton, where drinking and getting high are daily activities. April's aunt is an alcoholic, and a poor one at that. She constantly begs for drinks or cigarettes from anyone who has them. In her quest for a quick hit, she loses all concern for her niece. It seems obvious to me that she has no real concern for the child in the first place. Although I'm getting high, too, I never do so around small children. It bothers me a great deal, actually, so whenever April comes to the park, I ask her aunt if I can take April to the store or anywhere away from the drug use. I always see myself in the children of abuse. I'm cognizant of the damage it does.

I treat April as if she were my own child. I look forward to seeing her daily and miss her when she is absent. It turns out that she feels the same way, and would beg her aunt to take her to the park to see me.

---

14 Breaking and enterings.

After a couple of months, I meet April's mother, Adrienne. I think she's cute. And she whispers in my ear, "I want your sexy black ass to take me home and fuck me!" As vulgar and crass as that sounds, this is how we are living, and to me the offer sounds as proper as "Would you like to go out on a date?" Her reference to my "sexy black ass" causes me to realize that, for some women, my skin color is attractive. My self-esteem begins to rise, but the self-hate is still firmly rooted. Needless to say, I go home with Adrienne.

Her house is a complete mess! She's an addict, too, and it shows in the way she keeps her house. Nothing else matters in this house but using. I can't believe that April and her older sister's niece, a little girl I meet later, are living in this filth. It hurts me to my heart. April is only six, and the niece is just ten years old. I move in.

Caring for Adrienne and the kids sparks a purpose in my life that is powerful enough to make me want to stop getting high. Adrienne and I get married. I suggest that we stop using for the kids' sake, and I lead by example. She has no real desire to stop and, after a while, I become frustrated trying to get her to stop. What's the use? I start getting high again. I never do anything around the girls, but at the same time, my preoccupation with getting high and maintaining my ability to get high causes me to make a lot of decisions that have negative effects on their lives.

I regret not being there for them during that short period. The knowledge that I may have directly or indirectly caused those girls harm haunts me still.

TONY

"Tony, would you like some magic potion?" my sister would gently whisper.

In this little world of mine, where I had the freedom to roam, I was told by my mother that when I was a baby, my sister considered herself to be my mother. And at the ripe old age of four or five, Angela devised a plan that allowed her to obtain my unlimited trust. Me and my brother shared the same bed, but my sister had one all to her lonesome—that is, until the lights went out. The three feet over to her bed felt like a walk to the corner store. But when she asked me if I wanted magic potion, I crawled into her bed eagerly.

Now here's where the trust came in. In order for me to receive the magic potion, I had to close my eyes and stick out my tongue. The first few times, I tried my hardest to discover just what this salty, powdery substance was that made my sensitive taste buds ball up. Glimpse after glimpse, nothing was ever revealed until one night a small crack was left in the curtains and a beam of light squeezed its way into the room and landed directly on my sister's hand just as she was just about to administer a dose. I trusted my sister wholeheartedly, but my curiosity caused me to take a peek. I worried that she would catch me, because there was a chance that she would cut me off. But the payoff outweighed the threat of capture, because I could then supply myself with the potion, and the tremulous trek over to her bed could be eliminated!

At the very moment when the beam of light hit her hand, I cracked open my eye to take a peek, and there it was: a very fine, white, powdery substance, neatly packed into a meticulously folded piece of aluminum foil.

As badly as I wanted to know the formula, as hard as I tried to find out how she got it, I never could figure it out. It would be many years later before I'd realize that my zeal was not really for the magic potion. My sister had aroused in me that human longing to be a part of something. After twenty years, she finally revealed to me the formula. It was the greatly used and highly acclaimed baking soda.

* * *

When my mother was approved by Social Services to move us into a low-income apartment, my long bout with crime took root and grew nonstop thereafter.

I was in the second half of my first-grade school year when I met Terry. Both of us went to the same elementary school, which was walking distance from the apartment complex in Newport News, Virginia. At times, Terry and I would walk to and fro, looking for something to get into.

Terry was a rough, blond-haired, blue-eyed young lad who had lost two of his fingers by sticking his hand into a washing machine while it was on the spin cycle. He had a younger brother, but he only followed Terry's lead, so he was just a private amongst generals. See, both Terry and I had a handicap. Mine was a speech impediment, and his was his lost fingers. With Terry's handicap being more visible, along with his rugged features, other kids tended to shy away from him. True loyalty between the two of us quickly hardened like cement.

I could not pronounce certain words that contained the letter "s". It was worse whenever I got excited. Certain words took a lot of concentration for me to say clearly unless I broke them down into syllables. I got teased for all of this. The most notable one was "street." That word is widely used in the vocabulary of children because they're always trying to convince their parents to let them go somewhere, which usually requires them to cross the street. They also use it a lot when trying to manipulate their associates into going somewhere they have no business going, saying, "Come on across the street. You ain't got to be scared! Come on, man. Just cross the street so we can hurry up and get back before our mothers find out we left." I quickly figured out a way to utilize this much-needed phrase by simply replacing the word "street" with the word "road." This became my crutch.

We would start our days off with a cigarette butt hunt. Then came the task of finding a secluded area—virtually impossible to do in the ghetto, since everyone lives an ant's length away from the lap of a neighbor.

We soon devised a plan that would allow us to smoke first-class instead of the second-hand pluck that we so dearly despised. Not only were we depending on the trash of others, but it was also very risky: if an adult had seen us picking up the cigarette butts, they could've easily told our mothers. So we went to Plan B.

Back in the '70s, children could purchase tobacco products as long as they had a written letter from one of their parents stating that the purchase of the tobacco was for them. So there we had it: the answer to our problem. But this also left us with a new question. Who was going to forge his mother's signature? We finally agreed that we would take turns, but I quickly convinced Terry that his handwriting was more equipped for the task, and he graciously submitted to my request. We were then faced with the challenge of choosing the brand that was the most hip and didn't have a real bad smell or taste. We played the field in hopes that the store employees wouldn't question Terry's mother's unpredictability in brand allegiance. Finally, we chose Marlboros laced with the mint flavor of menthol to wet our pink little whistles.

Not only were we smoking cigarettes, but we were also dipping snuff. It became a regular part of our leisure time, and a key to our grandeur.

With good times come good things. It quickly spread throughout the playgrounds that Tony and Terry were the "who's who" when it came to tobacco products. In short, we were a two-man mafia.

With our newfound power and popularity, apartment doors opened to us—apartments with mothers gone to work and frisky girls itching to experiment with their gifts of seduction. They cheerfully welcomed us with their big, twinkling, Snow White eyes. Our time on the young pimping circuit was cut short, though, when we met a house full of well-tanned blondes with three sets of sky-blue eyes. It was as if we had stepped off the set of *Good Times* and directly onto the set of *Grease.*

They were sassy triplets varying in age. From day one, our supply couldn't keep up with their demand, and after only a few minutes of touching and feeling, they had us eating out of the seams of their pants. This couldn't have been the first time they had to use what they had to get what they wanted. But it was truly the first time in my short life that I was being asked to take off the Pampers and be a man. I could have gotten up and ran. But we were now the victims of self-satisfaction.

A call of distress was immediately sent out to our brains to devise a plan that would keep the smoke rings floating at this would-be "Bunny Ranch." The quantity of tobacco that our allowances and lunch money afforded us just wasn't going to meet our lustful need to be teased. But before we were even given an opportunity to display our fortitude, the tanned blondes of fun had retrieved three paper bags from under the kitchen sink. The oldest girl was about four years older than us. She hopped on top of the counter and placed the paper bag between her legs. Then she revealed to us the scam that she and her sisters had successfully executed to supply their daily fix of nicotine.

"The three of you will walk to the Winn-Dixie up the street. Before entering the store, you make sure that the paper bags are tucked away in your pants so that the store employees can't see them. After entering the store, find a cash register that is closed and walk into the small aisle. If no one is looking, take the paper bags out of your pants and fill them with the cartons of cigarettes that are there on the shelves. After every bag is full, make sure that you exit the store out of the door nearest to the alley. Make sure that no one is following you, and then walk quickly down the path that leads to the apartment complex. We will be waiting for you to get back." She folded the bag solemnly and presented it like a flag.

Things went well for about a week with this routine. Then one day when we had just finished pulling our paper bags out, the store manager approached us and asked what we were planning on doing with the bags. "Nothing," we replied. But the manager didn't believe us, so he just told us to leave the store. We never revealed to the girls that we had gotten caught stealing, because that would've meant the end of our sexual escapades, which had just begun to heat up and bake the oats that we were trying to sow.

For about another week, we lingered around the girls until our bouts of knocking on their door got longer and longer and the chuckles and sounds of bodies moving to and fro inside became our cue to leave.

Shortly after we shook off the reality that we were in the doghouse, the dung really hit the fan. I spent the night at Terry's house. His mother had turned out the lights, signaling to us that it was time to get some shut-eye, so we pulled the sheets over our heads, sparked a lighter, and lit a cigarette. Then out of nowhere, as if there was a hidden camera in the room, his mother appeared, snatching the covers and catching us red-handed in the act of puffing up.

I was allowed to finish my stay, but the next day when I got home, there was a surprise. I was greeted at the front door by my father. He lived about twenty-five minutes away. Sometime during the day, Terry's mother had told my mother. Then my mother evidently had seen fit to get my father involved. He didn't ask me many questions, but he did ask the one suitable for the occasion.

"Tony, were you smoking last night?" he asked, smiling.

"No sir," I began, but before I could finish saying the "ir" in sir, he rewarded me with a large carton of Milk Duds just for being his son.

There were five facts of life that I learned during my short episode of using tobacco to be hip and cool—using it to use people and ending up a foolish mule:

1. Power comes to those who splurge away their riches.
2. Crime may pay for a couple of days.

3. What comes around goes around. So when you use people, look forward to being used in the near future.

4. When you run out of money, you're sure to lose your honey.

5. And fifth and final: never think you have too much wit to be tricked.

BRAD

As I checked myself out in the mirror, getting my hair feathered back just right, I couldn't help but think that this was going to be the best night of my life. Brian and I were already drinking when Matt came to pick us up. Inside, I was going crazy, but I had to keep my cool. I was going to my first rock concert, my first big show, and I knew of no group that could top Rush.

When I was fourteen, there was nothing I wanted more than to be on stage and have the lights in my face, the fans at my feet. I didn't have dreams of being a famous sports star, fireman, or actor. I wanted to be Bruce Dickinson or Vince Neil. Those guys were my heroes! I've wanted to be a rock star for as long as I can remember. Hasn't everyone?

The show was out of this world, the immensity of it unimaginable. Walking out of the Richmond Coliseum that night, I was in a supernatural state of mind, intensely ready for anything—or so I thought.

The argumentative manner between the drug dealer and user was amazing; both pushing their point on how good it was and how good it better be, battling over size and cost. When all was said and done that day, I rode out of Richmond a changed person. Even though I didn't smoke any of the cocaine that was bought that night, I got high in a whole different manner, on the acceptance of being there on the scene.

* * *

"Brad, get up, man. I got some weed and you've been telling me you want to smoke." I had just fallen asleep a few hours ago after Brian and I had killed a twelve-pack.

"What the fuck time is it?" I mumbled to Eddie.

"Two-thirty. Now get up!" he whispered hoarsely, eyes flashing in the dark.

"All right, give me a second," I said, fumbling for my jeans.

"I got my dad's pipe," he said, hovering in the doorway. "Come in my room just in case Brian wakes up." Brian drank but he refused to mess with drugs, so we went into Eddie's room.

"Smell this!" Eddie beamed, holding the bag open.

"Holy shit! It smells like some kind of fuel!" But I was scared. I had never smoked before and didn't know what to expect.

Eddie proceeded to pack the bowl tight and hit it.

"This is good stuff. You're going to love it." I put it to my lips and hit it like there was no tomorrow.

"Why does it taste so sweet?" I asked.

"That's just how it taste, man!" He blew a thick puff of it in my face. I couldn't feel anything at first. Then the Mack truck hit me! I looked over at Eddie and saw that his head looked like a giant balloon. I was so high I couldn't tell reality from make-believe.

Later, I learned that we had smoked some very good love boat: weed laced with PCP. I believe any normal person would have freaked out under those circumstances, but for me it was quite the opposite: I felt free and powerful. Black Sabbath's "We Sold our Souls to Rock & Roll" played on for hours that night.

It would be some time before I was able to smoke weed again. But I was clearly hooked.

Shortly after the PCP experience, Brian's parents divorced. Eddie went with his dad, and Brian stayed with his mom. It was during this period that my social status seemed to override everything else in my life. I quit the Boy Scouts a year and a half short of making Eagle Scout. Girls and metal bands seemed to engulf my life.

My own parents' separation and eventual divorce came as no surprise and only made things worse. We sold the house in Bellwood Estates, and Mom built an even more beautiful home on the water just ten minutes from the beach.

Virginia Beach was a whole different ballgame for a guy like me, used to the woods: breathtaking and a little frightening. But it didn't take long for me to make friends and settle into our new house. When I found out that my father wasn't going to be coming home except on weekends, though, the reality hit me. It was just me and Mom. As music had always been my true love, I escaped into a familiar fantasy world at the beach. My taste in metal got heavier and heavier until all I was listening to was deathlike, speed metal. It was the deepest, darkest, most malevolent music on the face of the earth.

With my father never around and my mother having zero control over me, I began to do whatever I wanted. What started off as a little drinking and puffing on the beach turned into all-night trips on mushrooms and LSD. These would go on sometimes until mid-morning and take us on journeys that would leave us miles from where we started. Most of my friends from high school eventually faded away during this time, to be replaced with oceanfront deadheads, hippies, musicians, locals, and bums. We came together every evening at Flipper McCoys, and by 8:00 p.m., we were reinventing the world. But two things happened that summer on the benches in front of Flippers that would change my life forever. I heard the Grateful Dead, and I met my sugar magnolia. Both completely captivated me.

Colleen became my friend before she was my girl. I fell in love with her before I had her. The psychedelics were changing me, opening me up to a more holistic view of nature and why we were all here. My taste in music was getting deeper, and all my metal records started gathering dust. I was now listening to the Dead, Pink Floyd, Zappa, and Marley. To my way of thinking at the time, I was starting to settle down.

Colleen and I eventually fell in love, but it wasn't without obstacles. She actually lived in Long Island; Virginia Beach was just her family's vacation spot. With my wheels spinning and my life going nowhere, I decided to drop out of high school and move up north and go to work for my father.

That was good in the beginning. I was out of my mother's house and had finally found some peace. But then a leisurely afternoon of four-wheeling, target shooting, and drinking almost landed me in prison for life. An altercation at a restaurant parking lot had me shooting at this other car that was chasing us. That spur-of-the-moment decision would put me in front of the Prince William County detectives, facing attempted murder charges and answering a lot of questions I just didn't have answers for. My family's intervention set the stage for a long break in my self-destructive behavior. What should have landed me in prison for many years turned into a mere slap on the wrist. As my father had done before and would do so many times afterward—for years really—strings were pulled and my mess was cleaned up.

The reality of what could have happened that day frightened me to the core and forced me to inventory what kind of person I was becoming. Knowing there had to be a change in my life, I settled down and began to lay the foundation from which my marriage and career would materialize.

The next year was spent under the extreme supervision of my probation officer, and I mean extreme. I had to be in her office twice a month to report and give urine samples, so all marijuana use came to a stop for some time. Other than the occasional fungus or LSD at a show, I was clean of drugs for over a year.

At work I basically did what I needed to do and went home. I kept it up for three more years, but I think it's safe to say I squandered that time. The only aspect I had learned was application. As for rigging, management, bidding/takeoffs, and the social aspect of construction, I didn't know or care to know. I didn't take my career too seriously, and my addict behavior eventually caught up with me.

During a mandatory drug test, I tested positive for pot. I was offered a two-week drug program, the completion of which would get me back to work, no questions asked. But I ran and stayed gone for four months, spending part of that time on a winter Dead tour.

During the time I was following the Dead, I went months without calling Colleen. But as soon as I heard her voice again, it was like we'd never been apart.

Her senior prom in New York City was the most magical night. I'll never forget it. She looked like Cinderella, and I was just completely knocked out. We married in October of '95: a beautiful wedding with a beautiful bride. Our first bundle of joy, our daughter Molly, was already growing as we exchanged vows.

But my instability, infidelity, or just plain self-centeredness kicked in right away. I didn't think it was wrong for me to sleep with her coworkers or friends. Chauvinistically, I thought I was God's gift to women: "You should be thanking God I am fucking you right now" sums up my attitude back then. But Coll better not *look* at another man, let alone *think* about having a male friend!

Over time, work became a passion. I had a newfound willingness to always take on another job. I became really assertive, wanting to learn everything and absorbing as much as I could while I was there. Responsibility at the new company came fast, and it would be no time before I was running multiple jobs, which kept me busy from sunup to sunset. This responsibility helped me to justify my extracurricular activities when I was away from home.

Working out of town and commuting home for the weekends gave me plenty of time to "play." Brian and I eventually rented an apartment where I would stay during the week. It was a home away from home, my escape from having to be a full-time husband and father. Even though I had an active sex life with Colleen, I needed to be reassured that I could still pull women like I had when I was younger. I would hit the go-go bars in D.C. till all odd hours of the night with my friends, and sleep all day Saturday to recover.

I could never understand why Coll was so restless and wanted to go out and paint the town when I'd come home for the weekend. Today, I understand, and to be honest, I think I did a little back then. I was just too self-centered to do anything about it. She only had two days a week to spend with me, and she wanted some attention, time for her to be the princess. But she was only the center of my attention when we were making love. And while I loved Colleen with my heart and soul, I had only tapped into the flesh side of it. I had totally missed the spiritual.

Toward the end of '97, Colleen had become fed up with us living apart. The decision was made that we would move into a condo my father owned and try to fix our relationship. It failed terribly, and within a month, she was living back down at the beach. I tried to stop my security blanket from leaving, but this time it wasn't as easy as I'd thought.

Losing her for even the shortest amount of time was devastating, but finding out she'd been seeing someone else nearly crushed me.

"How much do you love me?" I demanded after abruptly stopping the car by the side of the road. "Tell me!"

She reaches for my hand. "You know how much I love you Brad, I'm sorry, baby."

"Would you do anything for me?" I challenge.

"Yes, you already know that," she says, trying to calm me down.

"Then get out of the car, babe!" I grin.

"Why?"

"I'll show you!"

In no time at all, I was exploding inside of her. The rush of the cars driving by made it a moment out of this world. But this control trip that soothed my inner self was really just a way of not facing the problem. It was a temporary fix, impulsiveness at its best—a vivid memory, even today, of the Brad we both used to know.

13

Mentor

The warden at Indian Creek won't answer my e-mails asking for special permission to visit Karl, Tony, and Brad. She won't return my calls either. She's drowned me with silence. I worry that I won't be able to keep the project going if I can't meet the men I'm trying to help. It's a worry confirmed when I happen to keep the warden's secretary on the phone so long that the warden herself passes through and is given the phone.

I state my case. But it doesn't take long for her to say no. Her cadence is slow and high-toned—so polite and impervious to disagreement, so Southern, I suddenly feel pushy and Northern. I guess I am.

"Will there be anything else, Dr. Coogan?" she asks breezily.

"No, thank you." I want to slam down the phone—give in to my growing conviction that people like her are the reason why prisons fail to help people grow. It's a problem I can't let myself think on too long, though. I know I only have but so much energy to stay positive. And I need it.

Dean has asked me to be his mentor in a program for ex-offenders. The first meeting with Dean, his pastor, and the other mentors and mentees—about a dozen of us—is at Harvey's Progressive Barber Shop, the place where Squeaky cut Andre's hair high off that heroin all those years ago. Around the circle we go, on the subject of mentoring: what it is, how we do it. Jeff is leading the discussion, signaling who should talk with his eyes. He's moving pretty fast. When he gets to me I start talking about the kind of dialogue that leads to critical thinking, which in turn creates agency—the ability to make choices, matching your words and actions. I go on about how the right choices can become your reality, and how the language you use to describe your reality matters. I'm going on, in other words, as if Harvey's *were* a classroom, and Jeff starts bristling with the bodily disgust of a man who knows more than I do about the boyish immaturity of the ex-offender (in this case, Dean). He's all but telling me to man up, ball up my fist, learn to curse, something! He realizes before I do that Dean wants me as a mentor because I won't scold, keep tabs on him, or tell him what to do. And he's right.

* * *

"Is that him?" Terence asks, hunching over the photo in my office. I nod quickly. "And that's your daughter next to him?" he presses, looking back and forth between the blonde girl and the black boy sitting on the porch of my house. He pulls the snapshot closer to his face. The warm light glistens on the photo.

Since Terence has come home from prison, we've grown accustomed to sitting like this in my office, talking about his writing, but also about the way we see the themes from our book in our lives. Before he fell into using and stealing a decade or so ago, Terence was a student at VCU. Sitting here, in a way, is like going back to college.

"How old's the boy?" he asks.

"He's nine—four years older than Lucy. *And* he plays on the same playground you did, right across from my house, always alone. *And* he goes to Bellevue Elementary just like you did, after your mom took you out of Baker. *And* he doesn't really know his father. He lives with his grandparents, but he only sees his grandfather on the weekends. And he loves being in my house. He'll turn down friends—other boys his own age—asking him to go to the playground, just to stay in my house."

"Doing normal family things," Terence finishes.

"Yes!" I exclaim, finally getting it. "Why else would a nine-year-old boy want to play with a five-year-old girl?"

"Ain't that something," Terence says, shaking his head.

"But you know what? He tells me some of those boys tried jumping him. I don't think he really has solid friends his own age. These boys, they're really not his friends, you know."

"I know. Believe me, I know."

"And when he does play basketball with these guys, he hogs the ball. He misses their jokes. It's like he doesn't know how to relate."

"I know. I keep tellin' you, I know!" He grins and nods.

"So this has been going on for a few months or so—meeting haphazardly at the playground with my kids, him coming into the house for a drink of water, staying for dinner, you know."

"So you're the father-figure," he says, grabbing a handful of almonds from the bag on my desk.

"I am, yes. I am your Mr. Mattox," I say flatly.

"Heh-heh!" Terence squints and smiles.

"You know this one time at the playground, Lucy came up on me to chase her. So I did. Then I picked him up—or tried to, he's big for nine years old—and he's laughing and all, but you know how kids just say what they're thinking?"

"Right. No censor. It just come out." Terence is munching and smiling, listening like he's at the theatre.

"So I put him down, and he just said, under his breath, like a comment on the whole scene—like he was looking down on himself or something. He said, 'I miss getting picked up.'"

Terence swallows and slides the photo across the desk. Then he gazes out the window, lost in thought. Together we tend the silence. I open the window. We hear the hollers and banter of students crossing campus, the thud of a skateboard, the distant, plodding beat of a car stereo.

TERENCE

Mother love. First love. The love you desire above all else. First heartbreak.

I never knew my mother's thoughts. Her intent was forthcoming, but her words and actions only created questions for me, none greater than the question of mother's love: was it there for me? I wasn't inclined to ask, for the obvious reason: I'm her son, so her love for me should have been implicit. But much of what guided her actions and reactions was a mystery to me. Not having a clear understanding of a relationship can either cause you to not care, or to care very much. For me, it was the latter. And I became lost searching for what was right there in front of me.

I was engulfed in the unknown. Cinder block and concrete: I dwelled in a mausoleum for the underprivileged on the welfare rolls, the single mothers and the low-income families. I never knew which of these labels my family fell under. Probably all of them. Yet I recall my mother working one, two, sometimes three jobs. Mother's handling of all the family responsibilities left her little time for the repeated questions of a boy.

* * *

The window is at ground level. The kids inside are painting on large pieces of paper, something I have never seen before. I'm roused to express my interest verbally, unaware that this is wrong. My correction comes by way of red: I am now covered in the paint that had captured my attention. The teacher was upset at my disruption. So she walked around without my seeing and let the paint sail through the gated window.

I do the only thing I know: run through the alleys and streets to my front door.

The shock registers every step of the way. It subdues my joy over my new discovery. Upon my arrival, the shock only deepens. No one is home. My mother is at work, my sisters and brother in school. Maintaining my excitement becomes arduous. Alone, I cry. Will Mother be angry with me? Up to this point, I can't recall a moment when she has been upset with me. Love still reigns.

My sisters arrive home, confused to find their baby brother already waiting, clothes ruined, face stained with tears. As I run to them, the oldest one speaks authoritatively.

"What happened to you? What happened to you?" Her voice echoes in my young mind.

"The lady, the lady." I speak through more tears. But I am unable to convey the information. "She threw the paint out the window and it got on me! I didn't do nothing!"

My sister grabs me by the hand in silence, and we go inside with urgency. She makes me go upstairs to the bathroom. In a brief moment that seems like forever, I am told to remove my clothing and get into the bath she is running. For some reason she keeps repeating to herself, "Just wait until Mom comes home." She can't believe someone threw paint all over a six-year-old!

Once I bathe, I change into another shirt and pants. Then we realize it is impossible to change the shoes. I only have one other pair, and those are for Sunday. This only heightens the frustration for my mother when she arrives home.

The next day she confronts everybody, from the teacher who didn't watch me on the playground to the woman who threw the paint, taking her case right to the principal's office. I'm clinging to her like a baby calf following its mother for guidance and direction. Then she goes back to work.

There is something wonderful, blessed, blissful, almost surreal about the gift of youth. You notice, then you don't notice. A problem can be there, confronting you, but there are big people dealing with it.

Once again I am in the care of these strangers. I feel scared but strangely empowered. The same command I had seen at home is now at school. This would all change in the next year or two when something called integration was introduced. My mother, seeking a better education for her kids, removed me from Baker Elementary School.

* * *

I don't recall what I did to earn my punishment, but I do recall being sent up to the room I shared with my three sisters. There was the waiting. A time of pondering my fate. Tick-tock, tick-tock. Her love was not what I was anticipating. Then there was her entrance. The punishment. A beating. Ass-whipping. Exit. The more this happened, the more questions I asked.

"Do you love me?"

"Of course I love you. Don't do it again!"

But I must have enjoyed her pain, because there I'd go again, doing something to bring about another beating!

The question about her loving me—I asked that a lot. Not of her, but of myself, even knowing that I didn't know the answer. *Who? What? Why?* become my battle cries. "Where is my dad? Why we don't we live in a house like Kyle, my best friend? Why can't I go there, do that?" If there was no answer except, "Leave me alone! I don't know. Ask someone else," it gave me even more reason to find the answers on my own.

Have you ever experienced being hit with a cord that leaves wounds even to this day? Or running from being hit, only to have the bed you are hiding under come down on you? Maybe you were told to go outside and bring in switches, you know, the tree branches that were everywhere in the projects. "You better not bring in no small branches!" It only made matters worse. Yes, I was whipped with those. I was a mess. The pain of discipline created within me a conflict between what I experienced and what I believed.

* * *

A playground is a field of unrestricted pleasurable activity. My playground was everywhere—school, church, the rec center, anywhere that inspired me to explore and find the answer to the big question: Who am I? I was *driven* to answer that question. My actions were governed by how I felt, and most times I felt like crap: confused, anxious, out of place.

Over time, I was placed in a number of group activities, but I never fit the bill. Boy Scouts was fun, but it was also just another grown-up telling me what not to do. Big Brothers? Who is this person, one visit and he's gone? Sports involved coaches. But I just wanted to play the game. I'm not a follower, and by all accounts I don't like authority.

Many times I was joked on for my limitations: a man-child from a single-parent home and low-income background, searching for his place in the world. My response was to joke harder. Humor became my escape. Since I couldn't be a part of the norm, I embraced the abnormal. I became mischievous, adventurous, ambitious, aggressive.

I could have accepted the dozens, a game of my era in which your mother was the target of the joke: "Your mother so broke, she pays her bills with food stamps." This game is directed mostly at those who cannot defend themselves. But instead of accepting the game, I toughened up and developed an "I don't care" attitude, which didn't help. I was—and continue to be—an introvert: alone, finding my way.

Growing up with my sisters, I developed a somewhat feminine philosophy toward life. Emotions ruled the day. But I refused to be walked over, pushed around, clowned. So I became the clown, but the joke was on me. Everybody loves the class clown, but no one wants to be friends with him.

If this all sounds irrational, you're getting the picture. I didn't know what to do, so I just did whatever came to mind. I did what I didn't want to do. These are the kind of choices you make when you have no choice. Fighting became my way to establish boundaries. I'd fight and then become best friends with the person I'd fought. It was crazy. My wonder years. But I didn't think so at the time.

* * *

He took a shine to me, this little kid from the other side of the tracks, unpolished and raw. When I met Mr. Mattox, I was a boy engulfed by the unknowns of being a male. My identity had to be forced out, but no one understood. I was being raised the only son amongst girls.

Mr. Mattox understood. He coached me: "Don't make waves. Do it this way. That's not how it's done. We have been doing it this way since I've been here." Knowledge validates a person and gives him the tools he needs to cooperate with others. I was like a kid in a candy store in Mr. Mattox's classroom.

I begin with Mr. Mattox because he was the first. Considering the fact that he was a father of sons himself, he understood the curiosity of the male child. He was a generous man with patience for my plight. He not only took time with me at school—he also spent quality time with me away from school, incorporating me into the fabric of his own family. Mr. Mattox's family became my second home. He became the father I never had. With him I started to experience training, learning what was expected of me. He did this with no expectation of gain, only the pleasure of allowing me to enjoy the workings of a functioning family. For the three years we spent together until the time I left elementary school, I was able to develop and perform according to recognized standards. I'd even begun to dream the impossible.

"But who does he think he is?" I can hear that question as if it were a moment ago. "Him thinking more highly of himself than what he ought!"

Mr. Mattox had encouraged me to be hopeful. Unfortunately, my peers back in Gilpin Court struggled against me over this, confronting my new state of mind. There were no fathers in most of their homes. Father figures came by way of mothers' friends—the occasional overnighter who played no role in upbringing or nurturing: "He's not *my* kid!" Mr. Mattox provided an unorthodox—or so it seemed to me—level of fatherly caring, but the continual reminder that he wasn't my father rang sharply in my skull. Because I had no real experience to rely on, his positive attention felt abnormal.

After Mr. Mattox, there was Mr. Parker, a single male, one of my teachers, more like an older brother. Then there was Coach Kouns, my swimming coach and the only white male to show me kindness. But none of these men, despite all they gave, made up for the fact that my father wasn't there. Nothing could cure the sense of longing. They could only fill the void temporarily, until another came and went. Stability was as elusive as my emotions.

I gained something from every one of my father figures, but the puzzle of who I am is something that only my father can know, for I *am* him. And though I can't remember missing my father, I know I missed a lot as a man-child and now as a father myself, yearning for the presence of my son. So I look toward the supreme Father of all for guidance, instruction, and correction. I've learned we are all challenged to provide wisdom, love, and support for the many among us who need a father, not a figure.

TONY

Not long after Terry's mom caught us smoking, my family was packing their bags once again to relocate to the east end of town, to an area in close proximity to the Social Services office, nickel-and-dime stores, more people with our same hue, lots of unskilled jobs, family, and friends. Once we had finally made a clear landing, it was evident that we had now entered the concrete jungle where only the strong survived and the weak perished. This was a world away from the manicured ghetto lawns we once knew.

Our new habitat was undergoing a major makeover, but from the looks of things, it didn't seem to be going as planned. Not only was the structure of the apartments being changed, but the name of the complex itself had transformed from "Chantilly Apartments" to "Woodsong Apartments." Including the word song in the name was suitable because there was always some type of crackling or clattering going on at any and all times of the day and night. It took a while to get used to all the sounds of gunshots and sirens constantly trespassing into my consciousness. But before long, I became so familiar with the sounds that I could tell the difference between the police, an ambulance, and a fire engine. It was a very useful talent because whoever decoded the sound first could then warn the masses, whose sole focus was on pimping, hustling, and killing. There were monetary rewards to reap if you helped people get away safely with their lives and their forbidden treasure (typically guns, money, or drugs). Nobody verbally schooled me to these codes of the streets. I just learned them by ear.

I was lonesome at first. My brother spent 99 percent of his time sitting inches away from the TV set, while my sister spent an equal amount of hers blowing her human humidity over the telephone receiver, holding up the line that I needed for more fruitful calls. It probably would've benefited me as well if I'd indulged in a few activities that required me to spend more time in the house and not down the street. But I was only focused on getting what I wanted when I wanted it.

My biggest want at that time was for a friend that possessed my same "living for the moment" values—values that seemed to tie in with my desire to be a self-made man. After several weeks, my hopes were answered when I met a young boy who went by the name of Lionel, but everyone seemed to call him Tony, too. It was very clear to me that he had been forcefully cut out of the country and pasted into the city. The reason for us not meeting earlier was because he had been visiting his grandmother in Smithfield, Virginia, to receive his fix of bare wiggling toes, corn bread, apple pie, fried chicken, and grass knolls. I couldn't blame him. Solitude was to be treasured if it could possibly be found amid the melee and "he-said–she said" that permeated the minds, bodies, and souls of those who wanted to play and those who suffered and prayed.

Located around the perimeter of the apartment complex, there was a very dense patch of wooded area, which held therapeutic remedies for a country boy's aching heart. Only minutes after Lionel and I had accepted each other's invitations to be country in the city, he took me on my first expedition in those woods. These artfully positioned trees, with their courageous limbs taking back privacy, inch by inch, from the drywall, brick, and metal—they sparked a daydream in me one day. In my mind's eye I saw the blueprints for a three-story clubhouse with all the amenities. I tossed and turned all night long, eager to bring to life what I wanted. But the darkness of the night took control. So sleep was the cure-all. And the morning could not have come sooner.

The next day, I was off to the races to find my new friend so we could salvage any and all of the usable materials strewn about the complex. Many treasures were found, and some warranted a second chance to fulfill their real purpose of bringing worldly prestige to us, their new possessors. A little hammering here and a little hammering there and, before you knew it, Lionel and I had laid the stained carpet, arranged the worn furnishings, and hung the printed pictures throughout the splintered corridors of our triple-decker clubhouse.

Then came the entertainment phase that goes hand in hand with being a bigwig. Snacks and utilities were needed for a party to be a party. It was out of the question for me to even consider raiding the refrigerator and cabinets at my house. My mother kept inventory, right down to each slice of bread, to ensure that the quantity of food met the demands of her kids' youthful appetites. On the other hand, Lionel was able to come up with a few items from home. That meant I had to go to plan B: to put my ten fingers on something that belonged to the 7-Eleven convenience store and discount it to the point that it was free.

The seeds of theft took root that way. I found myself shoplifting every day. The store was located directly across the street from the apartment complex. Lionel was too scared to steal anything. He just watched out for me as I filled my pockets with sweets and deli meats. I was forming two bad habits at one time and didn't even realize it until I was chin-deep into the first one: the buying of temporary popularity and not knowing where the money was going to come from to buy it the next time.

The funny thing about this popularity was that once I received it, I never allowed myself to become arrogant or conceited. What's the use of gaining favor and honor in public only to be truly hated when all the smoke clears? I really didn't have to think twice about the sincerity of the friendship that Lionel and I shared, because he never tried to persuade me to do anything for his own selfish gain. In fact, he would usually try to talk me out of doing whatever my mind was already cocked, loaded, and set on doing.

Because of the heavy flow of traffic into our clubhouse, the maintenance department for the housing complex was tipped off to its existence. They soon dismantled our house in the trees. It was sweet while it lasted. The number of people that I was trying to make happy increased after the clubhouse days. So I had to figure out a more productive way of moving the product out of the stores and into the hands of the needy and the greedy.

That was when I met up with two brothers named Noland and Chaka, who really elevated my shoplifting game to new heights. They showed me that I could triple my take by stuffing my briefs and my waistline. I knew that what I was doing could have gotten me into lots of trouble, but I figured that, much like I got in and out of the store with what I wanted, I could also get myself out of any trouble that I got myself into.

Noland and Chaka also took me from doing crimes that carried penalties of fines, to crimes that could've landed me in detention doing some jail time. The little convenience stores only offered snacks, but I was a big boy now. I had just passed to the fifth grade. Big boys had to do big things. I took their invitation and went with them to the local mall, which had lots of stores to choose from and thousands of items to steal.

It was only when I stepped out of the front door of my home into the mean streets of the ghetto that I felt a greed to please. My oily skin, combined with puberty, caused me to have acne breakouts on my face, and this added to my already injured ego. We all know that the bad guys always got the prettiest girls in school. But since I never wanted to be seen as a bad guy, it was very important to me to dress well, smell good, and give good gifts, in the hopes that the good, the bad, and the ugly could share the fame. I became very self-conscious about my physical appearance, as well as my speech. I was always the biggest kid in my class when it came to height and weight. So I quickly found out that when you please the desires of people freely, they tend to overlook the flaws of their fairy-tale Robin Hood.

The gift of giving, of charity, has been my most recognizable gift, and I learned it from my father. The defining moment that really sticks out in my mind was when he'd give me and my friends a ride to the Boy's Club. Before he'd allow me to get out of the car, he would always give me a couple of dollars to make sure I could buy me some snacks from the concession stand. What made this such a memorable moment was that my father not only gave *me* some money, but my three friends as well. And he gave them the same amount he gave me. At first, envy almost pushed me to question my father's generosity. But I quickly noticed my friends' overwhelming joy and happiness, the huge smiles on their faces—a rare sight to see, because they were three brothers from a very unstable home. What I also learned was that it was better for all of us to be able to buy our own snacks, because then I'd have more of my own for myself! That experience inspired me to always give more than I received, because whenever I gave, I felt a sense of worth and purpose that filled the void that echoed with the questions: "Who am I? Why am I here?"

But my greed to please almost got me in trouble when I decided to treat my entire fifth-grade class to Christmas gifts, compliments of Murphy's department store. The amazing variety in that store allowed me to personalize the gifts to whatever I imagined each person's taste might have been. Lionel and I were still hanging out with each other, but when it was time to make the people smile, I had to hook up with the crooks. So there I was in Murphy's, filling my pockets, waistline, and briefs with hair trinkets for the girls, and watches, wallets, and playing cards for the boys.

I never made it a habit to take the items that I wrongfully acquired home, because my mother knew every shoe, sock, shirt, and toy that was under her roof at any given time. But this was one occasion when I had to try my hand, so I smuggled all the items into my room without being detected. The key was to take the goods into the house at the end of the day when I was going in to stay, so that my mother would have limited time to scan her domain.

I wasn't really sure exactly how many people were in my class, but the next day when it was time to exchange gifts, I had enough stuff to give thirty people two items apiece. When my teacher, Mrs. Holloman, observed what was taking place, she found it necessary to give my mother a phone call to ask her if she knew about the gifts that I had given out. Mrs. Holloman never questioned me directly, but when I got home from school, my mother asked me about what had taken place and I told her I had given everyone a little something, but that it didn't add up to much. I guess the only reason I got away with it was because my mother always made sure we had a little change in our pockets whenever we left the house, so she probably figured I had saved it up and bought some candy or something with it. My teacher never specified the values or the descriptions of the items I gave to my classmates. I can't even remember if I received a gift or not, but it really didn't make a difference, because I got my joy from giving, not receiving.

When I told Noland and his brother what I had done with all the product that I had stolen, they told me I was crazy. Why would you give away stuff to people that didn't care anything about you? "What did you do with all the stuff y'all stole?" I asked back. And they said they gave it to their mother. That answer really shocked me, but after I thought about it for a minute, I recalled that the items that they stole were things like clocks, cookware, perfume, cologne, and lots of over-the-counter medications. And I understood better why they were stealing on a daily basis but never seemed to be happy.

We were hanging out one day when another one of the kids from the community told Noland and Chaka that their mother was acting real crazy in the hallway. So we hurried to see just what was going on, and to my amazement, the beautiful, soft-spoken woman that I was always greeted by was in her nightgown making sexual gestures and body movements. Her long, thick brown hair was being slung around and around as she twisted her head in circles, trying to release whatever it was that was causing her to act so strangely. This made her dizzy, and she eventually fell to her knees. No one dared to approach her, because during this entire ordeal she held two long, silver kitchen knives, one in each hand. She was rubbing them against her breasts and in between her thighs.

This wasn't the first time Noland and Chaka had experienced this type of drama from their momma. But it was for me. The wisdom they'd gathered in the past afforded them the understanding to know that only time or help from the authorities would set the matter to rest safely. After five minutes of her performing the tiring act—which deserved an Oscar, let me add—the police arrived and quickly subdued her without incident. The ambulance arrived shortly after, and they gently placed her onto the gurney and carted her off. I never saw her, Noland, or Chaka again. Word around the neighborhood was that Cheryl had ingested more drugs than her body could sustain and had lost control of her mind and body while she unconsciously fought for her life.

Before long I was in the company of a few more young ruffians whose stealing techniques surpassed Noland and Chaka's. These young hoodlums were so brazenly confident in their ability to steal *all* they wanted *when* they wanted it and from *where* they wanted it, that soon we were no longer stripping the New Market South strip mall. We decided to cross Mercury Boulevard to get to an indoor mall called New Market North. What made these stealing experiences intimidating was that once we had gotten out of the store with the merchandise, we still had to make it back out the building doors! These doors were usually being watched by cameras and security on foot patrol. I must have been good at what I was doing, because for the next several years I would periodically go on shoplifting sprees to satisfy my greed to please.

I focused a little more on money once I reached the sixth grade, because I now had the privilege of purchasing snacks during lunch, something that was not afforded to me when I was in elementary school. I used to sell Now & Later candy in class for five cents apiece, after only paying ten cents for a pack that contained five individually wrapped pieces. That little hustle kept me afloat during my tenure as a sixth-grader until I was presented with a new venture during seventh grade that lined my pockets with money to burn!

Instead of me going around early Sunday mornings and stealing bundles of Sunday *Daily Press* newspapers and knocking on peoples' doors and selling them for the full price like we had done in the past, I decided to ask my mother if she could cosign for me to receive a newspaper route of my own. Without any hesitation, my loving mother agreed to give me this opportunity to be my own boss and to make my own money. Fast money seemed to be the answer, and the hustling seed had been planted the year before with me selling the Now & Later candy.

My mother had just given me the go-ahead to corner the newspaper market, so I started off doing the Woodsong Apartments. This consisted of about two hundred and forty customers. When you do the math with regular Monday-through-Friday newspapers, which back then only cost twenty-five cents (and the Sunday paper was fifty cents), that meant that I was collecting roughly two dollars from every customer. So two multiplied by $240 equaled $480, if everybody paid on time, which unfortunately never happened. But on the average, I would collect between $280 and $360 a week. After proving to my mother and the *Daily Press* office that I could be responsible, I was offered a second route on the apartment complex located directly across the street from where I lived: Warwick Gardens, now better known as Brookridge Apartments.

There were about 180 customers on the new route, so my overall delivery was about 420 papers a day. The money was real good, but I had to share the profit with my two helpers, Lionel and Andre. On a daily basis, I would spend about twenty dollars on hotdogs, eggnog, cakes, and arcade games at the 7-Eleven. To make ends meet, every now and then I would call in to the *Daily Press* on Sunday morning and tell them that two or three of my bundles of Sunday newspapers had been stolen and could they deliver me some more? These would now be considered extras because nobody had really stolen the first papers. That really allowed the three of us to spend money like we'd gone mad. The entire time it seemed like I was on top of the world. I kept at least forty dollars in cash in my pocket at any given time, but I was really just creating a very bad habit of always doing what I wanted to do and not what I needed to be doing.

It all came to a head when one day Andre decided to go around and collect some money for himself to do what he wanted to do. But that just wasn't the way it was supposed to go. It was already understood between the three of us that I would be the only one collecting money from the customers. After I finally finished delivering the newspapers, collecting from the customers he had missed, and tallying up the names and the amount of money he had successfully collected, it turned out that $230 was lost. I now had to cover for it. I never told my mother what happened because Andre would've probably gotten into some deep trouble with his mother and the police. So I took it upon myself to go and question him to find out why he had betrayed me after all the fun we had had each and every day with the money being split equally among the three of us.

He really couldn't explain why he'd done what he did, but he did give me about seventy dollars' worth of checks. That helped, but it still left me about $160 in the hole, and like always, I had already spent the profits! Once I saw that I wasn't going to be able to live the same lifestyle that I was used to living on a daily basis, I gave up and just started spending all the money I collected from that day on. I didn't realize that my mother was going to have to pay back the money that I owed the *Daily Press* because she had cosigned for me to receive the paper route.

I was buying my entire seventh-grade class ice-cream sandwiches and cookies during lunch. I tried to run for class president and in doing so, I donated twenty-five dollars to the class treasury, which caused my teacher, Mr. Ross, to call my mother so that he could verify that this was all right. She agreed. But soon the *Daily Press* office stopped sending me newspapers. Then they mailed my mother a letter letting her know that she owed them $759, and it needed to be paid immediately or else she would be summoned to court. My mother had never had any dealings with the law, so she opted out and paid the money to avoid missing a day of work and being humiliated in the presence of a judge for no fault of her own.

So there I was, left with a spending habit that mirrored that of a child movie star. And now I lacked the funding necessary to hold up my ghetto-fabulous image. I tried collecting aluminum cans for a while, but the pay-off just wasn't enough. I had not yet realized that true happiness comes from within the person and not from material items.

The remainder of my seventh-grade year was a struggle financially, but I made it through thanks to the couple of dollars that my mother made sure I kept in my pockets and the little side hustles like collecting cans and washing cars. In the eighth grade I started opening up to the reality that there were serious consequences for my reckless behavior.

That year I participated in JV wrestling, JV football, and JV soccer. It really amazed me how fast the school year passed due to my constant involvement in after-school sports. The problem came when the school year ended, because then I had two entire months of free time before summer practice started for the JV football team. The first week or two were fine, until it dawned on me that my pockets were going to stay empty unless I got off my butt and did something about it.

That summer, I decided to take me a little walk around the neighborhood. There weren't too many changes to notice, except that the distribution of marijuana had moved from the second and third parking lots in the back of the complex to the first parking lot, where dudes could catch all the customers as soon as they entered the driveway. It seemed crazy to me that guys were willing to risk being seen by the police. The apartment manager's office faced the parking lot where the drugs were being sold, and the nosy older folk tended to live up front. I had to go and see it to believe it, because I had always thought that these fellows were a lot smarter than they looked. But I guess I was wrong.

I made my way to the front so that I could observe exactly what was taking place. I really didn't have anything to worry about because I wasn't a drug dealer. The police could question and search me. But they would've just been doing it for practice, because I didn't have any drugs on me.

I sat on the front porch facing the drug-infested parking lot, watching car after car pull in. Then a guy would run to the window and exchange the drugs for money, and the car would back right out and leave as if it had just received curbside service at Big Al's restaurant.

Not all the dealers had the guts to run out into the open and be seen by whomever happened to be looking or passing by. These guys would stand inside the complex hallways, and it was the customer's responsibility to get out of the car and walk up if they wanted to purchase some drugs. It was very dangerous for the drug dealers, but it was even more dangerous for the customers. They first had to pass the property, just to see if anyone was outside selling the type of drugs that they wanted. Then they had to worry about getting fake drugs, or getting robbed, maliciously wounded, or even killed, and make it back to the car without getting arrested. After making it to the car, they had to worry about getting pulled over by the police. If they were caught with the drugs, the police could confiscate the car *and* arrest them. Finally, if they did make it home with the drugs, there was a great chance that they hadn't received the amount of drugs they'd paid for.

I really wasn't eager to try my hand at a game that hadn't been proven to render the player more gain than pain. But in the midst of this open-air drug market, everyone who had a package of drugs was his own boss, and the normal rules of business didn't apply. It was an eye for an eye and a tooth for a tooth. In the ghetto, you had to have a strong will to survive; if you were weak, chances were you were going to die.

I weighed the pros and cons for the next couple of days, caught up in a melee amid mind, body, and money. My hope was that I could figure out a plan to get all that green without getting any of the jail or prison time that comes with crime. I'd been successful thus far in shoplifting, because I hadn't been caught, not once. The way things seemed to be going, I thought I would have the same success if I chose to become my own boss in the drug game.

Then one day, I was offered a chance to make some quick loot. All I had to do was drop off a package of cocaine, collect the money, and deliver it back to its rightful owner. I took the offer in hopes that I could get my feet wet in the drug game before I jumped into deep waters without knowing how to swim.

I was given very brief instructions to find two guys I had seen around the neighborhood. They went by the names Ricky and Black. You would never see one of these guys without the other because when they did their dirt, they did it together.

Ricky was known as the enforcer or muscle, and it was easy to see why. He stood about six feet tall and had arms the size of thighs. His chest was so big you could balance a twelve-ounce can of beer on his pecs without spilling a drop. And to top it off, he was pitch-black. When the sun hit his skin, he glistened like a new car straight off the showroom floor.

Black only stood about five-foot-eight and weighed about 145 pounds. His strength came from his ability to beat you mentally by convincing you that you had already lost, so there was no need to start the fight. I've never been fearful of man, so when it came to collecting the money and dropping off the drugs, I didn't think twice. All I saw were dollar signs.

It had been a while since I'd gotten that joyful feeling that giving to others gave me. My participation in school sports hindered me from hustling. I guess the reason why I hadn't thought of it in a while was because I could make people happy on my team just by giving them my all. Summertime, with nobody around, was different.

Finally the day came when I was given the chance to get my hands dirty and my pockets full. I successfully made the pickup, which consisted of two miniature ziplock bags full of cocaine. I know now that each bag had to contain at least a thousand dollars' worth of cocaine, but that was the least of my worries. My job was only to drop off the drugs and collect the money. As I started out on my voyage, it seemed as if everybody I came in contact with wanted to hold a conversation with me. I really didn't want to seem rude, but it was either their feelings or my life, so I chose to act as if I didn't hear half of them. The other half, I just told them I would talk to them later. I was hoping that I wouldn't run into Lionel or Andre because it would've been harder to get rid of them, and I didn't have no time to be doing any type of explaining.

I checked the area where I knew the majority of the customers would be, to see if Ricky and Black were hanging out. At first it didn't look like anyone was out there, but then several cars pulled in and drug dealers started coming out of hallways and parked cars. Ricky was one of them, so I approached him and asked him if he was ready to receive a new package of drugs. He told me that he had most of the money but we would have to go and see Black in order to get the rest. I was kind of skeptical at first. I was only fifteen years old and I was collecting drug money from two of the most treacherous guys in the neighborhood. So as Ricky and I started walking together, I asked him how far we had to walk, because I had the drugs on me and wasn't trying to get stopped by the police. Ricky told me that Black was in the crack house across the yard, which was only about three hundred yards away from where we were standing.

Ricky made the occupants of the apartment aware of his presence by knocking with a certain coded rhythm that didn't require a "Who is it?" response from the person on the other side of the door. The door quickly opened and we were greeted by the lady of the house: a very attractive, dark-skinned woman with a voluptuous body. Ricky told me to stay in the living room while he went to one of the bedrooms to retrieve the rest of the money. The attractive woman did not accompany Ricky to the back, but walked into the kitchen, about ten feet from where I was standing. I decided to try to get another peek at her beautifully sculpted body. She was standing over the top of the stove with a razor in her hand, cutting into small pieces what I now know (but at the time didn't have a clue) was crack cocaine.

"What are you looking at?" she asked calmly, with big puppy-dog eyes. That caught me off guard. Instead of telling her the truth, that I was trying to get another glance at her body, I told her that I wanted to try a piece of that stuff she had lying on a mirror. Even though I was only fifteen, I'd always been big for my age, but she seemed to see right through my size and straight into the eyes of a child.

"No, boy, I'm not giving you none of this."

But I dug my hand in my pocket and grabbed one of the two bags of powder cocaine that I was delivering to Ricky and Black and offered it to her if she would allow me to put one of her tiny chunks of crack on the glass stem so that I could try it. She gently told me no again, but I could see that the temptation of getting some of this powder for herself and making a little money on the side was weakening her resolve. I told her that she would have to hurry up and make up her mind because Ricky and Black would be coming out of the room real soon to get the drugs from me. She finally gave in and insisted that I hurry up because she didn't have no business letting me try that stuff.

I grabbed the slim glass tube. She placed the small rock atop the stem and coached me on how I needed to hold the glass straight up in the air toward the ceiling until she placed the flame from the cigarette lighter directly on it. Then, she told me, I needed to suck the smoke that was being given off when the flame caused the rock to melt, smoothly and slowly, until the white piece of crack was no longer visible, having turned to liquid.

"Tilt the stem down towards the floor, boy," she whispered. "Now, hold it horizontally so that you're facing me and the flame. That'll keep shit from flowing out the front of the stem or towards your mouth. It taste nasty."

I followed her directions and after no more smoke could be seen, I handed her the stem and inhaled into my lungs before letting the smoke out my mouth. Just then, Ricky came out the back room and handed me the remainder of the money for the new packages of fresh cocaine.

My smoking didn't hinder me from making the transaction; it was the first time in my life I'd ever smoked any type of drug. I had no idea what type of effects or feelings I was supposed to have, mentally or physically. So I counted the money, and after verifying that it was the correct amount, I then handed the two sandwich bags full of cocaine over to Ricky. Black never came out of the room to show his face, but he did scream to me that it was all right for me to give his package of drugs to Ricky because he was busy. I would later find out that Black and Ricky were both getting high off of rock cocaine on a daily basis.

I received my first pay-off for my first drug deal in the amount of one hundred dollars. It was about ten or twenty minutes' worth of work. I was surprised. But I wasn't about to start fussing with a drug supplier who was nice enough to look out for me. So I folded up the five twenty-dollar bills and told him to let me know if he ever needed my services again. He told me that it wouldn't be long at all. I didn't tell anybody who I shared my earnings with that day how I got the money. My friends who were spending that money with glee on candy, sodas, hot dogs, and sunflower seeds—they had no idea what I'd done.

I went on to make three more successful drug transactions with Ricky and Black. But during my last drop-off, I could really notice the terrible effects that the cocaine was having on their mental, emotional, and physical well-being. They were once very vibrant, outgoing, aggressive young men, whose actions and appearances warranted attention. But the rock cocaine had taken the fight out of them and made them slaves to the drug trade.

On my fourth attempt to collect the money, it was clear to me that Ricky and Black lacked the means to foot the bill for the package of drugs that I'd given them. They were two hundred dollars short of the twelve hundred dollars they owed. The supplier had previously informed me to give them the drugs as long as they had at least three-fourths of the bill and that he would take care of the rest later. I didn't even attempt to pressure them into explaining to me how they allowed a powdery white substance to rape them of their gangster mentality so quickly and effortlessly. Instead, I told them that I would tell the drug supplier that I didn't see them, in hopes that it would buy them a little time to try and scramble up some of the money.

Nothing ever happened to Ricky and Black for not paying the money. The supplier simply absorbed the loss and took his drugs elsewhere to be sold. Afterwards, I turned down his offer to trade my job as mule for the full-time job of dealer. I was very hesitant to turn down the opportunity, but after I witnessed what cocaine had done to Ricky and Black, I made the wise decision to walk away from the deal empty-handed.

I soon found myself looking for excitement. And it came in the form of a couple of guys from the neighborhood with a clever idea to gather together some money and purchase several twelve-packs of beer. I really wasn't with the plan because I knew I had to walk through my mother's front door later on, so I thought twice before participating. What I found out very quickly was that for every excuse I had not to indulge in negative behavior, my so-called friends had a solution that would allow me to follow them.

They showed me how to mask the effects of the beer in hopes that nobody would realize I'd been drinking. For instance, when I told them that my breath would smell like beer, they simply handed me Fireballs and told me not to worry about the smell. Then when I came up with the excuse of not wanting to drink because the slurred speech and staggering would definitely give me away, they simply said, "All you have to do is get a little rest before you go home and everything will be all right between you and your mother." After refusing to indulge the first couple of times, I found myself starting to nod in agreement whenever they justified their negative behaviors with phrases like:

1. This is my life and only I can live it.
2. Everybody gets high in one way or another.
3. The stores sell it, so it ain't illegal to use it.
4. I didn't steal it, so I'm not hurting anybody.
5. My grandparents drank alcohol their whole lives and they lived to be ninety-nine.

What I realize now is that they never spoke about the thousands of people who have lost their lives due to medical complications, drunk driving, domestic disputes, and physical violence: all results of alcohol use and abuse.

I finally gave in to the peer pressure and quickly found myself consuming all types of alcoholic beverages that didn't appeal to my taste buds at all. I was just drinking to be drinking because it was something to do to pass the time and it put me in the presence of my so-called friends. But it wasn't long before I was struggling to wake up for football summer practices, sweating all the alcohol out of my body on the field, and painfully building my muscles back up so that they could endure the strain of heat exhaustion and the hours of repetitive physical tasks. I didn't leave my newfound bad habits at the door. I was now justifying them. When we won games, I celebrated. When we lost games, I drank to calm me down.

The so-called "pleasure" I was receiving from alcohol overshadowed my knowledge of how much pain I would have to endure during the next football practice. My memories of that physical torture never manifested as usable wisdom. My lust for harmful behavior was winning the battle of good and evil within me.

I lost a lot of the drive I once had to excel in my academic ventures. I was gradually becoming an outcast, a teen constantly under the influence of alcohol. Along with irresponsibility, I adopted slothfulness and self-pride as my vices. My drinking didn't affect my home life at all, or so I thought, because the only reasons you would ever find me at home would be if I was sleeping, eating, using the bathroom, or taking a shower. I was the busy bee of the family, and no one seemed to care. I guess because it was one less person in the way of an already cramped living space.

My consumption of alcohol starting taking me to places that I'd never been. I found myself staggering into dance parties in private apartments and homes. I would be welcomed in, no questions asked, because of the twelve-pack of beer I had in my hands. That was my VIP pass. At those parties, I was seduced by young, drunk, carefree females, bumping and grinding their tender little bodies up against anything that held them up from falling.

For some reason or another my mother stopped me one day when I was making a quick pit stop in the house to use the bathroom and said, "Tony, don't be henpecked like your daddy." It was a very important moment in my life because my mother never talked badly about my father. But there was just something about the word "pecked" that didn't sit well with me.

Instead of me asking her what it meant, I just hurried out the house and sought the wisdom of these two older women I knew. They were always sitting on their porch sipping on some wine or beer and gossiping about everybody's business but their own. They said, "When a man is henpecked, he was no mind of his own, because he's blinded by the woman's love. He's given her total control over his thoughts and actions."

While I was party-hopping and coming into contact with more and more young ladies, I always kept the phrase "henpecked" in the forefront of my mind. This allowed me to stand strong against my heart's lustful yearning for companionship and commitment. Before I really became conscious of my father's failure to play the role of father, which was related to his being henpecked, I found myself sitting in the church pew, crying because he was dead. Unconsciously, I had made up my mind not to have any children if I wasn't going to be there to support them.

ANDRE

Coming to prison the second time, I knew that drama was the number one thing. Prison is designed to make you prove yourself or fail. I seen a guy get shanked up once—forceful hits to the man's body. They penetrated him so hard, I could actually hear the blade hit the concrete behind him.

Seeing a man get stabbed to death is totally different from seeing a guy get shot or me shooting a guy. Maybe it was the prison environment, but it made me wise up. I then took a look at myself: my inner self, and that inner beast in me. That was the day my blinders came off. A man got killed right there in the day room pod, because he turned on the TV. He just turned on the TV.

There are different rules in prison than in jail, and when you violate one, you just might pay for it with your life. I was playing by the wrong set of rules. So I started anticipating the good so that I might enjoy life. I started applying optimism and spending quality time with my family, friends, and loved ones in visits and letters. It was time for me to unlock the vault inside of me that held all my hidden treasures and talents. It was time to bring my life into balance.

Drug using and drug selling are heavy in prison, just like on the street, but I said "no more." I was reading books now. I had Maya Angelou poems, James Patterson, and my Bible. The door to my vault was opening.

My girlfriend at the time was LaKeisha. My Auntie Tammy introduced me to her when I was in prison. I was on the phone and she happened to be at my aunt's crib, so we did the introduction bit, traded information; she gave me her address and phone number and I gave her my address and state number. Soon after, I was calling her and sending her letters and cards. Then she came to visit me at Greensville Correctional Center.

It was her first time ever coming to a prison. She had two boys, and one was only a few months old. The visit was like a blind date, but she knew what I looked like because I had sent her some pictures. My auntie told me that she was cute, and when she walked through the door, I knew it was her.

She had on some brown leather pants, black boots, and a black leather coat, and her hair was a two-tone color. She was about 110 pounds, brown skin, and had the sexiest eyes a man could ever look into. I was truly happy. She was holding little Maurice, the baby, on her side. He looked so cute and scared at the same time. I gave them both a secure hug. I love kids, and I took to Maurice immediately. I held him the entire time while me and LaKeisha got to know each other a little more. We never officially asked one another to be boyfriend and girlfriend. It just happened. And when I got released, guess who came and picked me up from the Emporia gas station/Greyhound bus stop?

When I was released from prison, one of the first things that I wanted to do was visit my father. So my mother took me over there and, as we were pulling up to park, I took a look at the house. It was so run-down it looked like it didn't even belong on the block. It sho-nuff stood out, but for all the wrong reasons. My mom saw the sadness on my face and said, "He just needs some help. Your help."

Before I was incarcerated, my father's house was beautiful, inside and out. It was a burgundy two-story house with four large bedrooms, hardwood flooring throughout, a fenced backyard, and a small garage. It had been my grandfather's, and he had kept it up until his untimely death. I used to spend quality time over there with my grandfather when I was small. My favorite thing about the house was that in the wintertime we could use the wood stove. I got to put the chopped pieces of wood in the stove. I loved looking and listening as the fire burned.

Slowly, I walked to the front door, evaluating what I should say or do. Then before I knew it, it was showtime. The person in front of me was indeed my dad, but he didn't look like my dad. The years he'd spent abusing his body and mind with drugs and alcohol had caught up to him. A thought crossed my mind that if I wouldn't have stopped using, would I look like that?

I quickly hugged him. He was no longer standing strong and tall, looking and acting excited about life. My heart went out to him because, deep down, I knew he was suffering mentally and physically. When I was in prison, I would often write letters to my father, as well as send him Father's Day cards, Christmas cards, and birthday cards, never missing a beat. But unfortunately, he never responded. Still, I believed.

As I scanned the house I noticed holes in the walls, ceiling paint peeling badly, hardly no furniture, no lights. It looked abandoned. Then I looked on the shelf: all my letters and cards were right there. The strangest thing was they were never opened. My father never even attempted to open none of my letters. Automatically I was hurt, but I also knew he was sick, so me and him sat down to talk.

We sat near the wood stove, and it brought back pleasant memories. Of everything in the house, the wood stove still looked the same. My dad wanted me to give him some money to go buy some drugs. He said I was his son, so I was supposed to do it. So, reluctantly, I gave him some money. I knew it was wrong, but I wanted his acceptance. After that I wanted him to go open my letters and cards and read them, but I was too chicken to say anything.

I told myself after that experience that I wasn't going to give him no more money for drugs. I would bring him food and do my best to fix the house up to acceptable living standards. I also went to City Hall and talked to the tax people, inquiring on any back taxes that he might owe. Then I went to the John Marshall Courts building to check on the deed. I wanted to help my father get free from drugs, but eventually I came to realize that I was powerless over my father. Despite my vow, I kept giving him money to support his habit, until one day, when I developed some discipline from somewhere. But when I refused to give him money, the evil came out of him.

"Get the fuck out of my house!" he yelled. I came back again later on, knocking on the door, hoping he'd calmed down. But he refused to even open the door for me. He just kept on yelling, "Get the fuck off my property!" Then he said he was going to call the cops. He didn't have no phone service, so I pleaded at the doorsill. Then I seen him coming from the back of the house to the front, to go to the neighbor's house to use the phone. That got my undivided attention. I quickly got in my car to leave. He had to have the last word, though.

"By the way, I'm not your real father!"

This was the final blow. I was crushed by his words and his actions. But I will not give up on him, even though he has already given up on himself.

As I continued to deal with that dilemma, I lost my grip on change. Being in the company of my mother was still very challenging. I wanted to talk to her about my deepest feelings, but I was scared of what her response might be, so I said nothing. That was one of the reasons why I got it wrong in life with my actions and my choices after prison. The problem was that heroin truly made me feel like Superman, and there was no kryptonite to subdue me. I always seemed to escape death. I was shot and almost died. I took a lot of bullets and survived. So I earned the nickname Nine-Lives. "Nothing can dim the light that shines from within," Maya Angelou said. And that's how I felt, but in a negative way.

When I went back into that world of drugs, I lost my passion for life. I chose heroin over my girlfriend and family members. My friends were on heroin, so they felt just like I did. We thought no matter how full the river, it still wants to grow. I found myself needing to snort heroin up my nose as soon as I opened my eyes and put my feet on the floor, every time I fixed me something to eat, conversated, had sex, everything. My lifestyle started with heroin and ended with heroin. But couldn't no one tell me that I had a problem, because I thought getting high was the norm. Life is a series of strategic moves, but I'd forgotten that. I had to learn all over again I was the navigator in my life, and my success depended on me.

On my first attempt to give up using heroin altogether, I laughed at myself for even letting the words out of my mouth. Andre "Nine-Lives" Simpson giving up sniffing heroin? Never that! I would rather sleep on a bed of nails, walk barefooted on broken glass, give my girlfriend away, give my money away, even my freedom. Do you get the picture, how much heroin ruled my very existence? I didn't ever think I would be able to live without it. I had for the first twelve years of my life. That gave me hope, but it took a lot, and I mean *a lot*, of sinking lower and lower to even come up with the strength to move an inch toward change.

On September 6th, 1996, my birthday, instead of getting high and partying hard, I went to a drug program called Rubicon. No one knew I was there. I had to do a seventy-two-hour detox before I could be accepted into the program. Those were three of the longest days of my life. I went through so much pain and discomfort. They had nurses there on a twenty-four-hour basis to help you through it. But it turned out that it was one of the counselors, not the nurses, who would begin to help me define myself.

Her name was Angie, and she knew my father and me. I remember her because she used to come over to my grandfather's house to visit my father. She was addicted to drugs, but she turned her life around and got a job there, to help others. We talked a lot. Really, she did the most of the talking, because I was wrapped up in the bed, going through it. She had never known that I was on drugs, and it broke her heart when she saw me. I never told her it was my father who introduced me, but for some strange reason, we both knew that Gregory Simpson had introduced both of us to the world of heroin.

After my three days were up, Angie gave me a big, loving hug and told me something to the effect of, "It's going to be difficult to escape the grip of addiction, but just keep fighting; you will succeed." I wish that I could have stayed there with Angie, but I knew I had to move on.

For the next ninety days, I was living in a house run by Rubicon Rehab, with strangers with addictions of all kinds. Everyone was looking at me as I entered into the house, because I was the new kid on the block. I looked right back at them, trying to see if there was anybody I knew. I felt so out of my element that I was thinking of walking out. But for some reason I didn't. The program director was a tall black man, very imposing, with big hands. When you talked to him, he was very calm, honest, and caring. He knew some of my struggles. But I couldn't let him know them all. I couldn't let nobody know them all.

Rubicon was a structured living place with lots of rules, rules, and more rules, and on top of that, meetings, meetings, meetings. I was assigned a counselor. It was a lady, the only female counselor. She was really nice, but I gave her a hard time anyway. As the days went by, we got along pretty well. I even washed her car one day and took much pride in doing that job. It was so hard for me to believe that all the counselors were once former drug addicts and were now giving back. Would I be like them one day? Or would I fail?

I pondered thoughts like these as I lay in my room with three other guys. It was three or four beds to a room. I was the youngest person in the house, and for some reason, none of the positive-minded brothers in the house even tried identifying with me, taking me under their wings. To look at me then, you could see I was confused and alone. The negative-minded brothers in the house sensed it, and I was soon under their guidance. They told me how to duck the meetings, get high, pass the urine tests when you're dirty, and how to sneak in and out of the house. To sum it up, their motto was "fake it until you make it." So in turn, I broke all the rules at the house and made them invent new rules against the other things I was doing wrong. I was a full-grown Dennis the Menace.

After the first thirty days, they grant you weekend passes so you can go visit your loved ones, and my pass got denied. I was highly pissed, and I mean mugging at everybody in that room. I thought, how can a bunch of drug addicts govern me? I just walked out and went back to my room. Besides, I could sneak out like I been doing, so who was they hurting? But I didn't even want to sneak out. I was feeling left out and alone.

I decided to go seek answers from one of the counselors. Everyone was gone and only one counselor remained. So I went into his office. He was an old white man like my grandfather. His name was Sal, and we ended up talking for hours. I enjoyed this. He advised me that I needed to open up more and that ninety days of Rubicon would not be enough for me. I had to suffer some more to be able to successfully shoulder my drug addiction; otherwise it would ultimately destroy me. I told him that I didn't get it, and he just told me to stay diligent and I would be victorious.

I have encountered a lot of people in my life. Some I remember what was said and some I don't. Sal was one of the ones I remembered. One time he gave me the keys to a car, but didn't tell me where the car was. I had to locate it on my own. Then once I found it, I had to get insurance, title, tags, and gas to be able to drive it. I learned from this that a program can't change you. You have to want to change, and you have to do the work yourself. A program can only show you the necessary tools to use to assist you in fighting your addiction.

I relapsed while I was in that house. I thought I could I beat the urine test, but I failed, along with having other major rule violations. So I was asked to leave Rubicon. I was being kicked out. The feeling of hopelessness was compounded by the fact that the one thing that was bringing me relief, the one thing I depended on to remove the pain, was destroying me. As I left the house, I vowed to fight again. I had to keep fighting. I wanted to reclaim my life.

I only lasted about fifty days in Rubicon, but I did leave with some tools, and the knowledge that I can change. This was my first attempt at trying to stop. For some, it only takes one time, but for me it would take a few more tries. All I know is that I have to do something, and that by writing this, I *am* doing something.

I have found that the process of discovering who I really am begins with knowing who I really don't want to be. I still love my father, because he is my father. But I know he's still on drugs and that I no longer desire to be on drugs. And although my heroin addiction is like gravity, just waiting to pull me down, my commitment to remaining drug-free, and the love I have inside of me for others, especially my father, are like the forces that make an airplane fly. They only work when the pilot is doing the right things.

My patience, tolerance, humility, and love were tested by my father that day he turned on me and kicked me out of his house. But I'm not a quitter and never will be. I will not give up trying to help him cleanse himself from the slow death of drugs. Material losses you can get back again. Friends you can get back, or else find new ones. Girlfriends you can get again. But you only have one father. I only have one father, and I can't lose him. I constantly pray that God will restore him to sanity, and I know God's going to do it. My God is an awesome God.

14

My Story Is Still Being Told

"I need to call some folks up here that's a part of my journey," Ronald says into the microphone as he scans the figures in the folding chairs. Within minutes, he's lined up a dozen fellow addicts on the makeshift stage in the basement of the church. He moves down the line, saying a little something about each person while the applause laps like shallow waves around his words. Each hug bears the weight of an eventful week.

"My story is still being told," he tells the audience. "But today, I'm here to celebrate! Because today I been clean three years!" He glides into a game-show dance.

"Go, Ronald!" they cheer as he pumps his fist. "Go, go, go!" He twists his hips to their spontaneous beat.

Ron divides his time between this Narcotics Anonymous group, his job at McDonald's, and visits to see me at the university. He testifies to my students how writing has helped him in his recovery. His smile makes everyone smile. After class, I bring him to the office and pester him to write down the stories he's just told the students. He manages to squeeze out a screen-full each visit, and we share news about the guys we knew from the jail whom we thought would keep writing and stay in the project but who just stopped. I lament Larry, Bill, Anton, G, Marvin, and Raymond.

He listens patiently. Then he says, "You realize even some of us still in the book won't make it, right?"

The question paralyzes me. I hate even considering it. The whole idea of the project, I remind him, is to rewrite your life script. We're making progress, all of us! But he just smiles, tapping me gently on the back and agreeing that we are making progress, thanks to me, amen!

"All right!" he says at the NA meeting, rolling his shoulders in his loose button-down shirt. "All right! I also celebrate because today my grandmother can *rest*! I'm not hurting her with my addiction anymore."

He moves deeper into the center aisle and into a private confidence. "She didn't give me self-love," he says softly, as the faces in the audience lift in concentration.

"But she gave me all she had." He smiles. The people ease back into their seats, breathing with the speaker.

"Is Jerrell here?" Ronald searches the crowd like he's pressing up to a window. He scans the full room, starting at the right. But when he sees me standing there at the left, he jerks back like he's bumped his head.

"Man! I didn't know you was coming!" For a moment it looks like he's lost his script. He bows his head, praying.

"Everyone?" he says, raising his head at last. "This is Dave." He flashes a huge, boyish smile. "This is my writing teacher from VCU! My *writing* teacher!" he shouts, embracing me with his eyes.

* * *

He's just like Naji described him that day in the visiting room at Indian Creek. But I'm seeing something else when I see Brad Greene for the first time in person, in my office: a white guy from my side of the tracks.

"There were times when I was *crying*, Dr. Coogan!" He reaches up to touch his youthful face. "I mean *tears* just streaming down to the page!"

"I'm sorry," I say.

"No, don't be!" His voice jumps an octave. "In fact, I want to *thank* you— and Naji—for getting me to write. It's truly been a blessing, being a part of this project."

"What made it so hard?" I ask. He smiles the riddled smile of a survivor. The heat of the office in late summer is oppressive, but he pays it no mind.

"Addiction is a very selfish disease, Dr. Coogan. And when you kept asking me to explain how this led to that, it just made me realize how twisted my thinking had become."

"Like with Rachel," I venture, recalling his underage affair with his friend's mother.

"Yes!" he confirms. "Yes. When you asked how Rachel must have *felt* after I stole her car and went off on a binge? I had never thought about how she must have *felt*! Then I got to thinking. Her house is out in the country. And without that car, she was really stranded. And she cared about me. And I just didn't care, I guess. Hmph!" He hunches forward with shocked eyes.

"But she started it, right? I mean, couldn't you look at it that way? She was the one who took advantage of you, sexually, when you were . . . what age?"

"About thirteen, I think."

"She gave you the impression that you could have whatever you wanted whenever you wanted it. She was the one who taught you to see pleasure in everything. Maybe at some deep level, you wanted to show her exactly what she taught you?"

He sinks back slowly into the sands of this. "You know, at the time, I was just a kid. And I consented. I wanted sex. I wanted to be in control. And when I got into drugs, I had to be in control. My time with Rachel really was about control. Until I started writing, I don't think I really understood that. But I understand it now. So when I talk to guys in the hospital—"

"What?"

"Yeah, I volunteer to talk to at the hospital—you know, when they're first going through detox."

"Oh, I didn't know you did that."

"It's part of my program. I have to pass it on. It's just another way—like with this writing. Because really, Dr. Coogan? This is a huge, huge problem—addiction. And it affects so many different people! Drugs don't care what color you are. All they care about is how terrible they can make you."

RONALD

The truck driver is looking to score cocaine and asks me to get some. I don't even hesitate. I'm thinking maybe I'll freak him and run away with him. "You know, I live my life on the wild side," I tell him as I take his order. I have never gone this far for sex with a guy whose preference I don't even know yet.

Adolescent Ronald, at "sixteen" years old, is learning a new trade, living what he believes to be an adult life. "Fuck it" is his attitude now. The only responsibility he sees is to himself. Baby Ronald is still in there. He taught Adolescent Ronald how to deal with abandonment. Don't get attached to anyone or anything. With this insight, they live each moment as if it's their last.

The truck driver thinks I'm experienced with cocaine and asks me for the ingredients to turn the coke into rock. He wants to freebase. But I bring back baking powder instead of baking soda. So the first bag is lost. No getting that back! An expert is called in—a female ho. Now I have competition for sex! I still don't know his preference. I'm guessing female, but hopefully I can change that.

We get the right ingredients, park on the side of the street, and she cooks it up. Now here comes that taste. I don't know what to do, but I'm gonna attempt to be good at it. We finish and the youth in me gets naïve and gullible. I feel like I'm floating in the clouds. But I'm fearful I'll lose ground against the ho. So I stay in position, acting like I've been doing this for a long time. We argue about where to go score next. The young man doesn't really trust her. I am urged to travel with her to bring the package back.

My target is not comfortable using his truck as a front to get high, so the decision is made to get a room and set up there. We find a peaceful hidden motel room and my underage ass is asked to go in search of alcohol. I take a chance and walk about three miles down the highway with no success. When I return, she has done her thing and manipulated him for her personal gain. She's been given cab fare and money to score, but the reality is, she is not coming back.

He has some rock left and we start getting high. After about two hours, he is finally open to exploring oral sex with me. He really wants to score again but doesn't want to travel for it. After playing around for a few, we get some rest, and I try to persuade him to let me run away with him, but he is uncompromising. He decides to take me home.

I walk across the street to my building and run into my friend's mother, Barbara, who is going to score. She is overweight, dark, very loud, and unattractive. She asks me to come with her. To myself, I say, "Only if I can get some." Barbara does not hesitate. She urges me on. Confused, I ask if she's heard me. She keeps moving and I keep investigating. I watch as she prepares to go aboard the starship *Enterprise*. Then she takes another substance and puts it up her nostrils. "What was that you just did?" I ask.

The horse is a brown substance that can calm you and relax your muscles to a point of full extension. I'm eager to see the whole show, but she keeps denying me. Eventually, I wear her down. I don't feel anything at first, but as soon as Scotty beams me up, I become sick. I wouldn't know until later that that was the feeling of getting high.

I know that I can obtain money from my mother by doing little odd things for her. A few days later, I manage to get a few dollars and hurry downstairs to Barbara's apartment. The building we live in has many hidden compartments. The halls are hollow and sometimes spooky. But when Barbara opens the door, a big smile appears on her face. And it gets even bigger when I tell her how much money I have. She takes it to go score. I never got a chance to tell her I'm babysitting and only have about twenty minutes. And Barbara is taking a real long time. I'm getting anxious and panicky. Finally she gets back, and I tell her to hurry because I need to leave.

She cooks it up and Scotty takes my body right away. Feeling great, I rush back to my house. Fannie notices a difference in me and asks if I'm OK. I don't pay her much attention, but she is right on point. Eventually, she leaves and tells me to look after my brother, to make sure nothing happens to him.

While sitting in the living room watching TV with Boaz, I keep wondering. Did Barbara save me some? Then Walter walks in. He's a heavy man, a real charmer with the ladies. I don't really like him that much, but I tolerate him because he's Fannie's boyfriend, and Fannie is a means for me.

I ask Walter to watch my little brother. I tell him I'll be right back. I don't wait for him to respond. The White Girl is calling my name.

* * *

Barbara and friends in the neighborhood have been great teachers. For the most part, I enjoy getting high. Fannie is aware of the changes and tries to find a way to assist. She fears the outcome. I try to reassure her that I am not doing hard drugs and will let her know if I need help. But it seems everyone I meet is getting high on the down low, and I am just getting more and more caught up in this cycle.

I use getting high as a means to get some of the guys in the neighborhood to fool around on the down low. I am shocked that a few in particular give me a chance to have sex with them! Then this one guy, Eric, attempts to hook me on heroin instead of coke. Eric is a moody, thugged-out kind of guy who hates to be on the downside of things. But I like being with him, and every time I get a chance, we get high and fuck. I manage to keep things under control, but eventually, I have to distance myself from him.

Then, early one evening, the urge hits me hard to get high. I find my ash bowl with ashes in it and light it. OMG! That is *just* what the doctor ordered to get my mind churning around this money problem. I have already sold the things Fannie has given me as presents. So I decide to sell my little brother's television and get me some money for drugs. But something in my gut starts giving me bad vibes, so I tell Fannie not to go out tonight, to stay with me instead. But she still decides to leave.

Getting just enough to get me started, I get high only to want more. The plot thickens. No one is home. So I break into Fannie's room and steal her TV. It's bigger than my brother's. I know it'll get me more money. Later in the evening, when she still is not back and the high is wearing off and I'm still wanting more, I take the floor model television from the living room and sell it. By now, Fannie's boyfriend Big Walt is home, and guilt begins to settle in.

* * *

I can't say that I didn't see the signs. But it's too late now. The plane has taken off. And I'm just waiting for the pilot to announce our final destination. I hope he'll say that it's freedom, but I know that there will be delays and layovers. I will have to deal with people all too familiar in the surreal lands of courts and lock-up. This trip will be one of my hardest tests ever: an emotional roller coaster of fear, anticipation, scamming, larceny, pity, shame, and guilt.

When I arrive, I discover that I am late: check-in begins immediately. I am frisked and the flight attendant checks my papers. I sit through intake group, waiting for word about my destination. When it's over, I look for the flight attendant. She's approaching me with the police. They escort me to the back of the plane. First stop: Richmond City Jail.

I am put in isolation until I can be entered into the system. I can't believe I have no contact with the outside world. I contemplate ending my life. I don't want to face anyone, so I don't answer to my name being called. I never thought I would actually think of killing myself again, but today feels like my coming out the closet all over again. I want to take the sheets and put them around my neck and tighten the noose until there is no more air.

Silently, my soul is speaking to a force moving about in my body. It's a force that I failed to rely on before. I guess you could say I was praying, but I have no understanding of what is happening internally.

I spend two days trying to ignore my fate. Then I gather the strength to get up. I am taken down to the classification center, where I am interviewed for housing. They put me on E-2 and I am given a phone call. I call my mother to wish her a happy birthday and to tell her that I won't be there for the celebration. Fannie breaks down and cries as she wonders how I will endure another incarceration. I try to comfort her. Then the reality sets in that I must do something different this trip. I ask her to hang in there with me one more time and I promise not to be too much of a problem for her.

When I hang up the phone, I have no clue how to manifest a change. All I know is that I must find the way to wholeness. The emptiness in me feels like a black hole. Nothing can fill it. But I have to try.

After almost thirteen years of incarceration—one term after another—you would think I would understand the consequences of using drugs and people. But life deals your hand one card at a time. When you bet all you have on a losing hand, who is to blame? All you can do is try to play another hand, because in reality, it's never quite clear if you've lost. I should have been learning how to grow up, to be responsible for my own well-being and the well-being of people who have meant so much in my life. But I chose to let Adolescent Ronald take care of Adult Ronald.

Brad

She's sitting at the computer in the den. As I get closer, I can see she's talking with someone on the Internet. I can only read one sentence, but it doesn't leave my mind for many years: "I can't take it now that Brad's down here all the time, knowing he's laying next to you every night!"

Startled, Colleen reaches down to hit the power button on the CPU. The screen goes black—as does the next four years of my life.

The perfect father? The great provider? The perfect husband? Only in my mind. Of course, I am the greatest lover. We do it all the time. So is this the end of a perfect marriage that only I think is sublime? I try to talk some sense into Colleen—to try to salvage what I had slowly destroyed over the years. But it's too little, too late. The damage is irreparable.

As I sit back, sipping my beer in the home that was supposed to be for my family, a loneliness settles over me. Colleen has been my girl for almost a decade, and I don't quite know how to accept that she's gone, so I don't. I make a pact with myself instead: to win her back and make things all right. Empty promises to an empty man.

First things first: bury all of your feelings. Never let them see you cry. Shawn, Colleen's uncle, comes by later that night and we hit the bars, bringing all my problems deep under the control of substance. We become the toxic twins, feeding off each other's craziness.

I'm not the kind of addict that has to use every day. But under the spell of crack cocaine, I start doing things I normally never do. I call in sick to work. I pay bills late or just don't pay them. I jump on the trampoline with the kids one day and disappear into the drug world the next. Drinks at grandma's or family barbecues become preludes to my disappearing act with Shawn. I start to give away everything I own—vehicles, jewelry, stereos, computers, high-end construction equipment. I say "give away" because this addict *never* loses anything. Going into the summer of 2000, I'm coasting on fumes, living paycheck to paycheck. My living arrangements are crazy.

Colleen and I divorce, but we continue to see each other secretly. I corner her with tales of encounters I have had with other women in the recent past, ensuring her jealousy, so that she wants to prove to me that she is still the best. We'll have a quickie in the bathroom.

(I can admit now that these encounters, as much as I loved them, hurt me more than they helped me. They left me wanting more. And she knew that.)

Colleen remarries, but when she becomes ill in July of 2000, I move in to be with her and the kids. I want to take care of her. Her husband, who is on a six-month deployment with the Navy, never knows I'm there. I take a break from getting high and soothe my disease with alcohol instead. But when push comes to shove, when I hear the call, I answer. I start stealing from the people I love and care for most. Colleen is first. But they are all marked.

On my birthday, I am sentenced to three years in the Virginia Department of Corrections for grand larceny. I had taken Colleen's diamond ring from the house. But that sentence gets suspended for good behavior. Ten days later, when I walk out of the courtroom, I steal a car from a friend of mine and go on a three-month binge that ends in New Jersey.

Charges of possession of heroin with intent to manufacture and distribute are brought against me, along with warrants to hold me in Virginia. Deranged and delusional, I lie in a twenty-four-hour lockdown in the Ocean County Jail Medical Unit while the poison slowly works its way out of my body. I temporarily go crazy and contemplate suicide. But God is with me. My father comes three weeks later.

Forty-six days after that, on a $20,000 bond, the U.S. Marshals fly me back to Virginia to face the warrants they have on file. I am allowed to walk away again. My sentence—six months, to be served on weekends—ends shortly after it is given: a pre-Christmas binge has me running again.

* * *

Waking up in a drunken cocaine haze, with a drug dealer's gun stuck to my head, sort of seems like a blessing. I want to die. I don't want to face the mess I've created out of the last five days.

"Where's my money?"

"I don't have it yet," I slur. He turns to his partner, exchanges a glance, then tightens his grip on the gun.

"OK, you have two options. First one: we shoot you, get joy watching your brains paint the wall, then go have a drink and talk about how stupid this white boy was. Second one: you find a way in the next ten seconds to give us our money and explain to me why I shouldn't take option one. Ten, nine, eight . . ."

"All right! All right! Hold on! Shit!"

Five minutes later, I'm helping them rob my mother's house: TVs, computers, DVD players, guns, alcohol, camcorders, cameras, even presents that are under the Christmas tree for my children. "Just don't—please don't take my mother's jewelry." Amazingly, they honor this request. Even more amazingly, all I get is four months in a drug program at the Virginia Beach Jail.

I have drinks with my wife's family the first day I come home. In no time at all, I am lying, cheating, stealing, manipulating—doing whatever I have to do to make things go my way. I take a drive down to Norfolk during my lunch break to pay some fines. On the way back, I stop to get "just one" and stay for four days. I steadily withdraw cash until the ATM eventually keeps the card. Not long after, I am picked up and arrested for grand larceny. It looks like I am headed back to jail. But when I get in front of the magistrate in Chesapeake, the charges get thrown out on a technicality.

Once again, I am released. Colleen drops me off at a rehab center. From there I voluntarily do a twenty-eight-day program at Serenity House. Though I don't realize it at the time, I am still not ready to face myself. I haven't even peeled off the first layer. My focus is not on a continual program of spiritual recovery. I just pump myself up for *getting* clean. I have no plan for *staying* clean.

When an addict relies on himself alone, it's only a matter of time before his willpower runs out, and mine always seemed to run out quickly. Homeless, with little money, and charges pending again, I call my dad, as I always have. He helps me, no questions asked, and within twenty-four hours, I have funds in my pocket and a bus ticket to Vegas. In one week, I go from shooting low-grade powder to the best black tar a junkie can find.

I wake up in a wood shack a couple of blocks off the Las Vegas Boulevard, on a dirty mattress where tricks bring their Johns. The smell of piss is so strong I want to throw up. It's the middle of August, and the temperature is around 115 degrees. All around me are burnt spoons, broken bottles, and used needles. I haven't had a shower in over a week. I can't remember the last time I picked food over drugs. I've been wearing the same clothes for two weeks. I want to die just from the loneliness.

In a brief moment of sobriety, I get myself to the hospital. I'm dehydrated and malnourished. I have blisters the size of baseballs on the soles of my feet, from walking around all day and night.

The nurse wakes me in what seems like ten minutes. In reality, it's been six hours. "Unfortunately, you can't stay any longer, Mr. Greene. I'm sorry. I know you need to." I sigh heavily and close my eyes. "You're not from around here, are you?" she says soothingly.

"No, ma'am. I'm a long way from home."

"Is there anyone you can call? Anyone who can help you get home?" I can hear the concern in her voice.

"Yeah. I'm about to make that call now. Thanks for taking care of me." Then she gives me five dollars.

"Good luck. I hope you make it."

I make a collect call to Rachel and persuade her to wire me three hundred dollars. Walking out of the hospital that evening, I have peace of mind for the first time in quite a while. The U-Haul rental center, right across the street from the grocery store, looks like the perfect spot to crash. Plus, they have Western Union, so I can pick up the money first thing in the morning.

As I cross the street, getting ready to crawl up into the back of one of the trucks, I notice a gentleman sitting at the bus stop, smoking a cigarette. That's exactly what I need!

As I bum one, he asks me if I'm from around here. I tell him no, and I give him the condensed version of my story. It turns out he's in Vegas to get a rental truck so he can pick up some furniture from his father-in-law's house. He puts the offer up that if I help him, he'll drive me to Lincoln, Nebraska, and then shoot up to Madison, Wisconsin, where he lives. Quickly, I agree. The addict in me is thinking hard about how much money I can save by riding with him.

Every major city where we have a layover, I cop dope. When I get to Rachel's house in Virginia, I explain everything, and of course, she pampers me like a king, waking me up the next morning doing what Rachel does best. As I lie there, soaking it all up, listening to the wind chimes, the neighbors cutting their yards, the cool morning breeze coming through the window, it almost feels too good to be true. But sitting idle and sober for a week and a half, I begin to think and feel again, and what I feel is guilt and pain.

"What do you want for dinner, Brad?"

"I don't know. Why don't we get takeout? You've been cooking every night this week. I know you're tired."

"Sounds great," she says. "I'll call and order it, and you can take my car to go pick it up while I jump in the bath." Fifteen minutes later, I poke my head in the bathroom and tell her I'm leaving.

"Are you sure you don't want to get in here with me? There's plenty of bubbles for the both of us."

"Not right now. I'm going to run down and get the food. I'll slide in later on."

"Alright, honey. I'll see you when you get back."

The next time I see her, it's in circuit court. What was supposed to have been a night of partying in D.C. and just dealing with her lip when I got back turned into a month-long binge with no care of the circumstances I left Rachel in. Once again, I run myself right into the hospital. The infection in my arm from injecting has swollen to the size of a grapefruit, and the pain is really bad. After the operation, a team of doctors and students visits me to see how I am feeling and to tell me that the operation has been a success. The doctors removed and drained the infected area, but the infection had already spread to my shoulder, armpit, and chest. Three more days, they tell me, and the infection would have been in my heart.

"I can't tell you how bad that could have turned out for you, son."

"I don't know quite what to say, sir. Thank you."

"Oh, it's nowhere near over yet, Mr. Greene. You're going to be on IV antibiotics for at least a week. And we still have to go back in and remove the drain that we put in your arm."

After they leave, I fall asleep. When I wake up, my father is sitting in the room. Somehow he found me. What an amazing individual. My father's willingness to always help me has never been in question. And not just me. It doesn't matter if you need a cosigner on a car or if you're just having a problem with another man at work. He always finds a solution. He's a humanitarian, though it has its drawbacks. Years later, in trying to do what's best for our family, he will be undercut by the conglomerate of shareholders he's welcomed into his company. His thanks will be the complete and forced abandonment of the business he started years earlier. His thanks for trying to do what's best for me, for looking out for my best interests when I'm caught up in my own drug addiction, will not be much different.

When I come home from the hospital, I keep it together long enough to spend Christmas with everyone. But my disease is only sitting dormant, waiting for the right time to wake up. I begin by stealing from my father and the business. This time he kicks me out of the house. I end up at the projects in D.C., where I take part in a life I have always looked down on, with people I have always scorned. I eat at the soup kitchen, exchange needles at the needle exchange bus. I become a part of the twenty-four-hour drug house, constantly living on the edge in search of another fix. I get lost in the game of shoplifting, scoring, and ripping people off. I become scum, a waste of flesh and blood.

Tony

I became an out-of-control party animal on the weekends. I had nothing to lose but my virginity or my life. Then the school year ended, and once again I had to stand the test of idle time and overwhelming boredom. My curiosity seemed to have plans of its own, however.

A thrill-seeker wishing to indulge usually starts at the bottom, with alcohol and cigarettes, and gradually climbs higher, to harder drugs. I unconsciously positioned myself to take the next step on the drug pyramid when I went looking for some excitement on the block and ended up accepting a package of marijuana on consignment, in hopes that I could put a few dollars in my pocket.

While making my first hand-to-hand drug sale, I noticed how much bigger the two bags of weed I placed into the customer's hand were compared to the two bags of weed a rival drug dealer showed the same customer. I decided to take some of the weed out of my bags, to make fifteen bags out of ten. This plan also enabled me to smoke some of the weed I was selling, and at the same time make me some extra money. I was already familiar with the number one rule in the drug game: pay off everybody you owe first, then go play with what you have left over for yourself. So I followed that cardinal rule and went and paid my debts to the drug supplier. He then rewarded me with another package.

There I was, standing with a fresh package of drugs, my own money, and several bags of weed that I hadn't sold yet from the last package. I decided to stay on the block for a little while longer so I could pay off my new debt. I couldn't have made a better decision. After I got a guy I knew to roll me up a couple of joints and purchase me a beer, I found a secluded area close to the woods. I got high off of weed for the first time all by myself. It was really more than I'd bargained for, but with a few sips of beer, I got nice and mellow.

I really enjoyed the weed high better than the beer high, because it didn't make my stomach bloated. And it didn't cause me to stumble while walking. The only two problems I really had to worry about whenever I smoked weed were my eyes being red and half-closed and the strong smell of the smoke on my skin and clothes. I quickly fixed these problems by always carrying a bottle of Visine Eye Drops for my red eyes, and a small bottle of cologne to mask the smell left behind by the smoke. Both remedies worked: my teachers never questioned me, nor did my family ever suspect me of getting high.

During the next school year, things started to change. I went to my counselor to drop Spanish class and pick up another elective. The only available opening was Reserve Officer Training Corps (ROTC). The counselor asked if I would like to attend, and I agreed to give it a try.

The following day, he walked me over to the classroom. Immediately after I sat down, some students I knew and others I had never met started to talk amongst themselves about me. I never said a word, because I had already been told by the counselor that discipline was a key factor in completing the course.

The very next day, the counselor told me that the ROTC instructor did not want me to attend the class. The only elective opening left was home economics, which was just what I was looking for, because it had the two most important things to me at the time: food and girls. This incident, along with my memory of second grade, when I was accused of being disruptive when really I had just finished my work early and all the other kids wanted to talk with me, only strengthened my view that school was *increasing* my chances of failing in life.

The hand life dealt me in 1988 during the last summer vacation I experienced as a high school student wasn't folded and thrown back into the deck until the summer of 2004. The introduction of powder cocaine into my neighborhood allowed aspiring drug dealers to more than triple their investment in under half the time it would have taken them to sell weed. I didn't hesitate trading in the bulky bag of weed that netted me at the most $240 for the bag of cocaine that, if it was filled to the rim with tiny bags, could net me between three and four thousand dollars.

I really started to lose focus here. School and sports took the backseat to a new lifestyle that consisted of money, drugs, alcohol, and crime. I found myself justifying my negative behavior more and more, until it came to a head and I decided to quit varsity football.

When I think about why I made that reckless decision, I can now see how God has healed me since then, opening up my eyes. I can see and accept the truth for what it is. On that hot August day some nineteen years ago, during summer football practice, I chose to have more fun on the sideline, laughing and joking with a couple of my boyz that rode the bench. I decided to ignore my coach's request for me to get a quick drink of water and line up on the other side of the ball so that the second-string offense could get a few snaps of the ball. I really felt as if I was being misused, because I had just finished practicing on offense as a member of the first-string offensive line.

I thought it was very inconsiderate of Coach Lyons not to allow me a breather when he had twenty or thirty other guys with fresh legs on the sideline, eager to get some contact. He and I had a couple of words, and I honored his request by reporting back to the football field, but little did Coach Lyons and the rest of the team know that this would be the last request Tony Martin would be fulfilling as a member of the Warwick Raiders football team. Of course, Coach Lyons was just a pawn in my game of justification. I used his concern about making me into a better player as justification to quit.

Several players who I considered to be somewhat close to me came to me on more than one occasion, trying to convince me to return. But my decision was final, even though I stood a very good chance of receiving a scholarship. Why should I take orders from somebody who puts their pants on the same way I do?

So I put myself in a position to call the shots. I became an entrepreneur in the business of manufacturing and distributing ghetto pharmaceuticals: an expert in the processing, packaging, and selling of powder cocaine. The only thing on my mind when I made this life-changing decision was my lust for money, whores, and drugs. Not only did I resign from football; soon after, I found myself being kicked out of school and placed into an alternative school called Project Rehabilitation. This was the place where all the problem kids in school found themselves if they showed any form of aggression, lack of interest in school, or drug use. At the time, they also used the program for girls who were pregnant. I played the little game for a while, but the hours they set for us to go to school were in total conflict with the hours I'd set to run my illegal drug business.

The schoolwork assignments they gave us were so easy, I labeled the entire program a scam. I missed more and more school, gradually trading it for the streets. In a matter of a month and a half, me and my boy Orlando, aka "Doughboy" (who had also been sent to the alternative school by Coach Lyons), instead of getting on the bus, would simply watch it pull up and pull off. There were customers depending on us, and there was no way I was going to let them down. Doughboy was never directly involved in the hand-to-hand sale of powder cocaine. He was just an extra set of eyes and some muscle in case a problem arose.

My days as a dropout usually started with me waking up early in the morning and getting ready as if I were really going to school, in hopes that my mother wouldn't realize I was playing hooky. If she did, this would've been followed by an aggressive investigation into what was so important to me that it warranted my time more than school and sports. So my work was cut out for me when it came to avoiding my mother. Eventually she found out by way of the school counselor finally calling the house after 5:30 p.m. She informed my mother, who had just gotten home from work, that I hadn't attended school in the last several weeks.

I had never been in a heated conversation of any sort with my mother before that day. I don't remember any traumatic physical or emotional scars. I don't even remember what I said. The storm must have blown over. And I must have found it fitting just to go back out to sea to die gracefully.

See, it was never really about not feeling loved. There was more than enough for me whenever I took time out from my busy life to enjoy the comforts of home. My mother sacrificed a lot so that she could afford her children a loving, caring, and nourishing environment. But on the other side of the door, an entirely different environment awaited and lusted for my attention and indulgence. My sister and brother didn't care to leave home for the harsh struggles of the world that lingered several footsteps away. I associate their success with appreciating the comforts of home, which my mother, being a single parent, worked so very hard to give us.

Day by day, year by year, I saw the tears and fears of my worried mother, who stayed up listening for my staggering footsteps, which assured her that I was safe and secure. I now realize why she used to get so upset with me whenever I came to the house late at night and would grab some food and clothes and go right back out. My being in the safe confines of her house supplied her with a brief sense of peace. But she never received her reward: my presence. Sometimes it would be weeks that she'd sit, sadly waiting and worrying about her youngest boy, wondering if he was dead in a ditch somewhere or laid up in a hospital or jail without affording her the opportunity to rescue him. This was the untold truth that my sinful eyes failed to see. This is what allowed my heart to grow cold and my ears to become stopped and my face to become veiled, covered with foolishness.

* * *

The day started like any other, as we found out which police officers were going to be patrolling the neighborhood, secured a spot, and watched for customers. It was a Friday afternoon and business was moving a little slowly.

A customer that wasn't too familiar to me drove up into the parking lot. I observed his hand gestures signaling that he was looking for some drugs. But his drug of choice was only revealed after I made a gesture toward my nose, as if sniffing some cocaine. He nodded his head to let me know that it was cocaine he wanted. I then waved my arm, signaling for him to get out of the car, but both of us seemed to have a lack of trust for one another. Finally, I decided to take a chance, so I went to the car to see if he wanted rock or powder cocaine. When I got into the car, I sensed a tension that I'd never experienced during my entire eighteen years on Earth. Fear set off warning bells in my head. But when he flashed a handful of twenty- and fifty-dollar bills in my face, the bells went silent.

"I've got powder cocaine," I informed him. And he said I was just the man he needed to see.

"Man, is this stuff any good?" he questioned.

"Yeah, man. This the head banger," I assured him. I knew this was some potent-grade product, because I had tried it myself. He told me he was on lunch break and that he wanted to purchase three twenties for sixty dollars. After I exchanged the cocaine for the money, I told him to go ahead and sniff some.

"I shoot mine," he shot back boldly, like that was something to be bragging about. When he drove off, I noticed that he didn't make the left turn necessary for him to exit the apartment complex. I knew then that he was going to find a secluded area in the back of the complex so he could get his fix.

I continued to serve other customers, but for some reason I got this funny feeling in my gut about that man. He stayed on my mind. After ten or fifteen minutes, he pulled back up in his car. I made my way over and hopped in on the passenger's side. I could clearly see by the look in his eyes and the sweat dripping off his chin that he was satisfied with the product. He could hardly talk because the cocaine had made his throat and mouth as dry as a desert.

"Let me get four more of them," he stammered. I was concerned about the guy now. He had transformed into a drug-crazed junkie right before my eyes. As I exchanged the four bags of cocaine for the eighty dollars he had in his hand, I noticed the bloody needle and bottled water he used to mix and inject his drugs. I asked him if he was planning on going back to work, but he simply ignored me and ended our ordeal with a simple "Thank you, man." This time, instead of making the left turn, he made a right turn, which indicated to me that he was finally leaving the apartment complex and might be going back to work. Whatever type of job he had, I knew that the hundred and forty dollars he'd spent with me in thirty minutes must have put a dent into his little three- or four-hundred dollar paycheck.

The next several hours on the block went all right because as payday went on, more and more customers came to share their newfound wealth with me. By this time of day, I had already had my share of booze and drugs, so my alertness to the dangers that surrounded me were a little lax. My relaxation almost cost me my life.

The same customer who had caused my hair to stand up on the back of my neck only hours earlier drove up. He built up my trust by spending another fifty dollars with me and, once again, driving to the back of the apartment complex to get his fix inside his car. And, just like before, he came back to me after his fix. This time, though, he asked if I would take a ride with him so that he could get some more money to buy some more drugs. I honored his request, but not before my friend Doughboy asked me if I wanted him to ride with me. The customer quickly let me know that he didn't want any more people riding in his car, so I told Doughboy that I would be all right. But that couldn't have been further from the truth.

After a brief ride, the man pulled the car into a 7-Eleven and told me that he needed to get something out of the trunk. As he opened the trunk, I remember glancing over my left shoulder in the hopes that I would see exactly what he was getting. Something told me to get out of the car and walk into the store, but greed wouldn't let me. I was about to learn my lesson.

He slithered back into the car, but I was only able to see his right hand, because he kept his left arm and hand tightly against the left side of his body. As soon as he

181

sat down in the seat, he eased his left arm around the front of his body, keeping it very close to his stomach. And that's when I saw the gun. It looked like it was either a .38- or .357-caliber revolver. Whatever it was, I could see that it was loaded: the brass heads of the bullets shimmered like new pennies at the bottom of a swimming pool on a hot summer day.

He made sure to keep the gun low so that the car dashboard shielded it from view for anyone who might pass by. I didn't make any sudden moves because I knew he was still high off the fifty dollars' worth of cocaine I'd sold him twenty minutes before. I knew he was most likely paranoid. This was the first time I'd experienced not being able to do what I wanted to do when I wanted to do it. If I could've done anything, I would've gotten out of the car, went inside the store, and bought me a chef salad with blue cheese dressing and a fruit-flavored tonic water to wash it down. But that was a big "if." What I had to focus on was making sure that I followed all his demands in hopes that I would walk away from this incident with my life.

I was surprised when he only commanded me to drop some of the money and some of the drugs on the floor of the car directly in front of me. Some, not all. He also spared me by letting me keep all the jewelry I had on. So I calmly adhered to his request by peeling a hundred or so dollars off of the large wad of money I had in my right front pants pocket. Next, it was time for me to shuffle through the plastic bag that contained the small packages of cocaine. My whole mind was set on minimizing my losses by giving him as little as possible, while at the same time paying the price he'd put on my life.

"All right, you can get out of the car," he slurred. Evidently the glow of the green and his overwhelming drug-lust caused him to be satisfied with what he had seen, because I lived to tell about it. Other than my mother's "I love you," his words were the most pleasant I had ever heard. I was able to walk away with what was left of the money, the drugs, and most importantly, my life. I got out and didn't look back.

A feeling of triumph took over my entire body, leading me to verbally boast to myself about myself. I had successfully negotiated for my life! But with every stride I took, the triumph turned into embarrassment, because in all actuality, I had just been successfully robbed.

All of this was followed by the daunting task of having to decide whether to tell the truth or to lie. If I told the truth, then I might have been the conversation piece on the streets for several weeks. If I would've told a lie, and the truth was found out later about what really happened, not only would I have suffered embarrassment, but my word, supposedly as good as my bond, would've been made frivolous forever. So I gave my boyz a watered-down version of the truth that went something like, "Fellows, he got me for a little something but you know that's something small to a giant. Believe that!"

It surprised me when I saw that the guys were more concerned about my safety than they were about the loss of material goods. All in the name of greed and lust, I had allowed my life to take on the value of a couple of dollars' worth of change, a few bags of cocaine, and a useless form of fame.

After nearly losing my life in that robbery, whenever another risky situation presented itself, I always asked myself, "Tony, are you going to be able to negotiate your way out of this one, or are you going to have to pay for this chance with your life?" Even though that was a price I didn't want to pay, I considered myself lucky and would usually take the risk. To me, life was a form of credit, and I always hoped I could get away without paying the bill. This wasn't a question that just randomly came to mind. This was a question that was *engraved* in my mind because I lived a life of crime twenty-four hours a day, seven days a week, and three hundred and sixty-five days a year.

After a while I got used to the burden of playing the cat-and-mouse game of selling drugs. The streets were a maze, but I knew them. Day after day, I would enter at the same spot, in hopes that my sanity would lead me to freedom and not into the claws and paws of the law. But the police department has a database full of the names of young black men, and as soon as one turns eighteen years old, an e-mail gets sent to a policeman's patrol car in the area where a young Angus grazes. That e-mail notifies the officer that the time has come for this one to be herded, corralled, and branded with a number, transforming him from a young man into a con and eventually into an ex-con.

My day to be branded came several days after my eighteenth birthday. Me and a few of my friends decided to take a little stroll into the neighboring apartment complex, Warwick Gardens, which was right across the street from Woodsong Apartments. There was a public sidewalk that stretched along Warwick, interrupted every so often by narrow slabs of concrete, which formed an alley that led to a small parking lot. What my boyz and I didn't know at the time was that if we were to be caught standing on one of those slabs, the local herders could arrest us for trespassing, because that alley was considered private property. So there we stood, taking a vote on which direction to travel, when out of nowhere came this rookie cop known for his ability to run as fast as a cheetah. He had those rare EK glasses that made him look like a black RoboCop. We all stood there like deer caught in headlights, unaware of the danger that this man represented. With our armor of pride tightly strapped to our young, hairless chests, we drew our sensing swords, and the duel of words began.

I pierced the officer's mind with an insulting, six-piece combination: "Why are you bothering us, man?"

"Because I want to!" he returned, in a potent mix of arrogance and power. My pride was punctured. I was hurtfully shamed, and my ego piggybacked on these fragile emotions. I became pigheaded. Rather than wave the white flag, I challenged the officer's authority and ended up in jail for the first time.

I was released on my own recognizance. I didn't have to use my mother's love and protection to get me out. I only received a misdemeanor "trespassing" charge, which didn't even carry jail time since it was my first offense. But I was afforded the chance to see what all the talk was about: how the jail looked, and all the danger inside, lurking around each and every corner. It really wasn't that bad. My fears about jail just flew out the barred window.

Multiple misdemeanor arrests followed, but not until January 15, 1991, when I was sentenced to four years in the state penitentiary, did I begin to feel as if I had lost control of my life. I wasn't used to being told when I could and couldn't eat, shower, talk, and walk. In the back of my mind, I constantly had to convince myself that things could have been a lot worse. Instead of crying, I just made the most of each and every day. On most days I would just hang out at the poker table. It really didn't matter if I won or lost, because in my book, it was just a way to pass a little time. Almost every inmate who I discussed my sentence with reassured me that I would make first parole because it was my first time in prison. That meant that most likely I was only going to serve nine months instead of twenty-nine.

It became apparent to me that not only had I lost my liberty, but all the material wealth I'd gained was taking up space at the local landfill. The young lady whom I was involved with begged me not to end our relationship, even though I had broken it off a month before I went to court. She lasted about six months. Then, as I expected, lust landed her in the arms of another man. I could see the negative results of my incarceration, but my young eager mind kept reassuring me that I could quickly get back everything I'd lost. Just as I'd been told by fellow inmates, I did make first parole, and in October of 1991, I found myself back on the same streets where I had disappeared. I got back into the groove of things right away, putting my life on the line in order to feed my addictions and the addictions of those around me. The major difference this go-round was that my reasoning had grown more twisted. I figured that if I only hustled to feed my addiction, it was unlikely that I would be arrested again for selling. I hadn't realized that I was stuck in a lifestyle in which the rewards were poverty, jail, or death.

My addiction to cocaine never changed the love I had for people and the joy I received whenever I could make them happy. But now I was spending most of my time on street corners and in crack houses, getting high, trading drugs for sex, spending whatever time was left over with my girlfriend. The people who I was now making happy were drug addicts and prostitutes. I never lost respect for people. But I did lose a lot of contact with the world of people outside this lifestyle.

I did go to a local college called ECPI in the 1990s, where I received an A.S. degree in computer electronics. I didn't do any jail time during that two-year period getting my degree, because that would have caused me to graduate late. I graduated with my class, on time, with a very high B average. The sad part about it is that I was constantly getting high off of crack, weed, and alcohol. I had the ability to learn things quickly and follow directions. I had a keen eye for details. And this really helped in college, as well as in the two small businesses that I had before my incarcerations. One was a lawn care service; the other, a car detailing and car wash shop. It was easy for me to satisfy customers' needs to have their lawns manicured or cars restored with a thorough inside/outside cleaning. I've always enjoyed bringing smiles to people's faces, and these were just two more ways to do so. The more difficult the task, the more eager I was to attack it head-on, so that the hidden diamond that lay beneath the rubble could be given its due time to shine.

I never really thought that I was a failure. But, for the next seven years, I was constantly in and out of jail, losing jobs due to my addiction. I always understood that I had potential. That's part of the reason why I played Russian roulette with my life. I figured as long as I didn't die, then I could go cold turkey with my reckless lifestyle at the drop of a hat and rekindle my ability to learn anything, anywhere, very quickly. Bottom line: life was a risk. If I was going to win or lose, I might as well have some fun doing it.

What people outside the ghettos must understand is that if you're constantly surrounded by a certain type of environment, whether it's violent or not, you will gradually begin to accept it. It's just what you know. Once people get conditioned, they get into a comfort zone that may take generations to break out of. If you tell a child that he or she only needs to bathe once a month, the child will think that's normal until challenged to think differently. That's how it was for me when it came to my lifestyle. I figured that I was going to live by the sword and die by the sword, because the sword was what I saw all around me. And it's what I chose to pick up.

TERENCE

I was never tempted by drugs growing up. I was never around them, so they never became an issue for me. Most of my youth, I was involved with school and sports. It was when I turned twelve or thirteen that I was first offered a joint. It made me paranoid. During high school, I was reintroduced to marijuana, but this time it was in higher quantity and I had the ability to purchase it. Most of my peers were buying and smoking it, so it seemed like a natural rite of passage. My usage continued through my junior and senior years, in college, and in the military.

You never think about where life is taking you through your usage of drugs. They always provide an escape. It's only when they create a problem in your life that you become aware of their adverse effects. For me, that came when the army gave me a urinalysis. This was done at my first duty station upon arriving at the base. Until then I thought there was no negative consequence to my smoking pot. But I tested positive and had to go through what is known as the Uniform Code of Military Justice. It's a military tribunal that judges your guilt or innocence based on the evidence presented. No excuses could vindicate me. My punishment was to have my rank stripped and my pay deducted, and to be placed on restrictive duty.

I could have responded by refusing to smoke pot again. But that wasn't me. Instead I met a person who shared with me how to avoid getting another positive test result. During this period of going undetected, I was introduced to powder cocaine, but only on a limited scale. My drug of choice was still marijuana. I never again tested positive, but the result of my smoking was obvious. When I didn't have it, I would always go buy it. It was only after I was arrested and discharged from the army that my life seemed unmanageable.

* * *

I'm preparing to go home for the holidays. While washing the car, I smoke my last joint. Facing a road trip of several hours, I decide to go cop some more.

When it starts, the light rain seems like a blessing. The earth is coarse and dry, extracting every ounce of moisture from within to relieve its thirst. And just as the dusk of drought begins to gather, the clouds form. The sun is overtaken by the darkness of the atmosphere. It gets cooler, and the first drop of water hits the earth. Finally, the ground is saturated with refreshment.

As I approach the area where I normally purchase, I don't see anyone I know. The only person available turns out to be an undercover police officer busting individuals trying to buy.

The thunder roars. The lightning parts the sky. The wind blows harder and harder, causing the rain to fall faster, and suddenly the earth is overtaken, unable to handle the immensity of this relief.

Although I never again have a positive urine test, the nature of my charge—attempted possession—is drug related, providing the grounds for my discharge from the army.

Another crack of thunder. Warning! The stoplight goes from green to yellow, and just as the light turns red, here I go. The sky is bright with strips of electricity. The rain hits my back like I'm a car in the car wash—deliberate, purposeful, thorough. It's not me; it's fate. My choices are right. It's someone else's fault. I'm going to do me. Do what I do. Zoom through the light. I'm now knee-deep and I don't know myself anymore. I'm blinded by the clouds of the storm. I walk in the mist, searching for my smoke, trying to find some assurance where there is none. But the rain keeps falling from the sky.

I can't find any pot in the city, and I'm stressed. The weight of all my choices settles on me: guilt, pain, loneliness. In walks Character Number 1. His situation is no better than mine. He's looking for a way out. So he asks the question: Have you ever smoked crack?

The boom is so loud it momentarily deafens me. The lightning blinds me. I'm now waist-deep, screaming for help.

Yes, I've smoked coke before. But it was always offered. I never purchased it. That makes it different somehow. A truth develops from all the lies. Together with him, we smoke and smoke. Have you ever heard the saying "up in smoke"? My cares evaporate like that, but not the hopes and dreams. They stay rooted under the surface of chaos. For however long, just a few hours, my mind is no longer a part of my being. Escape! Or so I think—until the grip seizes me and takes control.

I travel with my associate to get the little white rock. Together, in a total of two days, my associate and I spend upwards of a thousand dollars. He is barely getting along. I'm on the verge of losing everything.

The wind picks up. It's now black as night. I'm cold. I'm wet. I'm now in chest-deep. I've lost my ability to maneuver. All I can do is tread water. Search for dry land. Fear, worry, doubt—they grip me in uncharted waters. There is no guidance. No direction. No aspiration. Doubting myself. My confidence is still high, but sadly this is only through my determination to say, over and over, "I'm OK, you're OK. Everything is OK."

I come to support a friend. His band is playing tonight in the Student Commons building at Virginia Commonwealth University. That's where I see her. I'm blindsided by her charm. My plans are still possible—even more, probable! Instead of starting another journey alone, unsure, and yes, even a little afraid, there she is, in spite of herself, I am later told. It's a one-night stand. I've never had one, especially on purpose, so naïveté reigns. I have known uncertainty all my life. Now she's having my baby. My first, a male. A beautiful, black, African child. I'm in heaven. Nothing matters but the love I feel.

It's perfect in no way. One after the other, a little at a time, the bricks of the dream come down. I miss all my final exams, receive all Fs. My grade point drops so low I can't pledge a fraternity. My ROTC program is suspended. I'm fired from my job that helps pay the rent. I'm living alone, feeling alone.

But it was my choice to fall. I had had enough listening, trying to be all I could be, not knowing, being the butt of the joke. It was as if everybody knew except me. No longer desiring, wanting, I fell down with the crabs in my basket. It happened fast. I wanted much in life. I still do. But things kept breaking out of my control. One right after another. And that provided the necessary pressure to weaken the foundation of my spirit. Not rich enough to have all the things the "haves" have. Not big enough to be a bully. Not man enough to take a stand. Only inquisitive, curious, eager for the knowledge of how to be happy.

* * *

A group of us go to a place that cashes checks. After cashing a check that is not any of ours, we proceed to go buy crack. Then we smoke until the money is gone. This experience makes a huge impression on me. After spending the little money I have with these people, I begin to hang out with them for company, not wanting to be with myself. But I get angry when I find out they're taking from me behind my back. Once I notice this, I leave, broken, upset, and frustrated. I'm not happy to begin with, dealing with my life, and I don't understand this game. So I decide to find a safe place to relax.

I go to an old friend. He's not in the drug game, so I feel safe. I can hang out without any trouble. I step onto the front porch, knocking to see if he's home, but there is no answer. As I turn to leave, I notice in the mail something that appears to be a check. I remember the hustle with the last check. I'm thinking my luck is changing. I'm not yet thinking clearly due to the effects of the crack. So I remove the check from the mailbox and proceed to the same place. I don't want to deal with the group. I don't want to feel cheated even though I am also cheating.

I walk up to the teller. She asks me to sign the check. I sign and push it toward her. My trouble comes once she asks for identification. I have ID, but my ID doesn't match the name on the check, so I tell her I don't have it. While I'm waiting, a worker comes out to tell me they're calling the police. In my state of mind, I tell her I don't care, and I don't leave. The police come to investigate, along with the person who owns the check. I have no argument and no hope and am arrested for forgery. This is my first felony conviction. I am twenty-eight years old and lost. It may sound crazy, but my arrest is a cry for help.

15

THE PRISON INSIDE ME

"Whoa!" Dean shouts, extending an arm to catch me as I stumble on the uneven pavement. "What are you doing, Dave? You can't trip here in the alley with four black guys!"

It's early in the evening, but already dark as we make our way across campus.

"'Cause if you got hurt?" he goes on. "You *know* who they'd come looking for!"

"Uh-uh," Ron chides, rollicking side to side. "They'd have *five* to choose from! They'd have to think on that."

"But they wouldn't pick *you*," Terence shouts over the fray. "Not with that sweater." Ron is wearing a plaid sleeveless sweater with a white button-down shirt.

"What?" Ron says. "We're going to hear Bill Cosby!"

The free tickets we have to hear Cosby came from the university, which, in celebrating its 40th anniversary, chose to honor projects like ours that engage the community.[15]

"That ain't no Cosby sweater!" Terence insists.

"He looks like Erkel," Dean says, assessing the ensemble as we reach the intersection. "Look at Dave back there, waiting on the light to change!" he laughs over his shoulder as he and Kelvin make their way across Broad Street.

"Dave, you got to learn how to walk ghetto," Ron says. "Like this!" He moves slowly at an angle away from the group, directly into the path of oncoming traffic a hundred yards away. He claims a spot on the cement island halfway across the street and turns around with both arms extended. Ta-da! Following his lead, I jog across.

At the door, we present our tickets and are directed to a back room for a reception honoring all of the community projects. Afterward, I start retracing our steps back to the gym.

---

15 Had I known in 2008 what I know now about Cosby's own criminality—the allegations about him sexually abusing women—I would not have attended the show, much of which focused on the kind of morality that Cosby's own history has made into hypocrisy.

"Dave, where you going?" Kelvin asks, furrowing his eyebrows.

"To the concert. Isn't it this way?"

"Look at Dave!" Kelvin shouts over the top of my head to Terence. "He thinks we have to go *all* the way back down that hall to get into the concert!" Terence starts snickering. Dean rolls his eyes. I look back and forth between the two of them. Then Kelvin stoops down to my eye level like he's addressing a nice but dim-witted kid. "There's a door right here, Dave!" He grabs my shoulders and twists me to face it.

"Oh!" I say. I had totally missed it.

"*Obviously*, Dave, you've never been followed." He leans into the explanation with some swag. "You *never* go back the way you come in! You always look to see where the other door's at."

"Makes sense," I reply.

Once in the gym, we settle into our seats and small conversations. Once the marching band starts, Ronald can't sit still.

"There he go!" Terence shouts with a wide grin, nudging me in the ribs and gesturing over to Ron, who is hand jiving, clapping, and shoulder-rolling in his seat. I smile with Terence at Ron's seat boogie.

Bill Cosby drifts in and out of comedy and essay. He sits. He stands. He makes little asides. And he takes his time with what he's saying, studying the horizon of our common morality.

"I had a *teacher*!" he begins in his inimitable guttural. "A teacher who I am still afraid of all these years later!" The teacher and his mother had made a pact with each other to make sure Bill did his homework. The story swells to a wholesome note: the teacher's dying now and Bill comes to see her in the hospital, still revering, respecting, and fearing the one who cared.

Then: "I went to prison!" he shouts, edging up roughly. "To *prison*!" He paces the stage until he finds the right spot. He looks at the ground. You can see him recreating the room they led him to in the prison. "The boy they brought before me. This young man." He pauses to contort his face into a stupor. "Sitting there barely seeing me." He lowers his voice and leans in gently, conjuring the young man in the faces of the audience. "Son, what's wrong?" he asks in a concerned, quiet tone. I sneak a glance at the faces of Dean, Terence, Ron, and Kelvin, listening intently. Then Cosby slips into the voice of the boy.

"Was up late. Gambling."

"Why?" he asks in the high end of his voice before changing character once more.

"Man's got to do what a man's gotta do." The words land like dull punches, sluggish in their reasoning. Cosby leans further into the fathering.

"Son?" he asks softly, asserting loudly with his eyes. "When does a man do what he *ought* to do?" He drops the microphone to his side, turns on his heel in the silence of the stadium, and finds a new spot to assemble a new trance.

STAN

"Count is clear, count is clear!" we hear one morning on the PA system at Lunenburg Correctional Facility. Every man's ears are tuned to that system. "Work call, work call!"

Doors start flying, men moving to their assigned spots on the grounds. But I'm waiting on rec call. All I want to do is dash at top speed toward the giant slab of concrete that houses 1,000 pounds of cold steel plates, bars that could rip the flesh off the palms of your hands, and benches stained with sweat and blood.

My first bit was done on that slab of concrete. What doesn't kill you can only make you stronger. This was our mindset: punish or be punished. Add another plate, and then when you can't handle that, another plate. Add another one: sweat, blood, and tears.

I'm a member of the dumb dudes club. We are the best-looking guys in here: rock-hard abs and chests, bulging biceps, legs like tree trunks, but with minds like babies'. We think how you look is all that matters in life—what's on the outside. We don't know what I've only just recently come to suspect: that life isn't always about "me." It's about discovering the beauty that lies dormant inside of your fellow human beings. It's about giving love and then receiving it. It's the solution to the prison problem that you never hear about.

Aren't they smart enough to understand our problem? They know the solution, but they whisper it among themselves, not allowing us to hear.

See, jail and prison are not really about bricks and bars to me. It's not about shackles and chains and guards and guns and razor-wire fences. When you look at me, you won't see any of the above, at least not on the outside of who I appear to be. But x-ray me with your mind. Listen to my words. Look into my eyes.

Here, let me help you. You'll need a light, because it's dark in my world. But trust me. When your light meets my darkness, you'll see the bars. You'll see the chains. You'll see despair, hopelessness, and gloom. You'll see things that chain me to childhood. You'll see the wounds that have been festering for years. You'll see the prison inside me. I've been released from prison over and over again. But I've never really been freed.

KELVIN

"Let's get this last point, man!"

"We need you to hit this last bucket."

"C'mon, Kelvin. One more rep! You can do it!"

But there's something terribly wrong with this picture. While I'm on the court or the weight pile, struggling to get this last repetition in, the man encouraging me isn't my father. The guys trying to motivate me aren't my brothers. And as I'm setting up to receive the pass and take the game-winning shot, there isn't one woman in the crowd—not my mother, girlfriend, or sister—just hundreds of men, most of whom I've just met. We are not playing in a gym in a high school, or a church or summer league. But these inmates around me are family, even if I don't want to admit it.

When you leave the people who depend on you, to come to prison, you change your life and theirs. But here I am, just one of millions of men—young, old, and in between. You learn to trust these men not to drop weights on your neck and kill you. On the court your team now depends on you, just as people did on the streets. It's the same feeling, but then again, different. There's so much wasted time.

You know the feeling that comes over you when you hear your favorite Christmas song on the radio? Mines is "Silent Night" by the Temptations. Every time I hear that song, I just want to look out for everybody, especially that part when they say, "In my mind, I want you to be free, for all of our friends, to listen to me." Whoever wrote that realized that at this time of year, even if it's only for a day, we *should* be free to give and receive love, to be all that our families need us to be.

I have to hold back a tear. It's this part of the song that really gets to me, and I'm sure that I'm not the only one. But there is no way that me or any of the other guys crowded around the radio is going to cry. If a man cries in these places, it's the beginning of the end, because now you are considered soft. The only thing to do now is to buckle down, forget that you have feelings, and get ready to go all-out. As I look back at the clock radio, I notice that almost everyone has walked away from the table and taken time to deal with the pain in their own way.

* * *

"Hey boy, look, you best to set your mind to working when you set foot on the body plantation!" That commercial comes to mind every day I get up at three in the morning to go to work in prison. I think of how similar it must have been to be a slave working on a plantation. Of course, there are a whole lot of differences in the two, but if you really look at it, there are more similarities.

In slavery, we as a people were sold by our own kind—traded for wealth and collectables to people on boats. With incarceration, we as a people are being sold out, snitched on by our own kind—traded for money to get high, for self-preservation, or as part of some kind of territorial conflict—sold to the people in white cars with the lights on top.

In slavery, we as a people were packed together on boats of all sizes, small and large; bound and shackled; bunched up side by side, without any room to move around and with no window to allow us to see the ocean. With incarceration, we as inmates are packed into vans and busses of all sizes and bound together by a linked chain, or shackled and cuffed, with no windows to see out. We're packed tight, with six, sometimes seven grown men on each side of the metal wall splitting the back of a van in half, leaving less than three feet of sitting space. That's twelve to fourteen men packed into a van that's not even made for transportation.

After traveling for days out on the ocean, slaves were delivered to the depot off the coast of the Americas—in this case, Virginia. After being taken to the depot, the slaves were taken off the boats, lined up, bid on, and taken away by their new owners. After countless hours of traveling, we inmates are delivered to a depot in Virginia, lined up, and called upon by our new pre-determined owners.

Slaves were made to work for free and were broken physically, emotionally, and mentally. They had to turn to God for stability and a means of support in a world and time where no one else cared. Some slaves were given a chance to earn their freedom after giving their masters years of service and loyalty, but they were ridiculed in the process. They were taken away from their wives and children to go out and do the master's bidding. Whenever the master chose, he could freely go into the slave quarters and take any female. This was done in front of the man of the house, the children, whoever. Women were impregnated, and the slave-men had no control. They had to accept the new child to prevent alienation. It wasn't the fault of the child!

Inmates are forced to work, prove their loyalty to their master, and show their trustworthiness (to become a trustee). The inmate is beaten down emotionally and physically by the administration. He's talked down to and treated as less than human. An inmate starts out earning twenty-seven cents an hour and can work his way up to the maximum pay of forty-five cents. Only by working for a privately owned corporation can an inmate earn more, sometimes up to a dollar. While incarcerated, the inmates' wives, daughters, and girlfriends are targeted by other men. Depending on the amount of time he's got, there's a chance that his loved one may get into a new relationship and also get pregnant. Accepting that new child is hard. But the inmate eventually realizes that it was his own fault, since he's the one who got locked up. Maybe it was meant to be?

After being released, slaves had to relocate north. The reason for this was that they were not educated enough to keep themselves from being captured and enslaved by someone else. Even though freed slaves were given documents saying they were free, most didn't know how to read, write, or speak up for themselves.

After doing his time, the inmate reenters society. Maybe he spent his time getting his G.E.D. But even with a diploma, most inmates lack the knowledge and understanding it takes to survive. Whether or not he's on parole or probation, the inmate is tagged as an ex-felon. Like being a former slave in slave territory, the ex-offender will continue to be a target for incarceration. Very few people relocate after being released, but those who do often find renewed success after moving someplace else to start anew.

TERENCE

I am on a bus, with chains around my feet and hands. This is incarceration. This is what it's like to be locked up.

My thoughts are far away from what led up to this judgment. My life had been planned out! In college I was pre-law. I was supposed to be on the opposite side of these bars. Keeping people out of jail was supposed to be my calling. Now I'm in jail?

I have no name, just a number: 194947. All personal items are stripped from me and placed in a box. And there I lie: bare, exposed for any and all to see. Nothing prepared me for the experience. Nothing within a household of women could have prepared me for being placed in a room no bigger than a garage with twenty men, none of whom knows me by name.

Fear, anger, hurt—so many emotions run through my body, my mind. All the while it's enemy against enemy, rival against rival, friend against friend. I've seen it right before my eyes: five, six, seven people on one. I am to live, not die! To be a man! To have dominion!

I find love for my fellow man in prison, but then I'm face-to-face with niggers. I have to avoid niggers. Hood niggers, street niggers, punk niggers, real niggers. Only by being a nigger, I am told, can I survive. So I make the change: the passive becomes the aggressive. I channel the anger of all who said no. I hear my mother's voice in my head: "You're just like your father, a no-good nigger."

Every time you compromise something inside you, your spirit dies. Will I say all was bad? The answer is no. Learning to bond and make friends was just as important. I'm just more blessed by those who became friends. One of them was Kelvin Belton, who was already involved in this writing workshop. We have been a part of each other's lives for many years, though we never really knew one another until now. He was the one who asked me to be a part of this project. His reasoning could be abstract, even to him; we don't always understand that which we do. So I have come from disorder to order. From the seen to the unseen: faith.

Sure, I've been to prison. I've seen its structure, influence, maturity, and religion. I've seen a world within all worlds. Yet to be with Man in any world is to know you are strong, weak, caring, sharing. That's our true dominion. That's how I became an alpha male.

NAJI

Musa is about fifty. Because he's a Muslim and believes in a "spook God," I attempt to bash him intellectually. But everything I throw at him rolls back as if I have said nothing! I never get the same results with him that I did with the others. He just keeps talking: "You're too intelligent to be hanging with them guys. Why are you wasting your time? Have you ever actually read the Qur'an? What is your purpose?"

The questions come quicker than I can answer them. Then Musa smiles, implacable. I have no idea what to say to him, and my face shows it. "Just remember," he concludes, "no finite mind can comprehend that which is infinite."

"What the hell is that supposed to mean?" I say.

"Keep searching," he answers before walking off.

I begin telling myself that he's crazy, and start treating him so. But he never takes offense to my arrogance and disrespect. He remains soft-spoken and level-headed. Secretly I envy not only his demeanor, but his knowledge. He makes the most profound statements that leave me awed.

"Here," he says one day by my bunk.

"What is it?" I ask.

"This is the Qur'an." I have heard of the book and long to read it but am scared for some reason. I take it and put it under my bed.

"I'll get it from you in the morning," he says. I nod my head, looking around to see if one of the gods has spotted me taking the book. Later that night, when I am sure everyone is asleep, I reach under my bed and bring out the book.

It's dark in the dorm and the only light that I have is the soft moonlight flowing through the narrow window at the head of the bed. I hold the book up to the light. I'm fascinated by the ornate, gold, Arabic calligraphy on the cover, dancing, seemingly alive in the dark. I open it, not at the beginning, but somewhere midway. At the angle at which I am lying in the bed, the moonlight streams through the narrow window, catching a small section, illuminating a short verse. I begin reading.

O mankind! We created you from a single pair of a male and female, and made you into nations and tribes that ye may know each other, not that ye may despise each other. Verily the most honored of you in the sight of God is he/she who is the most righteous of you. And God has full knowledge and is well acquainted with all things.

By the time I finish reading the verse, tears are streaming in torrents down my face! My heart is beating furiously in my chest and I can't seem to control myself. Reflecting on the verse, I look up into the moonlight, and in an instant my whole life flashes before me in relationship to what I've just read. It hits me like a shotgun blast to the chest. This is it! This beautiful verse, so simple and clear, confirms what my soul knows to be true! My heart is drawn into its depths and purified in its wisdom. It is the most profound thing I have ever read.

Here is a God addressing not any particular group of people, but mankind as a whole, regardless of color or creed, nationality or religious affiliation. Unlike previous scriptures that I have read, this cannot be misconstrued. He is speaking directly to me through this verse, and I feel ashamed and chastised like a child when he states, "We made you into nations and tribes that you may know each other, not that you may despise each other." But I'm walking around, once again being a follower, denigrating the European man even though I know that most of what I am saying is untrue!

According to Allah, the standard for "all" mankind in "his" sight is righteousness. But I have been living my whole life seeking the approval of man. Tears continue to fall because I know I am home. It's a home where my father is always present, providing guidance and support; a home where my mother smiles at me, embracing me with unconditional love and nurturing me when I falter and fall; a home where I am safe and feel secure enough to express myself, knowing that I will be heard and understood; a home where I am given a purpose for living, where I can rise out of the ashes of ignorance, and through righteousness, become a model of human excellence.

Sitting up, I wipe my face and look around for someone to talk to. Everyone is asleep. But I am so excited! My heart instantly swells with love for Musa. He didn't know what he was doing by giving me the Qur'an. Or did he? I need to talk to him. But it's lights out and I'm not supposed to be out of bed.

I sneak past the cameras over to Musa's bunk. Kneeling by his side, I shake him and whisper his name.

He turns over and smiles at me. "Peace," he says groggily. "What's up, bro?"

"Yo, I read a verse in the Qur'an and something happened to me!" I say, almost unable to contain myself.

"Al—humid—llila" he responds. Recognizing my confusion, he smiles and translates, "All praises are due to Allah." He tells me that I better get back to my bunk before I catch a charge.

"OK, but I need to know: why were you so persistent trying to get me to read the Qur'an?"

He looks at me with a knowing smile. "Aki, Allah knows you better than you know yourself. It is his will that you are Muslim. He makes Muslims, I don't. I was just his instrument."

"I'm not Muslim," I say, looking at him strangely.

"When have you not been?" he responds. "Now get back to your bunk. We'll speak in the morning."

I read the Qur'an the rest of the night. And when the sun rises, recapturing the sky, so, too, do I begin re-capturing my life, epiphany after epiphany, shattering my perceptions of self, my past, my present, and my future. The lies of the world crumble to dust at my feet. Although I am a grown man, I feel like a baby entering kindergarten in the school of universal knowledge. After breakfast I head outside.

"My brother!" Musa calls me.

"Hold on! There's something I needed to do." At the cipher of the gods, where the group meets every morning, I take my place and listen to the customary introductions, where you state your attribute and how you see that day's reality.

When it's my turn, I say, "My name is James Canady and I renounce the Five-Percent Nation!" To renounce the Five Percent is an affront, especially in their presence. But I am being driven and I never think about my safety.

"Now cipher!" fifteen guys bark out in disbelief. "Show and prove God!"

I'm not prepared for an intellectual challenge, but I'm not backing down either. As I step into the center of the cipher, the circle closes on me. It is incredibly silent. Things will go from bad to worse if I fail to prove myself here. I will receive a "universal beat down." But standing in the circle and glancing at the hard, angry faces of men who just yesterday called me brother, a sense of calm falls over me. I realize what I will say.

"In the 1–10 lessons, the first question is 'Who is the Original man?' and the given answer is 'The original man is the Asiatic Black man; the Maker; the Owner; the Cream of the planet Earth—Father of Civilization, God of the Universe.' Since we all agree that God never forgets and is aware of all things, my question to all the gods is this: If we are the creators of the earth and the universe, how did we do it? If any god here can tell me, then I remain. If not, I leave in peace."

I leave the cipher un-molested, renewed, and on fire! Hungry for more Islam, I go to Musa and tell him that I am ready to take the *shahadah* (declaration of faith). It is given to me that Friday at Jumah (the Day of Assembly).

For the next ten years I become a student of life. Everything I learn in Islam has a direct connection to my past, present, and future. I pour myself into the faith. I have never been so enthused about anything in my life. I am quickly moving away from being a passive, open-minded individual and becoming an aggressively active-minded one, becoming aware for the first time of how important it is to scrutinize knowledge and information before accepting it as fact, especially knowledge and information that becomes the make-up of your understanding of who you are and your purpose for being here.

In 1993 I change my name to Naji Faruk Mujahid. It has nothing to do with any ancestors being stripped of their family names. I instinctually know that there are too many negative images and emotions tied to James Canady. And a name is so important to how we perceive ourselves, as well as how others perceive us. It is important to me that the name characterizes and sums up who I will soon become. It works out even better for me because the name is chosen for me by a couple of Muslim brothers who think the name fits my character. Naji means "compassionate friend." Faruq means "one who distinguishes truth from falsehood." Mujahid means "soldier in the cause of Allah."

KARL

On March 4, 2003, I was sentenced to forty years with thirty-three years suspended for assault and robbery. My life, or so I thought, was over. In the courtroom all I heard was "forty years," and then all thoughts fled me. Sweat covered me in an instant. I was nothing more than a mass of cells and tissues. "Forty years" echoed in my mind. I listened. But it grew weaker and weaker, and then it was gone and the world came rushing back to me: the noise, the smell of my lawyer's cologne, the judge sitting above me like a sultan, the sheriff tugging me by my arm, and me craning my neck toward my family. I remember saying "I love you" as I was hauled off, but this could be a fabrication. I'd like to think I said it.

Jail was a blur: it came and went like a bad dream. I mostly kept sane because I was in a block with one of my old friends from Virginia, who was in for drugs. At the receiving unit, I spent most of my time reading novels, trying to get lost in long trilogies and sagas—fantasies about great warriors, conquests, crusades, and empires. These were my escape from reality. They were also a roadblock, because I accomplished little else.

Then I picked up *The Sword of Truth* by Terry Goodkind. It was definitely one of the best books I have ever read, but aside from the depth and joy that I found in the story, there was something more. Somewhere in those pages, I realized that I was not being true to my nature. I had built a wall around my true self. All that I showed was an elaborate façade. I was living a lie with such investment, and it really hurt to let it go. I was eighteen years old, in prison, reading a novel.

OK, Mr. Black, I thought, time to get back to the basics. What did I enjoy that was productive, educational? Two things came to mind: the first was computers; the second, biology. When I was in elementary school, I would put everything under the microscope my dad had given me: water from various places, bugs, blood, leaves, etc. It was a whole new world down there! So, at the prison library, which was horribly outdated, I searched for biology books. I immersed myself in the intricacy and beauty of nature. I now tore into science books like they were novels. The fact that I was totally ignorant of the scientific process escaped me. I was convinced that the complexity of nature indicated purposeful design.

I began to associate with one person, my bunky. We would talk a bit every night about poetry, which he liked; our futures; and how I could make it through prison. I studied a lot, and many of the older guys observed this and applauded me. I think that's one of the reasons why I was left alone, because of the old heads. They recognized I was trying to better myself.

I noticed that a lot of the people who had problems consistently had one or more of the following characteristics: too many associates, always trying to be in the mix of what's going on, chasing the drama, not minding their own business, and trying to be in the spotlight. I tried my best to avoid these characteristics. I tried to keep my associates to a minimum. I mainly talked to those I lived with, but only once I got comfortable. In prison there are boundaries that must be defended, some with violence. I quickly learned that sometimes an old-fashioned rumble was necessary, but not always. I only got in four fights during my years of incarceration. It could have been twenty, but I learned to be a diplomat.

During this time, I came across some sophistry from the Institute of Creation Research and the Discovery Institute. I read their pamphlets promoting the irreducible complexity of nature and the fine-tuning of the cosmos, as well as their evidence for creation. I also read books on the matter, such as Michael Behe's *Darwin's Black Box*, Lee Strobel's *The Case for the Creator*, James Gills and Tom Woodward's *Darwinism Under the Microscope*, and William Dembski's arguments about being able to detect design using his explanatory filter.

Though this material did not lead me to Christianity, it did lead me to the conclusion that secular scientists were wrong and that evolution was false. I even wrote some essays about it and shared these ideas; acts that I am now ashamed of, not because I was wrong, overall, but because my belief was founded on insufficient evidence and fallacious reasoning. As I studied more, I began to realize that the creationist argument for intelligent design had some fraudulent claims, quotes out of context, more than a little vilification of evolutionists, and no credible scientific research or data in its corner.

I decided to expand my horizons and read philosophy, psychology, sociology, astronomy, cosmology, and other areas of science. I learned things about nature, people, and myself. From that experience, I learned that I valued learning and the development of the intellect, not as a means to something else, but as an honorable pursuit in and of itself.

After many months like this, debating and studying on my own, I decided to look into taking college courses. I quickly learned how difficult college courses are, and they were that much harder because I was in prison. I had to cope with noise, distractions, a lack of privacy, administrative setbacks due to security and bureaucracy, correctional officer hassles, and disruptions from security staff and other inmates.

The Virginia Department of Corrections likes to put forth a front of fostering higher education. But most facilities, especially the lower-security levels where people will shortly be going home, are extremely indifferent to the desires and needs of inmates looking to further their education. Computer access for typing papers is denied at most facilities. Library access is dismal. Testing is sporadic.

I am glad that I was bamboozled by that creationist literature, and even gladder that I detected it. It taught me to see the scientific quest to understand the universe as noble, and to believe that one of the greatest achievements I can accomplish is to contribute to an intellectual arena of humankind, to help educate people. Today I am an atheist, which I define as an objective, rational, and chiefly intellectual position that obligates me to be well-read, informed, naturally skeptical, and a disciplined critical thinker.

ANDRE

My plan was to continue living drug-free and crime-free, and to do that I had to replace the drugs and crime with something else. The void had to be filled.

After my first bid, I began working as a salesman and getting myself God-centered. I chose to be a salesman because I already knew I was able to sell drugs to every walk of life. And out there, the competition was fierce. So I had to formulate a plan, and sho-nuff have a nice talk-game. If I didn't use my gift of gab, the other hustlers in the game would have climbed aboard my back and rode me 'til I stumbled and fell, stealing my air, my strength, my aura. So becoming a salesman on the right side of the fence made pretty good sense to me.

"You must do the thing you think you cannot do," Eleanor Roosevelt once said. I applied for the job, knowing I was a convicted felon, but I made the affirmation, and guess what? I got it and flourished! I became the best salesman GHH & Associates ever had. The boss even gave me the keys to the warehouse to run his business.

Change is an inside job, and slowly, I built awareness into my life. I learned to check my behaviors at the door. You can make a wish or you can make it happen, and I finally decided to make it happen. But immediately, peer pressure attacked me. I didn't want to be labeled a chump (aka "wanting to live right"), so I made drug deals. But I still held fast to not using the drugs. When I was by myself, though, I realized that I couldn't do wrong no more.

In time, I stopped, and the wrong truly subsided in my life. But I didn't have anyone to share it with. I didn't know how to meet new friends. So after work

I'd just drive around in my car by myself. LaKeisha and I would go to bingo or shopping. Our sex life was off the chain! All of her girlfriends took a liking to me and called me their big brother. But my girlfriend at the time was just that. I needed friends.

On those days when I was feeling alone, I drove over to Jackson Ward to visit with people I knew. But it really didn't fill me up, because they weren't my best friends. I would park my car by the graveyard and reminisce about my true brothers: Donnell, Weasel, and Toad. But the thoughts didn't last too long.

One day my car was unavailable. I could have caught a cab home or even the city bus. But I didn't.

All I was doing was chilling on my sister's porch when Lil' Darryl, Tiny, and Pete pulled up and asked me, "What's up?" I said I was getting ready to go home, and the ride thing came up. Now, where was my Lil' Dre to come to mind and say, "No, Dre, do not get in that car!" It was only a fifteen-minute ride, but in five minutes and a few seconds, the unthinkable happened.

It was nighttime on the Manchester Bridge. Police sirens and flashing lights hit the car's back window. My heart sank and I said to myself, "I have to be lucky all the time and the police just has to be lucky once." We didn't stop. Lil' Darryl threw his gun out of the window, and the police car behind us rammed us, and our vehicle almost went over the bridge into the unforgiving James River. But Tiny, a female, had Jeff Gordon NASCAR driving skills and got us off that bridge.

After that I just wanted the car to stop. But the police had a roadblock waiting at the end of the bridge and she drove right through it. Now I really felt I was in a Hollywood movie. I had experienced a lot of things in life, but never a police chase! The car finally stopped, and my heart was beating like the drums at the Gold Bowl game. Lil' Darryl and Pete got away, but they caught Tiny after just a block.

I got out of the car. It was a pretty Volvo four-door. I don't remember the color, but I knew it was totaled. I went to the police with my hands up, letting the officer know who I was. "My name is Andre Simpson, and I was just a passenger." The police was pointing a black 9 mm pistol at my head. He struck me on the side of the face, yelling, "Shut the fuck up!" I went to the ground. Then I was hit and kicked. More hits and kicks came when more police officers came to assist the first officer. I was placed in those old, familiar, cold silver bracelets and beaten unconscious.

When I woke up, I was lying on the floor in a room at the Richmond police station on West Grace Street, handcuffed, with the majority of my clothing removed—and mind you, this was in December. My face, ear, and leg were swollen. My rectum was also hurting and bleeding. They did an illegal cavity search, looking for drugs, when I was unconscious.

I immediately started complaining, asking what the hell they had done to me. No one would answer my pleas. No one. Then four different officers came into that cold, empty interrogation room. It looked like a padded cell for crazy people. They were asking all sorts of questions, like, *Where were you in the car? Who were the other two people who got away? Give us the names. We saw you throw the gun out the window.* I told them I wasn't driving, and that I just got in the car to get a ride home. Then I come to find out the car was reportedly stolen and had been in numerous robberies, and another gun was in the car.

Instead of the police focusing on catching the cats, they focused more on me. They let Tiny go home. Then they took me into another room, asking me more of the same questions. Police misconduct was not even the tip of the iceberg of what was to happen to me next. They asked me if I would give them my DNA if I had nothing to hide. I agreed. They had pictures, a gun, a hockey mask, and a coat. None of them mine. They started yelling, "You are the one!" and shoved the mask in my face. Then they beat me unconscious again. When I got to city lockup, I tried reporting all this and asked to be seen by medical, but no one would hear my pleas.

I was given two gun charges, three hit-and-runs, one robbery charge, resisting arrest, felony eluding, possession of a firearm in commission of a robbery, driving with a suspended license (I had a restricted license), and three counts of grand larceny. But now I had violated my parole, and I was sent back to prison.

The whole ordeal showed me that I don't need to revisit my old hood or miss any part of it. I still hadn't used, but it seemed God wanted to use me again, to show me that my life can go from good to bad if I try to mix good with evil, even if they are only thoughts.

Before I got in that car, I was still with LaKeisha and working two jobs: selling computer furniture, and delivering pizza at night. But having a relationship on the streets is different than it is in prison, because on the streets our communication skills didn't develop, so our relationship couldn't grow. I got her pregnant, but she never told me, and as time went on she got herself an abortion and never told me. I was clueless—had no idea—because I was working my two jobs, and when I got around her she was normal. So I believed everything was normal. Did her girlfriends know and didn't tell their big bro? What about her mother and her sister?

She told me the heartbreaking news when I got locked up on December 14, 2005, and she did it over the phone. Her reason was that she felt that *I* wasn't ready. My heart turned cold on her instantly. I hated loving her, knowing her. I even hated my auntie for introducing us. She was still on the phone explaining why, but I was in another world. I didn't hear the rest of what she said. But God was still with me, and through my growth and commitment to keeping my life in order, I forgave her and wished her nothing but favor in her life and in the lives of her three children. After I got locked up, months later, she got pregnant by someone else, and I heard she had that baby! The emotions I went through at the time only made this warrior stronger. I even wrote her a letter wishing her well with her new baby.

I was placed on Tier E-2 with one-hundred-plus inmates. I was facing thirteen charges. I had a parole violation. I was trying to heal up from my wounds, and I was trying to secure a bond. Usually when I got locked up, I would have to go through withdrawal, but I was drug-free this time and it surprised the dudes that knew me there. Instead of lying in my bunk under the covers and being looked after by the other guys, who would talk to me and give me sweets and pain pills because they had just gone through it themselves, I went straight into my killer mode of defending myself against all those charges.

* * *

July 30, 2007

Dear Dave,

It was nice to hear from you, and as always and when this letter reaches you, I know it's going to find you, your family, and your students blessed and highly favored. As for myself, I am blessed and highly favored. I love my story and what you wrote.

Dr. Coogan, a lot of bad has occurred in my life, and a lot of good as well. And one of my daily affirmations that I got from the gospel singer Yolanda Adams was "My Best is Coming, Starting Today." When I started this writing project, it truly opened up another positive side of me, and I'm remembering a lot of my past life, so this is a truly wonderful experience for me. Sometimes I be wondering to myself how the people I know are going to react when they read my story. Because a lot of this is a first-time sharing experience for me.

The sanity of my father is unknown. He looks like a black Bin-Laden, the hair and the beard. As for my mother, she just seems to not pick the right men, even after my daddy, but I think she really got one now.

So you drove past the house? My room was where those three little windows upstairs were. I used to sit there and stare out the window, looking at all the cars go up and down Chimborazo Blvd. This is a small world, my friend. You live right across from my old elementary school!

Dave, I will introduce you to Squeaky, the guy from Harvey's Progressive Barber Shop. I want you to see firsthand.

Listen, you tell your student, Clementine, I don't want her to ever leave the project. It's an honor to have her and her skills. I'm not disappointed or angry that those kids stole her stuff with my drafts in there. I got more work for her to type up. :) And tell her to be safe and careful and that she's in my prayers. Tell your new students that I said hello, and their thought for today is "Never try to figure out the mazes, just the mice."

I agree our project can reach a big audience, Dave. I see Naji is recruiting. I like that. Tell him and the rest of the guys that I said what's up and keep writing. We got a real moment going on, Dave. I'm telling you. I am so excited about this. When I write my sister, I'm going to put a letter in there for Anton. He needs to come back to the project. I believe when he went into the system, he lost focus. In the system it's quick to happen. It came at me, but I fought it and I won. I'll get some type of contact info on him. Dave, we do have a whole lot of feet to push our Flintstone car!

Your friend,
Dre

16

DREAMS OF CHANGE

"I'm still scrambling," Naji tells me over the phone. After finally getting an interstate compact for his probation and parole, he's moved to Phoenix to be with his fiancée. "You know, looking for a job, doing my coursework to become a substance abuse counselor. Oh, and I'm pretty much my grandmother's full-time caretaker. She's got Alzheimer's."

He reports it all with the weariness of knowing well the routine. I hear him walking through the apartment. A faucet cuts on. I try to imagine what he sees—a courtyard? The bedroom door where his grandmother is sleeping? His notes and books?

"So it's just you two together during the day?"

"Yeah, while my fiancée's at work." The water stops. He pulls a quick drink.

It sinks in what this must mean for Naji, all alone with his ailing grandmother day in and day out. All alone with his memories of how she tormented him and his brother growing up—memories that she no longer shares. "You can't talk with her about the past," I say.

"Nah, nah. She doesn't know what's going on." He takes another drink. I spin my chair to face the window and search the horizon, as if my eyes might reach Phoenix somehow.

I hear him set the cup down and I ask, "Do you sometimes think maybe it's better this way, not being able to get any closure on it?"

"Ahh! I've thought so much about that!" Then, more quietly, "I think about that all the time, actually." We each take an end of this puzzle, like two guys moving a delicate and heavy bureau up a narrow staircase.

"I mean, it's hard not knowing," I say, "but if she still had her wits, she still might not say sorry—or even acknowledge that it happened."

"Exactly!" And then he drops it. "How's Gina?"

"You remember Gina?" I'm surprised. Gina was a student who took Prison Literature, the course I created on campus to connect students like her and Clementine to this workshop and, more broadly, the field of prison literature. In the first few years of the course, I had asked students to take turns typing up the men's drafts—a popular assignment that exerted a quiet influence, this typing, dwelling on the writer's choices and the hard conditions they faced in life.

"Yeah, I remember her. She was the one whose place got broken into. She typed up my story about breaking and entering."

"And you wrote her a letter to say sorry—you know, that her stuff got stolen."

"Right, right." He pauses to reflect. "She was sharp. She worried sending me to prison wasn't going to help me solve my problems—to understand the things that trigger my addiction." He trails off in the memory. "Tell her I said hi!"

"Anything else?" In the pause that follows, I hear the emptiness of the apartment on the other end of the line.

"That I'm maintaining. For now."

Naji

Soon after my return to the drug world, I found myself behind bars once again. In 1991 I was sentenced to nineteen years for a couple of B & Es[16] and grand larceny charges stemming from my drug use. When I was asked before sentencing if there was anything that I wanted to say, I found it very frustrating. I was being asked to show cause—why I shouldn't be prosecuted to the fullest extent of the law. And I was about to be lectured on taking personal responsibility and not blaming anyone for the decisions I'd made.

I said that all my life, I had been hoping and praying for the "system" to come to my aid and rescue me from the abuse that I was suffering at the hands of my grandparents. No one seemed concerned when I spoke about the many days I went to school with bloody welts on my back. What about the personal responsibility of those who were charged with looking into the child abuse I went through? Was I being told as an adult that I was personally responsible for the abuse I suffered as a child, or was I being told that, although abuse may have been present, I was over eighteen and considered an adult, so none of that really mattered, because I knew stealing and drug using were wrong?

A very dear friend of mine was there to speak on my behalf. She was someone who had always been there for me when things were really rough. If it weren't for her speaking up on my behalf and providing the courts an intimate look at my life growing up in an abusive home, I would have been sentenced to much more time than I received.

Still, it's a very scary and intimidating experience for a black man to stand up in a courtroom and try to explain his actions to judges who have a fear of being

_____

16 Breaking and enterings.

perceived as soft on crime and who believe and support, without any personal vision, the idea of personal responsibility. After my bumbling attempt and the attempt of my friend, who went into more detail, I was sentenced to thirty-something years suspended, except nineteen.

As I stood there receiving the sentence, I felt like that little boy getting the blood beat out of him for wrinkling the place rug. Every beating, every harsh word, every put-down, every racial slur, all the indifference to my suffering growing up hit me in that moment, and a tear rolled down my face. As I looked back at my grandparents sitting in the courtroom before I was led away in shackles and handcuffs, what I registered in their eyes stung like a scorpion . . . nothing.

In 2002 I was released and quickly found out that the depth of my dysfunction was far deeper than I had assumed. Once again I made the mistake of assuming that if I just educated myself on financial matters more, or maybe got a trade, I would make it. I was overlooking the phantoms at the very edges of my consciousness: pain, anger, and resentment. Those three unresolved issues brought me back once again to where I sit now: Indian Creek Correctional Center (Civigenics Therapeutic Community). My violation, once again, was for involvement with drugs.

Coming home from prison in '02 straight into a serious relationship that I had begun months earlier was probably the first mistake I made in my attempt to remain free, both physically and chemically. The first few months out were rocky, but I had expected as much from times previous. It was hard finding employment. I had relocated to a new city, thinking that maybe a change in my surroundings would give me a fresh start. So problems with finding my way around and with transportation arose. I accepted help from my fiancée, but it bothered me that I had to rely on her so much. It was a challenge to my ego.

"Don't put a lot on your plate." That's what I had heard from the facilitators of the brief "life skills" class that you're made to attend before you're released from the Department of Corrections. This was a feeble attempt to give an inmate, in a few weeks, what should have been mandatory throughout his years of incarceration. Even still, that particular adage rang true in a very direct way.

My grandmother had become ill during my incarceration. I was unaware of how ill until I came home to find her living in squalor. At seventy, dementia had set in, and her once-immaculate house was in such a mess, it was hard for me to believe that it was her home. When I saw her, underweight, feeble, and filthy, lying in a bed of food crumbs and roaches, unwashed, with thick cobwebs hanging over her bed, I couldn't believe it! My heart immediately went out to her. I completely forgave her for all the things she had done to me. Mercy settled into my heart as I considered her life.

When she became pregnant with my mother at a young age, my grandmother left North Carolina. I've recently found out that her leaving may have been an attempt to escape the shame of rape by a family member. The complete details, I'm still probing. It seems a family secret.

When she went to New York to visit her aunt, and her aunt caught a glimpse of her coming down the street with a baby in her arms and, most likely, loaded down with whatever she could carry from her old life, her aunt screamed out to her, "You can't stay here!" But my grandmother explained that she'd only come to visit, to give them the opportunity to see the child. In that case, they told her, she was welcome. But being so rejected and hurt, not to mention embarrassed, she declined and turned around and left. She has never seen or talked to her aunt again. After that particular incident, she always concluded when she told this story to anyone who would listen, that she learned never to ask anybody for "shit."

Seeing her suffer, I knew I had to do something. My fiancée, also seeing my grandmother's condition, was the first to suggest that she come to live with us in Richmond. I was more than willing to take care of her. I really credit my fiancée for helping me with setting up her medical care. I took on the responsibility as her power of attorney. She became my ward. I soon found a job, and my schedule became hectic for both my fiancée and myself. I was up every morning at about 4:00 a.m., preparing myself for work and my grandmother for adult day care. It was a tedious routine to which I quickly became accustomed. It made me feel manly, taking care of her.

But trying to mold myself into a responsible family man, I lost focus on the foundation that I had been building before I was released from prison. I had told myself that the first real place I would go, even before I went home, would be the *masjid* (Islamic temple). This didn't happen. On some level, I became intimidated by my own faith. I remember my fiancée trying to encourage me to go to Jumah on one particular Friday. I offered some excuse as to why I couldn't go, but the real reason was that I was afraid of the responsibility of being a Muslim, as I understood it, in a non-Muslim society.

One of the most attractive tenets in Islam to me is the strict rule against intoxicants of any kind. Yet part of my socialization coming up was to "party" on the weekends. I didn't realize how ingrained that was in my psyche until I was released, trying to live a "drug-free, party-free" lifestyle. I found it difficult to associate having fun with clean living. Domestic problems began to arise at home. I was also attending night classes for welding. I wanted a better life for myself and my fiancée. But the stresses of everyday life began to weigh on my shoulders and it became harder to fight off the call to "Fuck it!" and go get high, to have some fun. This is how I had been conditioned in life, even though I knew that it went against what I now believed.

This contradiction is an internal struggle that I've now come to understand as a quintessential aspect of what it means to be Muslim. Jihad: to struggle. It's a tradition that the Prophet gave us after returning from war. He said, "Now that the battle is over, the greater struggle begins." One of his followers, who was unable to comprehend what could be a greater struggle than the one from which they had just returned, asked the Prophet, "What is the greater struggle?" and the Prophet replied, "The struggle with self."

I made a semi-conscious decision to put my responsibilities as a Muslim on the back burner. In doing so, I effectively cut myself off from the very help I needed at the time. I also felt guilty that I wasn't living up to the Islamic ideal I had created while incarcerated. Instead of "struggling" and relying on Allah's wisdom and the Prophet's example, I relied on myself. In doing that, I fell back into old ways and actions.

I have attempted to live by the principals of Islam in the past and failed miserably, not because of anything lacking in the tenets, but because of my own dysfunction. The comprehensive nature of the faith proved to be a bit much for the irresponsible, undisciplined life I had led up to that point. Replacing old ideas, thoughts, and beliefs was easy compared to changing the behaviors that correspond to those beliefs. This is where I found myself stumbling.

* * *

Indian Creek Correctional Center is hailed as Virginia's prize jewel in therapeutic rehabilitation within the Department of Corrections, and indeed, it is the largest therapeutic community inside prison walls anywhere in the world. On paper, the facility seems quite impressive. In real life, it resembles a large military compound set in the middle of rolling green hills of what is mostly rural farm country. This is indicative of the prison industrial complex when it comes to providing jobs to economically struggling communities in mostly white rural areas in America.

The camp is made up of six large dormitories painted beige and green. Each holds approximately four hundred inmates. Back in high school, during black history month, we had these posters of slave ships plastered all over the walls, with slaves aligned in tight rows foot to head down the length of the ship. The steel bunk beds at ICCC are set up side by side, sparing only two feet of space between them, and are painted the same drab beige to match the color scheme of the buildings.

At the head of each bed, attached to the sides, are old, stand-up gym lockers for storing personal items. This is the extent of living space that exists in the dorm, other than the two open areas at the front of the building that are reserved for watching TV and program meetings. Strangely, the buildings also resemble large airplane hangars reconfigured for the warehousing of human beings. For some reason, the two descriptive analogies seem to meld, creating, in my mind, a uniform, cohesive message. I wonder if old prejudices are at play in my thought process, or if I am being as objective as I can be.

On a daily basis, certain counselors praise the program, while others secretly let it be known to inmates that the program is full of shit! Every other week, dignitaries from various political affiliations locally and from around the world are paraded through the facility, and the whole inmate population is forced to put on a show that gives the impression that the camp is being well run and operated just like the private company, Civigenics, and the Virginia Department of Corrections claim. The reality is starkly antithetical to this.

I am one of the few here willing to open myself up to the reality that I have a problem. No denial! I am actually looking forward to educating myself about the dichotomous arguments relating to addiction and how they have, or have not, affected my own perception of the criminal drug lifestyle that I have been a part of for most of my juvenile and adult life. It isn't surprising to encounter inmates at ICCC who love that the program allows them to continue the vices that exist in every prison across the nation: drugs, gambling, prostitution, and extortion. But it's maddening that there is no real effort by the administration to stop the flow of drugs and other paraphernalia deemed contraband. How can a therapeutic facility be so infested by drugs and drug use? It's crazy! I almost feel like I am back on the "block."

Civigenics seems incapable of maintaining staff that care about their profession enough to keep a job for more than three to six months. The turnover rate is so high that inmates hardly have a chance to speak with a counselor. Counselors either quit because they are morally opposed to the fraud taking place in the name of a profession they're passionate about, or they are fired for "fraternizing" with the inmates. I think both groups would agree that the program is more about the funds it receives for each inmate forced into the program by the Department of Corrections than it is about the lives of the inmates who could actually be helped by drug counseling.

I don't want to sound like a disgruntled inmate trying to tear down the "system" by bad-mouthing their program—which is what the administration accuses me of—but once I begin to grieve about what I perceive to be a waste of time and taxpayer money (if they only knew!), I begin to view my own drug problem in a much broader context. It becomes clear to me that not only am I a perpetrator, but I'm a victim as well. I'm not a victim of a drug culture that fell upon me somehow, leaving me without any choices—I'm more like a victim of a system out of control, one that profits off the unfortunate mistakes and bad decisions I have made.

In no time, I begin to find myself at odds with prison officials, Civigenic staff, and inmates who haven't made the decision to turn their lives around and would rather be allowed to "*do their thing*" during and after therapy hours. I file numerous institutional grievances concerning the lack of adequate drug treatment and counseling, which is a shock to the staff. But why should it be? Hints are often given to inmates during speeches given by correctional authorities and Civigenic staff that to get through the program you have to "fake it till you make it" or "see and don't see," basically directing us to concentrate more on going through the motions.

Inmates are promoted to pseudo positions such as dorm coordinator or assistant dorm coordinator based solely on their ability to keep other inmates in check. It is necessary to have eyes and ears in the dorm after staff leave for the day, to report any dissension in the ranks, such as bad-mouthing the program, a capital offense that could have you stripped of your accumulated good time and sent to a more secure, restrictive prison.

Some of these inmates are brainwashed into believing that they are instrumental to the success of the program, but for the most part, the inmates chosen for these artificial positions understand the game and put on a show for staff and visitors when necessary. There are certain benefits that come along with these positions, such as being able to move around freely, which is vital for trafficking drugs throughout the compound. It is no secret that the so-called leaders of the community are just faking it to make it. It is a spectacle to see these same men stand before the community, espousing how they have changed, chastising other inmates who are not committing themselves to change, and then, later in the evening, after the ICCC staff has left for the day, smoking weed or gambling on the yard.

Visitors from all over the country come to the facility to see how it is run. This is when the real comical exhibition begins. The day before, the population is notified through the dorm counselors. We are told to be on our best behavior. There's a flurry of activity all over the compound. New towels and sheets are passed out to replace the dirty, dingy, ripped-up ones. Food that is never seen in the chow hall is passed out, giving the impression that we are being fed healthy meals all the time. Floors are buffed to a glass finish. But I should point out that the floors are always important. If the floors aren't shiny at all times, the dorm could lose all its privileges. Every dorm has an inmate that does nothing but buff the floors all day. These inmates are treated like royalty and are vied for and coveted by staff.

After the visitors leave, dorms are given points designed to reward those who acted in accordance with the wishes of the warden. These points accumulate over a month's period and the dorm with the most points at the end of the month is given the opportunity to order pizza or whatever fast food the dorm agrees upon, purchased with their own money of course. I can't understand these men degrading themselves like fools for petty rewards! Although I follow the rules and am considered a model inmate, I never allow myself to be played like a puppet. I find no value in anything the administration offers for my obedience.

Before I arrived, the person who seemed to be heading up the fight was Tony, or T. Martin, as he was called by other inmates. Shortly after arriving at ICCC, I needed help filing a grievance against a correctional officer (CO) who decided that because of his position of authority over me, he could cuss me out for asking him a simple question. I was told by another inmate that if I wanted to do something about the CO, I needed to talk to Tony, and that he could be found in the library. Because of the negative attitudes of most COs, I hated going to the security booth and asking for anything, including a pass to the library. In this particular case, though, I didn't have much choice.

I found Tony at the library, doing legal research on Civigenics.

"Yo, what's up, man? My name is Naji."

"Peace, bruh," he replied, standing, offering his hand. I immediately became aware of the suspicious glances from a couple of nosy inmates hoping to eavesdrop on our conversation. If it wasn't for Tony's clean-cut demeanor and wide smile, he could easily be perceived as an intimidating figure. It is indeed rare to see a person with a jovial attitude in prison, a trait that you are conditioned to view suspiciously, because as a rule in penitentiary, behind every smile is an ulterior motive. We sat down to talk quietly, and I explained my problem to him.

"I need to file a grievance on an officer for cussing me out."

Sliding back in his chair, he offered me a knowing smile. "That type of thing happens a lot here. This place is run very unprofessionally." In the next few minutes Tony filled me in on how corrupt ICCC actually was. On the table between us was a large pile of folders and manila envelopes. As we talked, Martin sifted through the pile to show me the evidence he had collected to back up his assessment of ICCC. Before we knew it, it was time to leave, and I found myself fascinated by what Martin had shared with me. But I was released before I could do anything about it.

* * *

I leave Indian Creek Correctional Center on September 17, 2008. It's an overcast morning. Expectations are high. Before leaving the facility, I am given the opportunity to address the therapeutic community I have been sharing my life with for the last two years. Immediately, as I approach the square, I am struck by a sense of grief that catches me completely off guard! This is supposed to be the happiest day of my life, yet here I am, feeling like I've lost my best friend. Looking at the ninety-plus faces staring back at me with indifference and agitation for having to assemble, I instantly feel an overwhelming empathy tinged with outrage.

The stress of trying daily to maneuver through this façade to obtain the treatment that I was sent here to receive has taken a toll on me. My physical and mental health have suffered. Doing the time is hard enough. But when you're being forced to participate in a prison-run program that is corrupt and basically operated and controlled by inmates, living by the same criminal drug lifestyle rules and expectations that you are running from, the stress is multiplied exponentially. What will happen to these men when they leave? When will the next generation of men who fill these bunk beds and polish these floors be challenged to do more than just fake it till they make it?

TONY

I am getting ready to open up a bag to receive my morning fix, just standing out there behind the local community center, when Motion, one of my boyz, walks up to me and asks what I'm doing. I tell him I'm going to sniff me a bag of heroin, to get the monkey off my back. He then tells me that he's tried mixing heroin and cocaine, forming what is known as a speedball. He wants to mix one right there. I agree. I understand that my heart will be subjected to an unnatural and unknown substance that will cause it to beat faster or slower than what it is used to. It's odd, but I've never really enjoyed getting high on just one drug. That's why, whenever I do cocaine, I will always have some type of alcoholic beverage to eliminate some of the paranoia that cocaine causes. And whenever I get high off heroin, I will have some cocaine present, because I don't enjoy the sleepy feeling, nor do I want the people around me to recognize that I am high on heroin by the head nodding.

We start to pass the bag of cocaine back and forth, trying to get the quantity down before we mix in the heroin, when an undercover narcotics vice officer approaches. I'm holding the bag of cocaine in my left hand, clinching it with my thumb, checking the seal.

"Excuse me, sir, can I speak with you?"

I quickly lower my hands. "Am I wanted? Do you have a warrant for my arrest? Am I under arrest?"

"No, no, and no." After he says the last no, I inform him that I do not wish to talk to him because I have to get back to work. I start walking away. That's when the foot chase begins. Of course, the odds are stacked against me because I have Timberland boots on, the boots are untied, my belt isn't tight (so I have to hold my pants up as I run), and I am sick because I have not yet had my heroin.

"Run, Tony, run!" the onlookers cheer. I run my sick little heart out, spinning on the vice officer, causing him to stumble into oncoming traffic. That buys me some time, but not enough. Several feet away from freedom, my legs lock up, my forward movement stops, and I hit the pavement. I try to hurry and get back up, but my legs won't move, so I helplessly watch as the vice officer slowly and tirelessly approaches me with his gun drawn. Not caring, and unaware of the danger I am putting myself into, I grab his arms in a last-ditch effort to get away by trying to sling him to the ground. I give it a good try, but my legs don't agree with the plan, so I stop tussling and comply with his command to roll over onto my stomach and lie still.

The vice officer uses his walkie-talkie to radio for help, which comes in the form of a uniformed police officer. They attempt to do an illegal search of my buttocks, pulling my boxers and pants down while I'm handcuffed, but that's foiled by the shouts of displeasure from the onlookers.

"You can't do that to him!" they say over and over. The officers abort that unlawful search and instead place me into the backseat of the patrol car. The first stop is to see the magistrate, where the narcotics officer goes to get a search warrant authorized. At the jail, they escort me to an isolated area and give me a direct order to remove all articles of clothing. I remove them as ordered. They then tell me to lift up my feet, so they can see the soles, then kneel down and cough, then bend over and spread my cheeks. I spread them a little bit, but they aren't satisfied. "Wider!" they shout. That's when I tell them that if they want them spread any wider, they will have to get the nurse, who has been observing the entire procedure. They deny my request and decide to get six deputies to assist them. When they arrive, they place me into handcuffs and shackles. I am totally nude.

One of the more humble deputies, who just so happens to be black, pleads with me to give them whatever I have so that the remaining five deputies, who all happen to be white, won't do what they are so eager to do. As he speaks, two other deputies, both around six-foot-five and a collective three hundred pounds, tell him to stop asking me, because they are going to get what they're looking for. I honor the challenge by telling the black deputy that I ain't *giving* them nothing! Then all the deputies put on black leather gloves and lay me on my stomach, directly on the cold concrete floor, handcuffs, shackles, and all. They try to pry open my buttocks, but their triceps and biceps are no match for buns of steel!

The same deputy that tried to talk me into making things easy on myself tells the other ones to stop because their aggressive method isn't working. He tells them to simply bend my legs so that the soles of my feet are touching the back of my head. It's as if they have suddenly been given a magic key, because as soon as they lift my legs, one of the officers simply reaches down and retrieves the heroin and cocaine from my buttocks. I have it wrapped in a piece of brown paper bag so he can't really see how much or what type of drugs it is. He walks around the corner out of my view, but I know when he's inspected the package, because he lets out a loud "Yee-haw!" of amazement.

There were times when I dreamed of making a positive change. But in 1997, when I was introduced to heroin, my days of being able to choose whether or not I'd get high were over. Heroin, I quickly found out, isn't only a drug that enslaves its victims mentally, but destroys them physically as well. There were times when I wouldn't get high off of crack for a few weeks because my willpower was stronger than the urge. But after a few weeks of constantly using heroin, I found myself experiencing bodily pains that made me get out of bed and go to the block. I had two choices: suffer stomach pains, a runny nose, and loss of my appetite, or go and risk my life and liberty to ease the pain and suffering.

DEAN

I'm staring straight up at the stars, suckin' on all the air I can, because it's hard to breathe with a bullet in your chest. One of my friends is telling me to hold on, to keep fighting, to think about my daughter; but at the same time, he's cryin' and holdin' me, wishing he could help. But it's in God's hands now.

I had the opportunity to kill the pussy motherfucker that shot me in the chest. Back in my younger, wilder days, when I didn't have a family, I wouldn't have even given a second thought about blasting this dude in the face, but I had to think about my daughter, and the baby on the way. Plus, was he worth doing twenty or thirty years in prison?

It's puzzling to me that after all these years of earning respect from my peoples, I still think I have to prove my toughness. When you're getting money from the drug trade, you begin to think that you're invincible and that people idolize you. But in reality, they don't want to see you do good. They talk behind your back. They think about hurting you, robbing you, calling the cops on you. They don't think twice about shooting at you. Over the years, I've been stabbed, hit with a baseball bat, had both arms broken and a leg too! I've been shot three different times in my life. Each time was because of some stupid-ass macho behavior.

There have been so many times when I wanted so badly to change the way I lived and my way of thinking. I knew I had to do things differently after prison, but something always seemed to get in the way. I needed money (no job). I needed a place to stay that I could call my own (not enough money). I needed a better-paying job (no car). I could go on for a hot minute, but I think you get the picture. I wonder about the craziest shit sometimes, like: *How do some people get the breaks that they need to get out of certain situations? Why didn't I get any? How come other people catch the luck of the draw when I work so hard at trying to move up in life but can't seem to get a foothold?*

I wanted the house on the big hill. I wanted the cash. I wanted the hottest cars and celebrity status. I wanted the world. I think that's where a lot of my mistakes came in. I didn't focus my attention on the bigger picture, which was education, and I didn't take full advantage of the opportunities that the Lord set before me. Instead I wanted to run the streets and follow behind my friends. I truly believe that God gives everyone special talents, but you must use what he gives you so that you may help others in need.

If I had played football or basketball, my life would've turned out totally different. I was clever using my hands as far as putting things together without instructions, too. The thing that killed me was that I didn't like to listen or take constructive advice, and I was in love with Harlem. I wasted half my life chasing a dream and putting my family through shit when I was smart enough to do something with myself. I never even got a chance to make my dad proud of my talents before the cancer took his life.

Kelvin

In November of 1992, I have just finished doing ten months for possession of cocaine. I am back in Dodge City, living with my son's mother and her family. I have the money to do what I want. I have my girl, my kids, and family to spend it on, but it just don't feel right. I go the club, get four numbers, make about $2500 dollars. I'm getting my share of women and fun with all the people I've groomed in the game, but I'm feeling just about as empty as can be.

The next night, I'm smoking some good weed on the porch when this guy I know pulls up in his red Jeep Cherokee. I jump up off the porch and tell him to give me a ride to the Chevron on Chamberlayne Avenue so I can get some snacks for me and my girl. That's when "Silent Night" comes on the radio. Even though I don't feel right, I still love my song, and I stay in the car to sing along.

I barely get through the first verse. *Now* I know why I wasn't feeling my same old feelings! Twenty-eight days after coming home and I have to deal with the Man again? Should I have jumped out as soon as I saw them blue lights behind me? Maybe I should have stayed in the house from the beginning? Does it really make a difference how I get locked up again? Can we change God's design? No. Destiny is already written and there's not a damn thing any of us can do about it.

You see, I don't really believe in luck. So when it comes to my problems with the police and with drugs, I believe it was fate. Or maybe karma: you get back what you give out. If you do bad, you get bad. I've always had these beliefs. But as you get older you think about things like this more. I wasn't feeling right that night on Chamberlayne because I knew inside that my story wasn't over. There were more chapters in God's big book for me to open up.

BRAD

It wasn't easy looking in the mirror. I had zero self-respect, zero dignity, and zero hope. I was six feet tall, 135 pounds—a walking skeleton by all accounts. Eating was a luxury I couldn't afford while using. I was sick, lonely, broke, scared, lost, hungry, and tired. I was tired of my life, of the person I had become. I was spiritually, mentally, and physically tapped—completely empty and ready to die. I didn't have one penny, one friend, one place to go, not a single supporting family member. They and the rest of the world had wiped their hands clean of me.

I was getting ready to repeat the daily misery once again, as I had every day during recent years—lying, stealing, and manipulating my way to my next fix. But then something came over me. A conversation I'd had with Colleen played like a tape loop in my head, along with flashbacks of our children and family. I'm not doing it! I just can't do it anymore! I would rather go and do twenty years in prison than keep living the way I'm living! I quickly panhandled fifty cents and called my mother's friend and asked him if he would please take me to the police.

After I got my sentence—fifty months—I decided I was going to do whatever it took to change my life. I began to work an honest and open program. I called it Complete Life Change. I was born again to Christ on June 20, 2004, at 9:25 p.m. My life once again had purpose. Even the prison food tasted good. Truly, I became freer behind razor wire than I ever was when I was on the outside.

Everything I had gone through was for a reason, I thought. Through the Word of God and the teachings of the twelve-step programs (NA and AA), along with the guidance of the Holy Spirit, I was transforming. I was learning to live life clean, on life's terms. And I was enjoying it! Lying, cheating, stealing, and manipulating transformed into being honest, trustworthy, caring, kind, loyal, and most of all, giving.

Every person who knew me and loved me let out a big sigh of relief. Even my mother let that hard wall come down. When prison became a reality, she was there for me. My mother got the chance to watch me grow all over again. She could see the changes in our visits and letters. In fact, all of my family could see it, as they were able to talk to the corrections officers and executive staff on a daily basis to hear how I was doing and to find out who I was becoming. When I turned myself in, I got honest with myself for the first time.

17

Character Witness

It's a strange experience to be subpoenaed: the deputy finding me in my office at the university and finding himself unable to resist grinning as he hands me the paper and utters the famous phrase, "You've been served." Has he ever subpoenaed an English professor before?

It is stranger still sitting in the witness seat at Andre's trial, seeing him, after all these many months, in a different prison uniform.

"You can't ask him that, Mr. Simpson!"

The judge has taken issue with just about everything Andre's said. "Now, I warned you about defending yourself. And this is one of the reasons why. A character witness can only comment on your character in the community. You can't ask him how he knows you. You can only ask him if he has some knowledge of your reputation. That's it."

"But he's my character witness," Andre protests. "That's why I called him."

"And I'm telling you how you question a character witness. It's not relevant how he knows you, only what he knows of you from your actions or behavior," the judge scolds. Andre leans over to his lawyer—active during the first two trials but retained here only as an advisor—who just smiles and shrugs.

"Aiight, then," Andre says, turning back to face me in the witness box. "Can you comment on my reputation in the community?" But now I'm confused which community the judge means. The only community I've known Andre in was the community of our workshop. If I can't say how I got to know him and what he's achieved there, how can I comment?

"No," I say to the startled faces.

"Mr. Simpson, this is your character witness?" the judge asks.

"Yes, your honor," Andre says, pulling in papers, ranging over stray leads and opportunities.

"But he's saying he can't comment on your character," the judge follows.

"Can I say something? Just a procedural thing?" I ask quietly.

"Yes, go ahead, Dr. Coogan." The judge shifts in his leather chair to face me.

"Because I think I was confused by the instructions. When you say 'community,' do you mean the one I know him from? Or do you mean the bigger one that other people came to know him in?"

"Just the one you know," the judge explains.

"Oh, OK. I'm sorry. The answer is yes, then. I can comment on his character."

"Resubmit the question, Mr. Simpson."

"OK. Can you comment on my character?"

"Yes."

"OK." Andre pauses, looking down at his notes.

The judge radiates impatience. "Any further questions, Mr. Simpson?"

Andre palms the table, looking up. "Would you have me over to your house?" I would.

"You can't ask that, Mr. Simpson," the judge says, overlapping the attorney's objection.

"Do you think I did any of these here crimes?"

I'm not sure, honestly. But it isn't mine to judge. It never has been—not with Andre or anyone else. I really can't answer.

"Objection!" the attorney says before I can protest.

"You can't ask that, Mr. Simpson," the judge continues in a voice like a nursery school teacher's. "Those are all conjectures or they're irrelevant. You can ask him if he knows you to be a truthful person in the community, but he can't comment on the case at hand or talk about the future." Andre absorbs the instructions quickly.

"Aiight, then. Do you know me to be a truthful person in the community?" Was he forthcoming about his struggle with heroin, his addiction to street drama, his desire to live differently?

"Yes," I say quickly. "Absolutely," I add, finally figuring out my role in the conversation.

"That's it, then, I guess," Andre says.

"No further questions," the judge corrects, eyeing him sternly. "And the Commonwealth?" he asks, pushing his glasses back up his nose.

"What kind of practice do you have, Doc?" the prosecutor asks.

"Professor."

"At which institution?"

"Virginia Commonwealth University."

"And your subject?"

"English."

He moves his tongue over his bottom row of teeth like he's moving a piece of chewing tobacco. "No further questions, Judge," he finally says.

"OK, Dr. Coogan. You may go now. And thank you for your time." He squints into a smile, holds my gaze a polite second, then looks down to mark a form. I walk past the weary jury, weary myself, unsure what any of us have just witnessed.

ANDRE

My attorney, Dennis, comes to visit me, wants me to take a plea bargain. The Commonwealth is asking for ten years. I immediately say NO. I will not plead guilty to something that I didn't do. Dennis is losing faith in me, because he feels that we can't win, and we argue in good measure, like he's a father and I am his son. We fight over it for hours, and after our meeting, it's still unresolved.

In the courtroom, I see the district attorney: a very young-looking white male with dark features that make him look mature. But he also has the look of an opportunist. He refers to me as an evil person and a pathological liar. Then it's my lawyer's turn. Dennis stands up with his dark-colored suit, looking very poised and professional. His words are lucid, and I can clearly see that the jury is moved by what they are hearing. "The police charged the wrong man. My client was beaten and sexually assaulted by certain police officers. Police misconduct took place with the DNA evidence, too." I look at the jury and get the sense that they are losing faith in the criminal justice system, just like me.

The Commonwealth Attorney shows pictures of the guns and the crime scene. Then he brings out the white hockey mask and black leather trench coat and starts showing them to the jury. It's scary, because they are looking at all these items and then looking at me. The Commonwealth Attorney seizes the moment, showing that my DNA has been found on the mask, which clearly looks like a Jason mask from those *Friday the 13th* movies. The DNA evidence has a 1 in 6.5 billion chance of belonging to someone other than me.

The witnesses who were robbed take the stand next. One is an elderly couple. The other is an old man who reminds me of my grandfather. My heart goes out to them. I am informed that he is very ill, and I advise my lawyer not to attack him on cross-examination. To me, their testimony has veracity: they describe who robbed the cleaners. I understand that a lot of robberies took place in the County of Henrico, and I feel truly sorry for what happened to them people. But I'm a victim in this as well.

The former Richmond police officer speaks next. He's the one who struck me with his gun that night. He denies it under oath. I scream out, "Why are you lying? You know you hit me!" But before I can finish, I hear the gavel slam and get a stern warning from the judge. The Commonwealth has tried getting the female that was driving the car to testify against me, and lo and behold, even my own mother! Neither one would do it.

Dennis advises me not to take the stand when it's my turn. He says he has it 85 percent won, but my gut tells me that the jury needs to hear from me. I take a special look at three of the women who have been writing everything down. Then I go to the stand. I tell the jury all about my criminal past, to go that route and show them I have nothing to hide. I need them to know that I have never been convicted or charged with any violent crime in my life. Then I speak on the physical and sexual ordeal, and the Commonwealth objects. I don't let him cut me short. I quickly tell the jury what happened and, again, the judge hits her gavel for me to stop. I make sure I get it all out. Now the Commonwealth gets his turn to cross-examine me, and for some reason, he knows not to attack me.

The jury goes to chambers to deliberate, and I am handcuffed and sent to a holding cell. The deputy brings me a dinner tray, but I have no appetite. I just start pacing the cell, back and forth, for what seemed like eternity. An hour and forty-five minutes later, the phone rings. The deputy answers, then just as quickly hangs up. "Verdict's in."

That's when I learn the true meaning of walking the green mile. As I make my way down the long hallway to the courtroom, I picture the people in their offices saying, "Dead man walking, dead man walking." Dennis whispers in my ear, "No matter what happens, don't yell out nothing."

The jury is led in and I am told to stand up. A professional-looking black lady, the jury foreman, gives the verdict: "We the jury find the defendant not guilty of all charges." I look at all of them as they are exiting the courtroom, thanking them all. I thank Dennis and tell him I'm proud of him. I am so happy! But it's short-lived, because the Commonwealth didn't try all the cases at once. They broke them down into three trials. I have two more to go. Dennis tells me that the Henrico Commonwealth hasn't won a jury trial all year. Upon my acquittal, as I leave the courtroom, the attorney shoots me the look of a madman.

The newspaper details the outcome of my acquittal. It's more lies, taken mostly from the policeman who abused me, including this nonsense that I'd been wearing a skirt when they found me. I write the reporter, challenging these alleged facts. Then I just let it go.

I have a new awareness of life now. I have already grown emotionally and intellectually. I not only have peace with God, I have the peace of God through active God consciousness. Change only occurs when we change our minds, which ultimately redirects our behavior. And I have been making a conscious decision to grow. There is no roller coaster or race car, no bungee cord or game that can give me a thrill that compares to the wild ups and downs, the twisting curves of this thing we call life. And my boat has been sunk a time or two.

I ask myself, "Why am I still alive?" I've been in car crashes, gunned down, addicted to drugs. And I am the only one left now from my crew. The only one. God don't make mistakes. He took me through all this to become his stronger warrior, so I can now help, uplift, change hearts, restore lives, show them a walking miracle, and honor the name that my Virginia Commonwealth University professor, Dr. David Coogan, gave me: "Teacher." I was taught the wrong way, taught others the wrong way, and now I'm going to teach the right way.

When I'm finally released from prison, I will be going to my mother's house. I plan to tell her all about my heroin addiction and that my father was the one who began that process in me. I do love my mother, and I want to give her back her son. I know that I'll have good days and bad days, being tested by people who are still in that lifestyle, people who have not yet made the conscious decision to change. They are going to be saying things like, "Is Andre still getting high? Is Andre just fronting for society?" You see, the pill of acceptance is going to be harder for some to swallow than others, especially those who have traveled down the same road as me. But I love a challenge. So when the peer pressure comes, I welcome it! No one will be my judge, jury, or executioner again. I answer only to the Lord.

18

The True Ending

"Yo, we could pool our money together! Self-publish!" Dean's voice is breathy, each phrase the grind of a slot machine.

"Man, why are you walking around like you have an eight ball in your pocket and needs to unload it tonight?" Kelvin blurts, his stutter a far memory. He steps back from the huddle and swings around, shoulders back. His eyebrows threaten to furrow down his nose—he's that angry. I sit there, stunned, imagining our manuscript like a pile of cocaine and these dealers' wheels turning clockwise and counterclockwise. Andre has the same deep look of watchfulness, passiveness. He isn't talking. But from the sidelines he keeps tabs.

"Where's your mind at?" Terence asks me.

"Just listening," I say, clearly outnumbered in a debate that feels more like a street fight.

I've asked them to meet me on campus so that we can talk about the way I've edited and arranged their stories together. Everyone who's been released from prison has come, except Brad, who's stuck in a commute as he comes home from a construction job in Washington. I'd imagined we'd find a classroom in my building and pore over the work for a few hours. I'd given the men copies in advance, but when everyone arrived at the office, no one wanted to sit inside. It was too nice out. And they all liked the manuscript. They could see that they've all gone through more or less the same dramas. They didn't have much else to say about it.

Instead, Terence argues that we should channel what we're doing with our writing into what he dreams of doing through a nonprofit: helping other ex-offenders in their reentry. It's an idea I like and that Kelvin likes, but it's just that: an idea. Kelvin reminds Terence that we've asked, repeatedly, that he write out the plan so that we can study it and see how we might all contribute, and that he still hasn't done it. Terence dismisses this right away with a sneer that implies that we're either too dim to recognize an obviously good plan, or that we're just being difficult by insisting on seeing it in writing. Dean questions why we would even want to start a nonprofit to help other people when none of us have sufficient jobs or money to help ourselves. Again he brings up the idea of self-publishing, and again I deflect it, rehearsing the reasons I've already given him privately.

I see publishing as making something public, not just making a product to sell. Publishing should have a critical impact as well as a commercial impact, and I know of few self-published books like ours that have had a critical impact or have even been reviewed. I list the titles of books about writing workshops in prisons and jails that are within our orbit—all of them published by university or commercial presses. And I remind him that, as the guy putting everyone's writing together into the format of a book, I want the advice of reviewers, editors, and copy editors. I don't just want to print it. And I definitely don't want to pay up front to print it. But no matter what I say, I am accused of just sitting on the mountain of our manuscript and doing nothing. Just sipping tea and staring, I guess.

And so, like a reluctant boxer tired of blocking his face, I am pulled into the ring, swinging, by Dean's jabbing accusations. I itemize my time on the project since it began, in 2006, when we were still meeting at the jail. I detail the progress we've made since 2008, when everyone finally finished writing their drafts, more or less, sharing the feedback I've gotten from publishers, agents, and colleagues and how I've learned from it. I remind him of the other classes that I teach, the work I do at the university beyond the classroom, and the life I lead beyond my work. I keep talking like this until my eyebrows look like Kelvin's. By the time I'm done, I'm glaring at Dean. Satisfied by this strong defense of my dignity, he lets up.

I tell him we should focus on his own book instead, the draft I saw so long ago. We should meet tomorrow to get that one out and reviewed, write a proposal and cover letter. And to Terence, I make the same offer—suggesting he come and meet with me to draft out that business plan. They accept what I've already offered previously.

I mention that soon we'll need to line up some talks to promote the book. Everyone should start making a list of places we could contact. Finally, Andre speaks up, reminding me of the Library of Virginia event: the reading by Dwayne Betts, another ex-offender with a memoir, whose talk we heard. We could speak there. Soon everyone's nodding, shouting good-byes and little jokes and promises to holler. And the meeting breaks up like a huddle, the manuscript still cradled in my arms, and the writers fanning out toward their own end zones.

* * *

Tony sits at the head of the seminar table in my classroom at VCU, looking crisp in a light-blue button-down shirt. He works through the jitters, adjusting his seat, intertwining his fingers. It took a year to arrange this visit after he was released from Indian Creek and living an hour away from Richmond. After he finishes reading, we reminisce about our correspondence in front of my students.

"I really got it wrong," I concede. He studies my face. "I theorized you must have felt unloved by your mother—that you were compelled to buy friends and later sell drugs so you could belong, to feel some love. You remember?" Now he's nodding.

"I sure do. And then I wrote back—I put that in the next draft—that it wasn't about not feeling loved. I knew my mother loved me." He leans back in his chair, shaking his head. Then he looks up, a little smile, until he can pull down the words he wants. "I just didn't like TV!" The students laugh. "I had to get out of the house!" We snicker along with him.

I flip through the manuscript to find the scene of him visiting with his family in prison. I tell him what I'm doing and am about to hand it to him to read when he waves it off to improvise.

"I really blew their minds that day. I said it straight-up. 'I never loved you!' And they all were like, 'Huh?' But that was good. It got their attention so I could explain that, 'If I *had* loved you, I wouldn't have *hurt* you.'" His voice levels up, a little edge in it. "'Nah! I didn't love you! I only *cared* about you. If I was *loving* you . . .'" But he can't build beyond this. He covers his face with one hand, holding up one finger with the other. A trickle of tears we can't see cools the heat, and in a moment the interlude passes like a TV commercial that suddenly seems more vibrant than the show.

After class, Tony and I walk back to my office, catching up on the news from Naji, Brad, and Karl. "Naji tells me there's a video of Karl on YouTube bench-pressing something insanely heavy," I say.

"Hey, I don't have to see that to believe it. Karl's a strong dude. Yes, sir!"

"He called me last week after class when his semester was just about over."

"Karl's in school?"

"College. Yeah. Computer networking. And he's got a job as a physical trainer. His only problem now is that the girl he was seeing Googled him. She found our website."

"This isn't going to end well, is it?" Tony shakes his head.

"And he hadn't told her yet about doing time. She ended it right there."

"Was he pissed?"

"Not really. We laughed about it. He was like, 'Well, you did warn me about putting our pictures and names on the web. People are going to figure out who you really are.'"

"And some won't accept it," Tony adds quickly. "But others will. Like with my woman now. I told her straight-up about my past. And she can see how I'm working my way beyond it."

"You're just being honest about the struggle," I elaborate.

"That's all I can do, man. What else is there?"

TONY

After sucking the contraband ketchup out of their packets in a desperate attempt to ward off starvation, I get into the swing of things. My mind and time are now available to indulge in all the lust and temptations that Portsmouth Regional Jail has to offer. The choices are poker, dice, chess, Scrabble, spades, and basketball. They're all used for gambling. Then there's lottery, football, and basketball pools, and football and basketball parlays. My sin of choice is the high-stakes poker game. A man can easily win or lose a hundred to a hundred and fifty dollars before getting up once. The only real reason to get up is to go to the bathroom, and believe me, if it would have been possible to bring the toilet to the table, some men would pay to piss right there!

I spend 95 percent of my day just sitting around the poker table, talking trash. This is also the place where guys share tips on how they're planning on bettering their criminal enterprises. Being that drugs don't agree with my staying free in society, my new criminal enterprise upon my release, I decide, is going to be prostituting women. I even go so far as to have a tattoo drawn up: KHPT, which stands for "Killers, Hoes, Pimps, and Thugs." Yes, I am a boy inside a thirty-three-year-old grown man's body. Insane is the only way I can describe my way of thinking during my brief eleven-month stay at Portsmouth Regional Jail.

My number is finally called and I am transferred to a road camp. We take care of lawns and pick up litter on the area highways. One evening after work, this guy asks me if I want to smoke a joint with him, free of charge. I don't know why the word "free" has such a profound impact on my decision-making. I tell him no, but seconds later I am sitting on the toilet, passing the joint back and forth.

Immediately after smoking the marijuana, I sit in front of the TV and watch rap videos. With all these negative criminal behaviors playing out in the videos, I find myself coming up with a scam to get some heroin on the camp. The plan doesn't seem too far-fetched, because the same guy I smoked the joint with has a heroin connection. While the plan is still fresh in my mind, I hurry to find him and reveal the idea, and he agrees without hesitation.

The next day, after the marijuana high has worn off, I realize that he is actually going to contact his brother to let him know that I'm going to be sending him a money order of $150.00. I don't know how to go about telling him that I've had second thoughts, but I know I have to change course fast, because I have five and a half years left on my sentence, and I am about to get some heroin inside the prison!

It really scares me when I realize that I might end up spending the rest of my life in prison if I don't change the way I walk, talk, and think. For two days, I avoid the guy who's going to get his brother to bring the heroin. No money has been exchanged, so the drug deal hasn't taken full shape anyway. Two or three days later, on June 23, which so happens to be my birthday, I go to this guy I've seen reading the Holy Bible and ask him to assist me in giving my life to God.

I fall to my knees. At this moment, I truly believe that Jesus Christ died, was buried, and then on the third day, God the Father resurrected His son from the dead. Sin was condemned to the flesh. I understand that if I want to receive the promises that God has made to His children, I have to be obedient to His commandments.

And I never got high again.

I remained associates with the guy who shared his marijuana for about another fourteen months until he was released, but not once did he or I mention that incident, nor did he ever ask me to get high with him again, though he continued to do so. I began to seek God in other ways, because I believed that He rewarded those who sought Him. I got rid of my pornographic magazines. Instantly, the stress from the lust and temptation to sin was gone. My faith in God was strengthened, because He rewarded me for my obedience. I had been committing adultery in my heart. I finally realized that by lusting I was causing my heart and body to burn and long for the fulfillment of desires that usually ended with me pleasing myself through masturbation. I grew stronger and stronger each day that I denied my flesh this pleasure. I know that suffering produces perseverance; perseverance, character; character, hope. And hope does not disappoint, because God has poured out His love into our hearts through the Holy Spirit.

I was always one of those people who had to see something to believe it. Now I was finally able to recognize that, through obedience, trust, and patience, I would reap the rewards of God's wisdom.

During this time, I realized that my loving, God-fearing mother was not to blame for the sinful life I lived. It was my decision to take the love that she gave me and turn it into a tool to destroy myself. My misuse of her innocence, fairness, and genuine love caused her to inherit the label of "enabler." But my mother was very involved in her children's well-being. She made sacrifice after sacrifice.

The clearest evidence of how God has changed me lies in my actions. When my family came to visit me in prison, I acted in a way I never would have before. I told the truth. First, I admitted that I had a drug problem. Then I drew their attention to the core of it: "I never really loved you all. I merely *cared* for you. If I had *loved* you, I would not have caused you all this hurt and pain through my selfish behavior." Take away all the other visitors and inmates in that prison visiting room at ICCC, and you could have heard a pin drop.

Ever since I was a little boy, I've loved giving to others—craved making them happy. I can see now that my gift of being able to give, no strings attached, is a spiritual gift. And I will no longer use this gift to administer death in the form of drugs to impoverished communities. I understand that a friend, neighbor, or associate is a person who will show mercy, compassion, and sympathy. Mentally, physically, spiritually, or financially, they will be there for me, and I will be there for them. So if my so-called friends are still living the worldly, sinful lifestyle that rewards the struggle until death, then I won't consider them friends anymore, even though I will be more than willing to share the Good News with them. It would be reckless for me to think that a nonbeliever would respect the laws and moral principles of life that God requires me to follow.

I'm looking forward to doing volunteer work during my leisure time, showing mercy to orphans and widows in their afflictions, ministering to young people lost in sinful lives. The way I'm going to do so is by creating businesses that will allow me to offer them good-paying jobs in return for them giving up their ways and means of supporting their negative lifestyles.

I believe my true purpose in life is to serve. I'm not looking to make great profits. But I don't wish to sell you any dreams about what I'm going to actually do once I'm released from prison. The true ending to my story can't be put into words now. Readers won't hear any more from me, but they will see a miracle being worked out before their eyes when God uses me for the good of mankind.

KARL

This writing project has increased my self-awareness of how I came to be involved in crime, instead of just letting that story fade over time. Instead of saying, "Well, that was my past," which is essentially a cop-out, I have examined my life, thoughts, and development.

Why did I commit my crime? I keep coming back to simple stupidity. A lot of times our decisions have a risk-return trade-off behind them, but some of us don't stop to consider our actions or what's at stake. Our mental calculators are either broken or were never programmed. If I'd had a significant investment in something that required my freedom, and if I'd been educated enough to think about what I do, then I would have been less likely to commit an act that would jeopardize my investment. Many people confine themselves to the standard sociological reasons for crime: education (in a formal, "school" sense), poverty, race, or culture. But it's even more basic.

I was just sixteen when I committed my crime. At that time, I would do things for people because I wanted them to do something for me. I would keep a line of debits and credits in my mind, and I would try to keep people balanced. I would engage in a primitive cost-benefit analysis and try to make sure my benefits exceeded my costs. I think most people do a little cost-benefit analysis in their relationships, however subconsciously. And they do it for the "right" reasons. But as a man named Rochefoucauld said in the seventeenth century, "We would often be ashamed of our finest actions if the world understood all the motives which produced them." Indeed. Sometimes we get so caught up in what we want, we forget just who we are. As teens, we try on identities and experiment. We are like actors on a stage, playing different roles. But sometimes, we fall into a role so deeply that we forget who we are and fail to grow as individuals. We get too comfortable in our costumes.

Who is to blame? No one. Blame fixes nothing. The problem has been recognized; now we have to fix it. How? Learn to think. Lofty morals riddled with absolutes are easily forgotten when they become inconvenient, or when no one is watching. But, if we change the *way* we think and really *own* morality, well, that's not as easy to disregard.

I often hear people say, "I don't change" or "I will always be me." But what constitutes "me"? A physical body? Mental states? Both drastically change over time. Thus the "me" of five years ago may have very little in common with the "me" of today. I think it should be obvious that one's emotional states change, and these states influence thoughts and actions; thus you are not always the same. You develop over time. Everybody does. We are in constant flux.

When my mother died on November 29, 2007, I was flung into emotional turmoil, despite months of preparation in prison. My mother, the woman who loved me and cared for me when I was hard to love, was gone. I'd lost a confidant, a friend, a mother, the one and only. Even into my incarceration, we maintained a close relationship. I am happy I got to let her know how sorry I was for being so much trouble. But I am sad that our relationship did not extend into my adulthood. I will miss our letters and talks, our nights out, conversations over sushi, lounging by the pool, being beach bums together. I will miss her at Christmas especially, singing songs and getting the house ready. Though we came to view things differently and I disagreed with her religious beliefs, this does not lessen my love. We always made amends.

I wonder how my old self would have reacted to my mother's death? Could my jar have held such emotion, or would it have shattered? I used to think that all strength ought to come from within. So I repressed whatever I was feeling and acted in anger instead, which is precisely what led me to my crime. Since I've been incarcerated, though, my cousin Brianna has helped me open up, to understand more about familial love, loyalty, courage, and fortitude. Why shouldn't people help each other and offer support when needed? Why suffer weakness longer than necessary, when help is right there, waiting for you to ask for it? It is amazing how much people can change.

Since my mother's passing, I've grown a new appreciation for life and a new respect for its vulnerability. I've also gained a new level of emotional empathy and emotional understanding. Some people, I know, view prisoners as disgusting, unprincipled agents of low education, with low chances of success and low empathy. Well, some of us prisoners are as soft as cotton! Despite what my father taught me, I no longer try to seal my emotions in a jar. I am now able to embrace difficult ones, almost revel in them, and then if I'm able to, I dismiss them. I do not dwell on them or allow them to control me. I know my father is disappointed in me. But I also know he is happy for me. He knows I have more potential than I did yesterday.

I look at the possibilities in my life: I am only twenty-three. I came to prison a teenager, a boy, and soon I will go home a man. I have never lived as a man does, dated as a man does, or worked as a man does. I am lacking those transition experiences. But I can almost say that I do not regret my life. To regret it would imply that I wish some part of it had not happened.

RONALD

Early in the morning, I get up for breakfast. I have not yet been called, and the tension is rising. Are they going to release me without any problems?

I return to the dorm where I have lived for many months. My heart beats fast and unsteady. I take a moment to pray and reflect on the things that have helped me to make it through this experience.

My memory gives me much to be grateful for, and I am now at peace. The many days I spent wishing to be released have finally brought me to the moment at hand, but I find myself wanting to stay a little longer. I think about the many guys locked up who I want to pleasure. I wonder about the guys who have begun to open their hearts to me and let me in. I feel relaxed here. No one here would lift a finger to hurt me. I will be leaving a place of comfort to meet the uncertainties of life. Who will assure me that everything will be OK on the outside? Out there I know I must live on spiritual stuff, without the loving embrace of certainty.

After fourteen long months, I hear my name being called, and I quickly grab my things. I travel to the mess hall, where a sergeant is waiting to receive me. This is my final walk to freedom. My excitement is mounting. I am given a pair of brown slacks and a brown shirt to put on. The voice in my head says, *My past is done and will not change, but today is my present, a gift from my creator, and my future is not yet. Stay in today. Make positive choices so tomorrow will be brighter. Let's go and take on the world.*

I take my last breaths of confinement and gaze at the fences of sharp steel that have been daring me to cross them. Then I say goodbye forever. The gate is opened and the officer allows me to walk through without him following.

"I wish you well and hope you never come back," he says seriously.

"Thanks, and you take care, too. And remember, we're not all criminals," I say over my shoulder.

A female officer is there to transport me to Richmond. Now I *know* I am truly free, because they trusted a female to carry me by herself! I want to cry, but instead I stuff it away and proceed on. I have my clothes, a box, and a few dollars in my pocket. I purchase the bus ticket only to find that my bus is late. Wanting a cigarette, I go outside. I try to control my desire to roam the city and find something or someone to get into.

A man appears in the bus station, and we strike up a conversation. I tell him I'm trying to reach my mother and he lends me his cell phone. Finally, a familiar voice! I tell my mother that I am free and in the bus station in Charlottesville. I'm hoping she has made plans to come pick me up from the bus station, but this is a difficult task for her these days. Fannie no longer has a driver's license or a car to drive. I know she will do everything in her power to help me, but I have to do my part to make it a success.

I thank the gentleman for letting me use his phone. The bus arrives and we board for Richmond. There are two seats available and we sit next to each other.

"Excuse me, no offense, but did you just get released from a penitentiary?"

I am surprised but relieved when he says he recognizes the clothes. This means he's either been there or he knows someone who has. I close my eyes and try to isolate myself because I have this feeling that everyone knows what I've done and is watching me.

But this man is a God-sent angel. He was sent to relieve some of the pressure I'm feeling about making it on the outside. He shares with me his testimony since he's been home, the struggles he's encountered on the streets, the low points, high points, letdowns, and successes. After talking with him, I feel more assured that I can be a conqueror—that success is mine for the taking.

There is no sign of my mother at the station. I take a seat. I position myself in thought. All of a sudden, a correctional officer and an ex-offender walk through the side door. Immediately I want to run and hide. Then, just as suddenly, I embrace the fear. The brother who has just arrived is a bit anxious to get back out there, just to experience freedom. I gather the nerve to go speak with him like the gentleman on the bus did for me.

"Say, man where's the closest store?" he asks before I can speak. He wants to get a beer. I tell him where to go and to be careful. I wish him well. We part ways as our new lives start on the same day: two strangers graduating from two different schools.

There was a time in my life when I would have done just what he's doing. But not this time. I take a look at the choice he's making and decide I want to take advantage of the opportunity being given to me. And the only way to do that is to practice some patience. Adult Ronald tells Adolescent Ronald to chill out. He takes advantage of the moment, gives thanks to God, and proceeds to the pay phone.

Dealing with all three people inside of me took great courage and strength. I was truly relying on prayer and for God to show up in my life and direct me on my path. Baby Ronald needed to be nurtured because the feeling of abandonment was strong. Adolescent Ronald was in a state that said, "I don't care, fuck it." But Adult Ronald was sustaining and maintaining with the love of God. I was learning to live above and beyond what I thought had to be.

NAJI

I never expected, at the beginning, to find a sense of therapy in revisiting my past on paper. Being able to participate in this project in prison has allowed me to do an analysis that I otherwise probably wouldn't have recognized needed to be done. And I'm grateful that I had the chance to do it—to scare off the black ghost, that tormented phantom, James Canady. At this point, the blame rests fully on my shoulders for any criminal decision that I may make in the future, because I know that I have compulsion issues stemming from years of abuse. I have no illusions. I know the hard work is ahead.

Life has curves and quirky paradoxes that consistently show the *conscious* human being that, as much as he would like to be in control of what happens in his life, the truth is he is no more than a spectator who has been granted the privilege of viewing the glorious masterpiece called existence. The only constant that I have found to be absolute in this life is the universal law of reciprocity: "What you do will always come back to you." Trust this! But I once heard someone say, "Pearls are not made because the oyster is a creative artist. It is because a grain of sand gets in its shell and makes it uncomfortable." Similarly, through affliction, a great character is made. It's going to take time, but time is what it takes to change the essence of a man, to become Naji Mujahid.

BRAD

When I came home from Indian Creek Correctional Center, I lived with my mother for a couple of months. I think it's hard for her to understand, but then again, she doesn't have to. I don't think anyone, other than another recovering addict, can fully understand this way of life. I learned to let go of old resentments. I haven't forgotten them. I've just released them.

My son was pretty angry with me for all the years of his life that I was incarcerated. And my daughter, Molly, may be doing more than just skating down at the rink. But Coll and I have talked with her about drugs. And Brad Jr. has had his time to yell and cry. We're moving on now, as a family. This Father's Day weekend was one I will never forget: mom and dad were down for the whole weekend, and all three of us did projects together around the house like we used to when I was younger. With time, my relationships are repairing themselves, because of living right and the willingness to surrender.

If I had to sum up my life in one word, "surrender" would be that word. My day started today as all of them do, with me on my knees praising God for the wonderful life I'm living and the grace he pours out onto me, using me to shine a light in the dark. Some days I'm not grateful to put in fourteen hours at work, but I know this is where I'm supposed to be in life right now.

I am just taking baby steps into my new life, but I would never change my past. Writing has helped me see that my errors were not just about drugs, but alcohol, women, and money. I am forever grateful to Naji, my friend, for introducing me to Dr. Coogan, who I have great respect for. He taught me to love writing, something that never came easy before. And this has been the most powerful, life-changing kind of writing, too. You have to put your sweat and blood into it. Otherwise, it's cheating. Without a doubt, this has been the deepest, fullest searching I've ever done, enlightening me on my shortcomings and character defects and helping me look at things I'd missed.

TERENCE

Now my thoughts are in transition. My emotions, too. I'm a son home, a son apart. I'm dwelling in this home, but I'm far away. It was just recently that I learned for the first time what my mother thinks about many of my choices in life, from the early age of fifteen up until my return home from prison four months ago. That happened when Dave asked me to write about it.

She was proud of my going to college. She tells me I was immature for getting married when I did, and she didn't know about my divorce. She was saddened by my prison time, and glad and amazed that I am home. I'm glad and amazed to be home myself. I love you, mother.

But as I was, I am: a child, a man, a man-child dwelling in the valleys and alleys, the by-ways and no-ways, dreaming of a way out of this long meander. So listen to my voice, the sound of my becoming.

KELVIN

The smallest crime in my life was stealing a large bottle of glue out of the library at Ginter Park Elementary School. My punishment was humiliation. But honestly, I didn't see it coming. We had a song that we sang in class called "Who Stole the Cookie from the Cookie Jar?" The class would sing the chorus and every one of us, one at a time, would reply after hearing our peers say our name. When they said, "Kelvin stole the cookie from the cookie jar," I felt like I had taken the cookie for real! I felt so stupid when I said "Who me?" And the class said, "Yes, you!" It felt like they really *were* pointing the finger at me. I then had to say, "Couldn't be!" and they all said, "Then who?" I was humiliated that day, but there was no real consequence. So I didn't learn my lesson. That was my smallest crime.

I can't say what my biggest crime has been. Sin is sin in the eyes of my God. But I will say that selling drugs to people is just about as bad as anything you can do without causing anyone any real physical harm on purpose. This last time around, I've had almost two years to think about all of the things that I did get away with, and after doing so, I've come to realize that most of us will pay for our wrongs in one way or another.

I'm sure that everyone's heard of a compound misdemeanor. That's when the law takes three or more misdemeanor charges and compounds them together into one felony. It doesn't matter if you are religious or spiritual or not. Real is real. We can call it God, or karma, or coincidence. It doesn't matter: our wrongs will be compounded. Of my thirty-eight years of life, I've spent ten of them since the age of eighteen behind bars. I know some men would look at my numbers and laugh, but I could have done much better things with my life.

I go back to when Moms said, "Do as I say and not as I do!" She told me I didn't have to follow none of the examples I saw around me. But it wasn't until I started writing for this book that I realized I never really took her advice. As a matter of fact, besides my Moms, who left every now and then for a few months for stealing, I was the first in my family to go to jail. The consequence of my not learning from those few *months* my Moms did was the *years* I did. I have been in Richmond City Jail more than twelve times for more than fifteen different charges. And I was in denial most of the time.

It wasn't until my firstborn, Lil' Kelvin, wrote me a letter in prison and told me that he needed me that I made up my mind never to sell again. That letter was— and still is—my motivation. It reminds me that I have people out here that depend on me whether they're my children or not.

When I got out of prison, I wanted to switch how I was living on the streets. Before my release date I continuously told Skinny that I would stay with her if she would change her ways. I wanted to change most of the things I was doing, or at least put a different twist on them. But after coming home and being under the same roof with her for maybe ten months to a year, I didn't see any change. She not only picked up my bad habits, but added some of her own.

Skinny and I had a son, Kentrell, my second son and the one child I have that's just like his daddy. Rell laughs like me, shoots ball like me, and gets street respect like me. He's very smart in school, but too stubborn to deal with authority. Rell got it on both sides, because most of the family was rolling with me. As a collective unit, we did enough damage to lay down the red carpet to a life of crime.

There are a few people I have known throughout the years who sold drugs and worked, and managed to understand how to balance the two. But for some reason, I could never seem to get my priorities straight. I put the quick money in front of the sure money and benefits every time. That was my dope-man mentality. I didn't put any money into the bank, college, or nothing. I've heard people at Narcotics Anonymous say that their main problem wasn't using drugs or selling, but themselves. I have to admit that while I haven't learned much of anything from being around those meetings, I did learn that one: I am my biggest problem.

I thought I was going to change when I came home to Rell. I tried, but I hadn't totally changed, and he must have sensed it. Though I wasn't *out there* like I was before, I still had most of the same acquaintances. I was in transition, but I hadn't moved fast enough. I know now why my mother used to blame herself for how my life turned out. No matter how much she tried to explain it to me, I wouldn't listen. I kept saying, "No, Ma, I make my own decisions." But anyone looking in at this now, including me, can easily see that kids follow the examples of the people that raise them. And my kids are turning out just like me.

By the time I came home, it was too late to stop Rell from testing the waters. I was being called to school all the time. He was wide open, going fast. We fought for years until he turned fifteen and started running away from home. We went through that for a long time until I came to realize that unless I physically chained my son to the house like a pet, he was going to have to learn the ways of the world on his own. During this time, he went through something that not even his streetwise daddy has been through. My son was in the backseat of his cousin's car, and someone shot the car up. He was slouched down in his seat, leaning to the side, when the bullet came past him and hit his best friend and killed him. If not for poor posture, my youngest boy might not be here today.

Now, some things don't change once you're released from prison. I'm still playing ball and still willing to take that crucial game-winning shot. The difference is that out here, I *do* know these guys, and they know me. Their sincerity is genuine and we have years of bonding and friendship behind us. It's the same scene, different scenery. There's another difference from prison: girls and women are out here cheering us on. The only problem is, none of them is my favorite girl. As I write this,

I look at the clock and realize it's after midnight on November 18th. This is when my favorite girl died. I've tried to block out the exact day, date, year, and time. But sometimes it's all I can think about. As I do, however, I also remember that my mother raised me to be strong. She wanted me to make it through. So I'm going to make the best of this, my second second chance at life.

STAN

For entirely too many years, I have allowed a creation, a by-product, something I am not, to lead my life. But no more. I no longer make excuses for my pain, my shortcomings, my weakness, or my vulnerability, because history could too easily repeat itself.

I no longer find myself connected to the umbilical cord of negative thinking. I will not masquerade behind slogans such as, "You are a product of your environment." Nor will I attend your pity parties, channeling phrases like, "It's because I'm black." The people who shared those thoughts with me were handing me high doses of poison. Those times are over, and as long as I allow myself to hold onto those anthems from the past, I will never muster the power that lies quiet and dormant inside me.

But let's not lose focus or heart. There is a task at hand, a transformation waiting in the shadows of who I really am. FrankenStan does not want to be destroyed. He's been enjoying the comfort of living inside of me.

Shh! Stay alert as we walk through the forest of my emotions, where the creature has been known to feed. I'm going to roll back the leaves of my memory. There! I can see him! He's just on the other side of my dreams! This is what we have been searching for. For too many years, this creature has hidden in the jungle of addiction, the tall trees and thick bushes of insecurity, prowling through my inner being, devouring every good and meaningful part of my life.

Mr. Coogan has been a worthy guide in this exploration, this safari to track down the source of my madness. He called it a creative writing class, but we were actually tracking a beast.

I realize now that I've been selling myself short. The Bible says I am the temple of the living God. I can't even begin to imagine the value of God's temple. If a man is willing to protect his home with his life, to kill over material things, what sort of obligation should he have to defend God's temple? Now I understand why I shouldn't do drugs, why I shouldn't smoke, why I shouldn't participate in any lifestyle that would bring harm to the temple of the living God. I don't want to lose the spirit that lives inside of me.

This makes me rethink who I am. The Bible says God *is* love. So if God is love, and God resides in my spirit, then God's love is overflowing in me. Why, then, wasn't I walking in love before? Sometimes people think they are sharing love, but there's no clarity to their definition. I loved my son, but I didn't know how to express that emotion correctly. The Bible says God so loved the world that he gave it his only son. Based on that teaching, love is about giving. But that's not the way I did it. My love took and took until it couldn't take anymore. But no more.

Carefully, I shift the position of my heart. That allows a fresh supply of oxygen: colorless, tasteless, odorless, but very empowering. Pure air, like love, never fails. And I can feel a fresh supply marching through every fiber of my body right now, like a legion of well-trained soldiers, conquering all my fears and phobias. It exposes my heart beating away in the dark cellar of my chest. It shines a bright light to the spot where dysfunction meets the truth.

* * *

"Look! It's a bird!"

"No, it's a plane!"

"No, it's Superman!"

Whenever Superman showed up, things always got better. He made himself available. He had heart. He was the ultimate man.

But just like us, Superman had a weakness. Kryptonite could drain his power and leave him weak and vulnerable. Then Superman would be in need of help himself. Someone would have to remove the kryptonite so he could renew his strength, rejuvenate himself, and come back to win the battle.

What is your kryptonite? What has been draining you of all your strength and stopping you from being the superhero God created you to be?

Superman would transform himself in a phone booth. He would remove his outer suit to unveil what lay beneath, the best of who he was. As I sit writing in this phone booth of a cell, I, like Superman, have to remove my garments: my suit of selfishness; my shirt of foolish pride; my necktie of greed; shoes that walk in addiction; and my hat of dysfunctional thinking. I must take it *all* off in order to become what has been hidden from the world.

Dave asked me to write about how my life is now, after taking off these garments. My first feeling is that I have been wearing something that was not designed for me. On too many occasions, I was told to wear it, pressured to clothe myself in the characteristics of a villain.

"Look, it's a thief!"

"No, it's a con-man!"

But for those whose lives I have touched in a positive way, they would say, "No. That's my SuperStan. He came to my rescue with his positive words. He saved me in my physical distress. He found a way to get over all the obstacles that were placed before him."

By being involved in the lives of others, Superman stood for righteousness. Today, I find myself standing for righteousness. My ministry isn't in a church with beautiful stained-glass windows and fine carpets. My church is the weight pile, and as I work out with all these young men, I find myself teaching them not only how to develop their muscles, but how it's equally important to develop their minds, to free themselves from the past.

I no longer slay your dreams, but support you, because I have a need for your support as well. You see, I firmly believe that every person has an opportunity to become a superhero or to help someone else become one. I am not alone in this world, and I don't choose to live my life as though I am. And so I reach out from behind these prison walls. My words fly like a bird, like a plane. If you need me, look to the sky.

19

Open Minds

Following his first not-guilty verdict, Andre ends up beating all of his charges at the remaining trials, confounding just about everyone. When he's at last released in the late summer of 2009, he comes to see me at my office. He's wearing what looks like a thrift-store army surplus jacket and an impassive stare as he relates his experience this afternoon: just now, as he was walking to meet me, he witnessed a robbery at the Rite Aid by the campus. The clerk, a woman, ran out of the store to chase the guy, and Andre warned her to stay put and call the police, because the suspect could be armed.

"Dr. Coogan, would you believe the police questioned me? I mean, why would I do that after I just got done fighting all them charges for over a year?"

I can't imagine why, and I don't know what to believe. I feel like I did when he showed me his wounds in Redemption Chapel three years ago. All I know is what he shows. If it were me, I wouldn't risk another incarceration or trial, which is what I say to him. And with that, I push away any thought that maybe he took part in that robbery.

We take pictures. Reminisce about the trial and the workshop. I ask why the judge was always talking down and condescending to him, suggesting that maybe he was being racist. Andre disagrees. The judge was just upset because nobody had ever insisted on defending himself in his court before.

I ask if he misses heroin.

"Not really." He laughs. "Except what it did for my sex life!"

But he seems to be talking about someone else, someone long gone, the man he used to be.

Not long after we meet in my office, we meet again with Brad at the Library of Virginia to hear Dwayne Betts read from his prison memoir. Afterward, I drive Andre to his grandmother's house, just over the bridge on the south side, not too far from where the car crashed in 2006, the event that led to his incarceration. He shows me the spot.

Andre joins Brad, Terence, and Kelvin as one of the guest speakers in my prison literature class on a Tuesday toward the end of the semester. Having studied the published literature of prisoners for months, along with earlier drafts of this book, the students are excited to meet the authors who were once incarcerated. Andre recounts the story of that night on the bridge when he got arrested, and of his court trials. But he's more focused on where his story is going. His childhood dream was to become a fireman. So when he shares with us that he has passed the written portion of the test to become a city fireman, I can tell he's proud.

Later that weekend, I will look down from Libby Hill Park at the twisting road below. I'll cry as I conjure the deadly car crash of forty-eight hours prior. And I'll hold my phone to my ear as Kelvin tries to feed my hunger to know why Andre would risk his life in a robbery all over again.

* * *

The coffee shop near campus is filling with students as Jonathan, a dealer-turned-prisoner-turned-actor who knew Andre years ago and who read about his death in the newspaper, locks his neck a little to the left, stares past me, and sprints around the bases of his former life.

"The DEA said I was one of the most successful drug dealers in America at the time, in the top fifteen! That's why I got federal charges and did federal time." He speaks loudly, and his words draw a few heads up from bagels and laptops. "And you know how I did it?" He lowers his voice to a withering judgment. "It wasn't by standing out there like Andre! I didn't even *live* in the city. I got me a home in the county. I joined the neighborhood homeowners' association. I did all that to insulate me. In fact, it got so bad with Dre that I wouldn't even let him or people like him come *near* me. They had to go through others. I understood the Andres of the drug world—standing out on the corner, using and chasing women. That wasn't me."

He goes on to tell me how he renounced drugs, partly through an acting program in prison that inspired him to write his own plays. He's pursuing a new life now as a writer. He wants his work to help all people, not just former addicts or prisoners, but everyone struggling to remember the American dream. He teeters at the precipice of his new empire—first this play, a venue in downtown Richmond; then a bigger venue; maybe later, a movie. His hands rest lightly on a Malcom Gladwell book. We talk about Lee Daniels. Michael Jackson. Oprah. Then I remember how little vision and ambition Andre had attached to selling drugs.

"I remember him telling me during the workshop that his father gave him an eight ball to go make some money, but he gave most of it away," I offer.

"He was a bad dealer, Dave. He wasn't thuggish *at all*! He'd give product away, half-price, whatever. He'd get robbed. Everyone knew that about Andre." I lift my coffee cup. Set it back down. I shift in my seat, remembering Andre's passion for our project, and another guy who called me at the office last week—someone Andre had done time with in Halifax—who had promised Andre he would help promote our book. He and Andre had vowed solemnly to dedicate the rest of their lives to stopping kids from making the mistakes they had made.

"So why do you think he did it?" I ask. This is, after all, what I'm aching to know—why, after coming so far, Andre would gamble it all for a few hundred dollars from the cash register of a Fas Mart.

Jonathan leans back, shakes the ice in his drink, and strokes his shaved scalp with the other hand. "One thing you need to know—maybe you already know—is that Andre was a follower. It might have been he wanted to help that other guy out, the one driving."

"So you don't think he had some master plan?"

"Followers don't make their own plans, Dave. He followed you when you were around. But you weren't always around, right?"

I frown as I try to swallow this reality. It touches: if I had become the kind of mentor that takes on a caseload of writers, would Andre still be alive?

Many months have gone by and I still can't answer that question. Eventually I let go of what I cannot know and what is not really mine to know. Andre's death marked the limit. With each bit of news from the others—a job here, a new relationship there, another year sober, a brief detour back to jail, and so on—I realized I can no more pat myself on the back for the good news than I can beat myself up for the bad. Unless I live their lives, I can't take the credit or the heat. This is the limit of writing. It is also the limit of teaching writing. When the class ends, the students have to find their own ways home. They have to stop writing and start living.

* * *

Several years after they finished their memoirs and had been released from prison, Dean, Kelvin, Terence, and Naji were all re-arrested. I met Kelvin at court. Though he had wanted me to testify, Kelvin's lawyer persuaded him to skip the jury trial. So there was no role for me to play as the character witness. Forced into a plea for possession with intent to distribute marijuana, Kelvin got ten years with eight and a half suspended for work release—an arrangement that meant he would have all those other years hanging over his head in case he got caught with drugs at work. This arrangement also meant more of his custodian's paycheck would go to the Commonwealth than to his family. And he could not spend time with his family: when he was not at work, he would be in the lock-up downtown.

To me, this was a case of mistaken identity. What the court saw was the Kelvin of several decades ago, the one who used to sell cocaine—not the forty-two-year-old grandfather with a little marijuana in his car. In his defense, Kelvin told the judge he had gone back to smoking because he had gotten depressed when his son, Kentrell, had been incarcerated, leaving Kelvin with his grandchildren and not enough money to raise them. It's the kind of reason that might drive another man to drink. It's not the kind of action warranting ten years in prison.

Naji, Dean, and Terence's re-incarceration stories differ only in small details. They, too, had fallen back on old habits, spinning their wheels, disappointing their loved ones, but ultimately harming no one. Had their lips touched blunts in more liberal parts of America where marijuana laws are finally starting to change, their habits would not have been cause for incarceration. Had their skin been white, it's less likely they would have been incarcerated. White and black people in America use drugs and sell drugs at more or less the same rates, but as civil rights activist Michelle Alexander has shown, African Americans are far more likely to be incarcerated for it. The problem is not necessarily drugs. The problem is the War on Drugs that has targeted African Americans like Kelvin, Dean, Terence, and Naji.[17]

At the time of this writing, all the men are free. Kelvin works construction and, in his free time, he coaches basketball for kids in Richmond who need the kind of mentors he never had growing up. Terence and Dean are writing again and laying the foundations for nonprofits that will help ex-offenders and at-risk, African American boys. Tony is engaged to be married. Brad moved to Virginia Beach and works in the building restoration industry. After prison, Karl got a bachelor's degree and a job in information technology with a Fortune 500 company. Ronald moved to Baltimore to be closer to his family. His Facebook pages are filled with prayers. Naji found his high school sweetheart, Sandy, on Facebook and now lives with her and her children in Virginia; he now has the family he longed for as a boy. And not long before he was finally released from prison, Stan discovered the identity of his birth mother, and his given name, Maurice Jackson. At long last, he learned the facts of his identity, but he's chosen to remain Stanley Craddock.

My life changed after this workshop, too. But unlike my coauthors, my change came when I went back to jail to build from this experience something new. In 2010, I helped to create Open Minds, a program that enables the incarcerated to take classes in the arts and the humanities with students and faculty from Virginia Commonwealth University.[18] In these courses, people come together as equals to touch the elephants in the room: these creatures of crime, faith, addiction, incarceration, gender, sexuality, race, family life, violence, work, the American Dream, and so much more. But unlike those blind men in the parable, who each touch a different part of the elephant and argue over what they know to be true—

---

17 Michelle Alexander, *The New Jim Crow: Mass Incarceration in an Age of Colorblindness* (New York, NY: The New Press, 2010), 7.

18 See www.openminds.vcu.edu for more about this program.

convinced that the part they touch is the *only* part—we assemble to touch the diversity of experience. We assemble in humility. We write with vulnerability. And we grow, knowing this is only the beginning. We won't know just how partial our view of the world is until we learn to see through others' eyes. This is life in the light of inquiry.

When I pass the spot in Libby Park today where, years ago, those boys raped the woman and beat her boyfriend, I see the danger of broken community. But I see so much more than those four boys, whose names and faces I never learned. I see the faces of writers I know today. And before I leave, I imagine them in a circle with me, facing each other, pencils moving, writing their ways out.

DAVID COOGAN is an associate professor of English at Virginia Commonwealth University, where he teaches courses in writing and literature. He is the founder and co-director of Open Minds, www.openminds.vcu.edu, a program that enables college students to take courses in the arts and humanities with men and women incarcerated at the Richmond City Justice Center, formerly the Richmond City Jail.

Coogan is the co-author of *The Public Work of Rhetoric: Citizen-Scholars and Civic Engagement*. His essays on the teaching of writing have appeared in the journals *College Composition and Communication*, *College English*, *Community Literacy*, *Public: A Journal of Imagining America*, and in the books *Active Voices*, *Texts of Consequence*, and *Working for Justice*. He is currently working on a new book, *Memoirs of Mass Incarceration: The Rhetoric of Revolutionaries, Witnesses, and Survivors*.

To learn more about the writers in this book or to schedule a reading, please visit www.davidcoogan.com or www.brandylanepublishers.com.

SEP   2017
(2016)